STEVE WAUGH

ASHES DIARY 2001

STEVE WAUGH

ASHES DIARY 2001

**With highlights from Australia's
remarkable tour of India**

HarperSports
An imprint of HarperCollinsPublishers

Harper*Sports*
An imprint of HarperCollins*Publishers*, Australia

First published in Australia in 2001
by HarperCollins*Publishers* Pty Limited
ABN 36 009 913 517
A member of HarperCollins*Publishers* (Australia) Pty Limited Group
www.harpercollins.com.au

HarperCollins*Publishers*
25 Ryde Road, Pymble, Sydney NSW 2073, Australia
31 View Road, Glenfield, Auckland 10, New Zealand
77–85 Fulham Palace Road, London W6 8JB, United Kingdom
Hazelton Lanes, 55 Avenue Road, Suite 2900, Toronto, Ontario M5R 3L2
and 1995 Markham Road, Scarborough, Ontario M1B 5M8, Canada
10 East 53rd Street, New York NY 10022, USA

ISBN 0 7322 6444 8.

Cover design: Nine Hundred VC
Internal design and layout: Graeme Jones, KirbyJones Design
Front cover photograph: Hamish Blair / AllSport
Sir Donald Bradman photograph on pages 22–23: Hulton Getty.
Printed and bound in Australia by Griffin Press on 100gsm Matt Art

6 5 4 3 2 1   01 02 03 04

To the Anzacs and their spirit,
which lives on

Acknowledgments

As has been the case with all my books, I am very grateful for all the help I've received in making this one. First of all, I must thank my wife Lynette and children Rosalie, Austin and Lillian — their love and support during my career has been unstinting, and their help and patience as I wrote *Ashes Diary 2001* are much appreciated.

Special thanks to:

• The guys in the Test and one-day squads (and their wives, partners and friends), for giving me so much support, for allowing me to describe many of the events, on the field and off, and for letting my camera snap away in the dressing-rooms and elsewhere.

• Gary Hayden, for writing the foreword. I was keen for Gary to pen his thoughts on his experience touring with the Australian team, because I've never met a bloke who loves cricket more than he does.

• Pat Rafter, for allowing me into his dressing-room at Wimbledon so soon before one of the biggest matches of his life. An unforgettable experience!

• Lt Gen Peter Cosgrove for organising our time in Gallipoli, and Col Don Murray for his efforts and guidance when we got there.

• Errol Alcott, for his help taking photographs with my camera, and more importantly, for all his support during the final four weeks of the Ashes tour.

• Jock Campbell, for providing one of the photographs in the book (page 231) and for sometimes taking control of my camera and snapping some of the photos in this book.

• Ray Phillips, for providing a photograph of the most amazing set of fingernails you'll ever see (page 32).

• Brian Murgatroyd, our media manager, for his professionalism, support and advice.

• All at the Australian Cricket Board and the Australian Cricketers' Association, plus all the sponsors who supported me during the tours covered in this book.

This is my ninth book, and the ninth time I have worked with Geoff Armstrong in putting a book together. He knows cricket, is project manager, editor and photo researcher, and always gets the job done despite some pretty tight deadlines. I appreciate his continued excellence and professionalism.

Once again, many of the photographs here come from the magnificent resources of Allsport, a division of Getty Images. I am very grateful to all their photographers, especially Hamish Blair, who took the front cover shot. Thanks, too, to their staff in Sydney, especially Ruth Gray and James Nicholls, and also to Mark Skarschewski.

Ashes Diary 2001 also needed the legendary expertise of Graeme Jones, who designed and produced the final pages, and Chris Magus at Nine Hundred VC, who did an excellent job designing the front and back covers. Thanks also to the queen of commas, Sarah Shrubb, who helped put the words in the correct order, to Ian Russell for making sure the facts are right, and last but not least, to everyone at HarperCollins for giving me the opportunity to write this book.

Steve Waugh
September 2001

Tour Itineraries

Introduction

By Geoff Armstrong

Since World War II, 26 Australians have taken part in three or more full-scale Ashes tours. Only five — Neil Harvey, Doug Walters, Rod Marsh, Allan Border and Steve Waugh — have gone on four tours. Only one, Steve Waugh, has written and published diaries about three of his Ashes adventures.

This is Steve's eighth diary, continuing a run that began with the 1993 Ashes tour, and his ninth book — surely a record for an active Test cricketer. His original brief this time covered only the 2001 Ashes series, but that was before the Australians' pre-Ashes tour of India evolved into one of the most remarkable and talked-about of recent times. Steve has developed an affinity with India during his career, and earned the respect of the Indian people through his runs and his off-field support for worthy projects, so it seemed proper and appropriate to include his recollections of that eventful tour here.

Thus, this is now a book that covers eight Tests, two one-day series and features a couple of the greatest matches and a number of the greatest cricketers of the modern era. Because of the sheer depth of cricket covered and the constant demands on the Australian captain's time, it has been impossible for every day of touring between mid-February and late-August to have its own entry. Consequently, for India the events of a number of days feature under one banner — so, for example, Steve's reflections on the epic second Test in Calcutta, where India fought back from an impossible position to win, appear on March 15, the match's final day. In England, the daily diary entries are much more regular, but there are occasions — especially when Steve mounts his comeback from what was at first thought to be a tour-ending injury, and also when he enjoys short breaks from the tour with his family — when the happenings of several days are grouped into one. Still, no event is missed, every match and talking point is analysed, and there's a laugh or three along the way. There are reflective moments, too, especially when the one-day squad visits Gallipoli on the way to England. The huge impact that stopover had on the team comes through as Steve describes his emotions, and asks each of his comrades what the experience means to them.

The real beauty of this book, besides its worth as a souvenir of an exciting time in cricket, is that it offers many valuable insights into Steve Waugh's approach to the game and into the team's philosophies and strategies. Steve's ambition is not necessarily to be the best of all time, but to get the absolute most from his men and himself, to be aggressive and to entertain, and to learn and grow along the way. The results, of course, have been outstanding — although sometimes, such as in Calcutta and at Headingley, opponents can rise to the occasion. Read on and you will learn why when Australia plays, they so often play well, the cricket is more dynamic, and the public's interest in the game and the Australian team continues to grow.

Foreword

By Gary Hayden

IT WAS ALMOST AS IF by magic that the plan came together. Passport ready, flights sorted out, family looked after . . . I'm going to England! Now a holiday in another country should be enough in itself, but the thing I was looking forward to most of all was having a bowl in the nets. Yes, the rumours are true — I really love bowling! It costs nothing, there are plenty of nets around and the prospect of challenging someone's technique and temperament during a lengthy net session is irresistible. My goal when bowling is simple — get them out. Just once will do. A little nick behind, a caught and bowled, an obvious lbw, anything. Furthermore, I'm not ashamed to admit that I stack the odds in my favour by bowling over the wicket, around the wicket, through the wicket and from less than 20 metres away. Whatever it takes to get that 'skungy' little edge is all fair go. If I bowl on concrete I have a favourite ball which bounces so well that even Joel Garner would be satisfied with its performance.

Anyway, there was a problem — it was winter in Australia, which meant that the cricket season had finished and I hadn't had a bowl for some time. Fortunately, a mate at work generously gave up his time and agreed to face me in the nets. Some 1700 balls later and I was ready to go. In fact, bursting to go. My wife could see disappointment and disaster written all over the adventure if I didn't get a bowl. She said, 'Don't worry if you miss out — just enjoy the trip.' I couldn't believe it when my parents said the same thing, word for word. What's going on? Surely I'll be OK. I'd heard Slats and Lang are two players who will hit in the nets until the cows come home, not to mention the young pup (brother Matthew).

So there I was. Brisbane Airport and the last thing I heard as I was going down the elevator through to customs was the concerned voice of Kellie (Matt's wife) saying, 'Oh . . . Gaz.' You see, I'm really a 'bushy' at heart. I love the wide open spaces of North Queensland and I'd never been overseas on a big trip before, so I was as green as they come. Kell could sense my fear. In my mind this was all a bit of a big deal, especially as I'm a nervous flyer at the best of times. However, 24 hours and one sore neck later, and I touched down in Manchester.

I had to catch a train to London straight away so that I could see the last moments of the one-day final, and it was here that I had my first cultural lesson. I asked someone for directions to the platform from which the train was leaving for London and, although I was sure he was speaking English, I couldn't understand what he was saying. It took a couple a minutes to sort that out but then I was on my way. After the train pulled into London, I had my next little experience when I got off the train with my luggage and walked to the underground. I remember being surrounded by thousands of moving people as well as lights and signs. I looked up at the information boards and thought to myself . . . what have I done?

Well, I managed to eventually get myself to the right platform and was surprised by the lack of people around me. So I was thinking that this isn't too bad. Not wanting to be run over by a train in my first few minutes of being in London, I stood well back from the line. In the next couple of minutes, people started arriving on the platform in droves. The train came and they're just piling on . . . where was I going to fit? I looked in front of me and I just couldn't see a way. It was all too much, so I decided to miss that train and gather my thoughts. Then I remembered a bit of last-minute advice from Kell. She warned me that the underground might be a bit busy and that negotiating a space might be a bit of a situation. She said, 'You might have to shuffle on and be prepared to push a little.' So I waited for the next train and was comforted by her words of wisdom and the fact that I was bigger than most and was prepared to barge with my backpack — no worries, a few moments later I was away and soon I was at Lord's — the Home of Cricket.

It was hard to believe. Teaching one day — at Lord's the next. All those times spent in the backyard playing cricket with my brother as kids . . . now this! What a feeling, walking out onto the ground after the game, and also into the 'Long Room', where most of the paintings are hundreds of years old . . .

Next day, we went to a place called Arundel, south of London. It was, most surely, the perfect English setting and everything I had imagined England to be. Splendid countryside, green and lush, little stone houses and even an enormous castle overlooking the cricket ground. This was all very beautiful, but I was starting to think to myself: too much look, not enough do, when am I going to get a chance to roll the arm over and maybe take a couple of scalps? As things went, the Australian top order had a bit of a shocker and so a dose in the nets was prescribed for after play. The nets were installed on the grounds (most grounds don't have nets behind the fields) and my moment of truth had arrived.

Here I was, about to bowl my gentle medium pacers to the 'big boys', and I suppose I felt a little nervous because I didn't really know what to expect. I mean, I can pretty much put the ball where I aim, but the last thing that any bowler wants is to be belted out of the ground and reduced to a jibbering, twitching mess left to contemplate the mysteries of life from an obscure part of the ground. Thankfully, this didn't happen and I was able to sleep straight in bed without being bothered by the night demons.

The next day got even better. The Earl of Arundel took the team for a look in his castle and, let me tell you, his castle is something else. It's got the lot — trophies from hunting expeditions, huge fireplaces, paintings, drawbridge, enormous billiards room, swords — wow! Perhaps the best part of it all was the fact that the Earl has these dams that are stocked with trout, so after training that day, Matt, Buck and I headed out to have a whack at these fish. I don't know how all of this was organised, but sometimes it's best not to ask questions. Matt got a strike but, fortunately, he dropped it. This saved us having to clean it, which would have ruined an otherwise perfect day.

After Arundel, things started to get really busy as preparations for the first Test at Edgbaston got fully underway. To be honest, it really surprised me just how busy each team member was. Training, stretching, extra fitness work, meetings, media commitments, bat signings and autographs all make for a frenzied time, and their schedule doesn't have many rest days. Even 'days off' are a bit of a fallacy. Work still has to be done and autograph hunters lurk from the boughs of every tree. There was only one game left before the first Test, but I decided to do the tourist thing and see London before heading up to Birmingham. Besides, my neck was really sore from that nasty plane trip and it needed a couple of days to settle down. In just three days I saw Wimbledon, the Tower of London and all the other sights from the tour buses that go through Central London, as well as the third and final State of Origin game live at the 'Walkabout', where the better team obviously won. Queensland! On yer, fellas! You made life tolerable over here for plenty of us.

Three great days, but enough's enough. It was time to really get back into some hard-core bowling, so I was Birmingham bound . . .

At last! Edgbaston has practice nets. Armed with my plastic bowling marker and my little piece of string (which I put on the pitch as my radar) I had three mornings of bowling bliss. And I must say that the groundstaff did everything to help my cause by preparing wickets with slow and unreliable bounce. But as I've said, if it gets me a wicket — it's all good! My wife often says that I'm in a different world when I have a ball in my hand or if I'm watching Matt bat on television, and when I stopped to consider where I was and what was around me I had to concede that she's right. The perimeter nets kept the media at length, but there were heaps of them, and I thought to myself that I could have been anywhere in the world and it wouldn't have mattered.

Finally, the big day arrived. The first day of the Ashes. England were dismissed mid-afternoon and it was time to sit back and be terrified as I watched Matthew and Slats walk to the crease. Now as much as I love working in the nets, there is no substitute for the centre. After all, it is the only place where the runs are put on the board. The boys got away to a flyer and things were going along swimmingly well until Matt was caught by a blinder. It was a great catch and I was disappointed, but these things happen, and if you read the lips of batsmen as they walk off the ground, I think you'll see that this is what they're saying as well. This is actually the only time I've seen Matthew bat in a Test, so it was a special day for me. It was also a great day of Test cricket, with over 400 runs being scored.

Unfortunately, all good things come to an end and it was time to head back to the grindstone. I had a terrific time. Everyone was so friendly and welcoming, and I'd accumulated experiences that I'll remember forever. England is an amazing place, full of history and rich in multiculturalism. But I returned home with an even deeper appreciation and love of our own magnificent country.

Gary Hayden
Ingham, Queensland
September 2001

Prelude

THE AUSTRALIANS
IN INDIA 2001

Welcome to India

Well done to everyone on being selected. Congratulations to Kasper, welcome back. This is going to be a great tour to be on, the challenge we need. We've had a relatively easy home season, but we must be ready to play tough cricket here in India. There will be times when I'm asking a lot of you, but I'm not going to ask anything that is unreasonable or unrealistic.

WHAT I WANT US TO BE

- Mentally and physically the toughest team the Indians have ever played against. That means no bad sessions, guys being able to bat all day, bowlers being able to produce long spells if needed.
- The hungriest and most uncompromising side they've ever seen. Never give them an inch; if we get a sniff, we go in for the kill.
- The closest knit, most determined unit they've ever come across. Think about Kasper, the inspiring way he's come back from injury, or Junior in Australia, the way the team backed him.
- The most positive, self-assured and aggressive side they've played. Remember our wins in Hobart and Hamilton.
- A side with the strongest body language and most intimidating aura they've encountered. Never take a backward step. For example, the way we took on Lara in the recent one-day finals, when it was 11 versus one.
- A team with self-belief and the will to win, no matter what situations confront us. If you don't believe this or you can't feel it within, then make it happen or you're on the wrong team.

We must focus on what we can control — our planning, practice, preparation, not the facilities, wickets, umpires or crowds. Keep whingeing to a minimum. If you haven't a solution to a problem, don't bring it up. We must have fun and enjoy it. We will celebrate and we will win.

THE KEY TO OUR SUCCESS IS OUR ATTITUDE. WE MUST SEE THE POSITIVE AND NOT THE NEGATIVE IN EVERYTHING.

Our tour motto: 'Attitudes are contagious, is yours worth catching?' Let's be the first Australian team in 31 years to beat India. Let's be the first team to win 16 Tests in a row, doubling the next best by an Aussie team. Let's create our own history. But always remember: 'The PROCESS to ACHIEVE the END RESULT is what counts.'

February 15 *Mumbai*

IF THERE WAS ONE BLOKE'S face that I was most pleased to see above all others two days back, as we gathered in the airport lounge for the flight to Mumbai via Hong Kong, I reckon it was Kasper's. The lion-hearted Michael Kasprowicz is just the sort of strong character we'll be needing here in India, and I was especially pleased for his sake because I know how hard he's worked to earn his seat on the plane. Like everyone else who was part of the Australian team that lost in India in 1998, I'll never forget how Kasper toiled so bravely and magnificently and what a key role he played in our third Test victory on that tour.

Commentators like to talk about the high-profile guys in the team — Glenn McGrath, Shane Warne, Adam Gilchrist — but in many ways it is less heralded men such as Kasper who have been the key to our recent success. What we always want this Australian side to be is a strong unit full of guys who are tough, smart, resilient and, above all else, put the team before themselves.

Of those not on the plane, the bloke I felt sorriest for was New South Wales leg-spinner Stuart MacGill, who had missed out again because in Shane Warne and Colin Miller he was competing with two superb spinners for just two spots. Stuey bowled extremely well in the recent Test series against the West Indies, when Warney was out injured, and is a tremendous bowler who loves the big-match occasion, but there are always going to be unlucky players when you have got a strong side and a strong squad.

Photographers, fans, media, officials and security guards combined to make the walk from the arrivals lounge at Mumbai airport to the team bus a tricky one. Shane Warne is the focus of attention here, with long-time physiotherapist Errol Alcott right behind him.

The same could be said for a number of batsmen, including Simon Katich, Michael Bevan and Darren Lehmann. You can often judge the quality of a team by the players who have missed out.

Some critics said we should have preferred MacGill to Warne. I know Shane is looking forward to a return meeting with Sachin Tendulkar, who had far the better of their duel in 1998 (when Shane bowled with a troubled shoulder). I also know that Shane has delivered many more times than he's failed during his career, so it won't surprise me one bit if he has a big tour. He knows a great challenge lies ahead, and he likes proving people wrong.

On a personal level, I'm keen to get a Test hundred in India, something I've never done before, but most important of all I want to win a Test series in India. I've never won in India, or Sri Lanka for that matter, but I've been part of winning teams everywhere else. Looking beyond the Test series, I'm keen for us to build further on our reputation as the No. 1 side in international one-day cricket. As World Cup champions, I think it is important that we stay at the top of the tree. And I also want myself and the team to enjoy the country and the culture rather than complain about it as some teams have done in the distant past.

Our attitude will be the key.

We actually arrived here yesterday, Valentine's Day, but I soon learned that there is supposed to be little love between the two teams. Part of this media speculation is, I guess, my fault, as the local media have leapt on my pre-tour comments about the possibility of Indian captain Sourav Ganguly putting undue influence on the local groundsmen. My remarks were prompted by reports emanating out of India that this was exactly what Ganguly was doing, and he reportedly responded with some intriguing statements about what I should and shouldn't be saying, the quality of the Australian team, and how the Indians were looking forward to any on-field verbal sniping that might unfold.

Vice captain Adam Gilchrist and I answer questions during the first media conference of the tour.

It was all very interesting. My original statement was on an issue that I had raised at an official meeting of Test captains in Melbourne on February 12, a get-together of eight of the 10 national captains (only Ganguly and England's Nasser Hussain were unable to attend). I want the practice of Test captains trying to influence groundstaff to be prohibited, and the general consensus was that this was a good idea and something that the International Cricket Council should legislate for in the future.

Such a rule would remove the temptation for a Test captain to say to the groundsman that he'd like a turning or a bouncy pitch. The groundsman's job is to produce the best wicket he can and it's the players' job to go out there and play on it. The rule is not in the ICC's code of conduct at present, but I think it will be by 2002.

Of all the Indian skipper's reputed statements, the one I found most amusing was his theory that Australia had only beaten 'weak' sides during our record-breaking undefeated Test-match run.

'He forgot India was one of those sides,' I said before we left for India. 'As a leader of a side, that's not a real good thing to say about your own side.'

So at our first tour press conference, at the Orchid Hotel, the local media was clearly looking for a way of escalating this story. But I didn't want to play that game, not after a long flight.

Next came a question from an Aussie journo, about brother Mark and the ongoing 'bookie' scandal. You could hear the ears prick, the tape recorders buzz a little quicker and the pens move closer to the pages, but I had no problems with the answer. Mark had been interviewed by the International Cricket Council's chief anti-corruption investigator, Sir Paul Condon, in Melbourne a few days before we left for India. And that was the end of it, at least until Sir Paul submits his report. For now, Mark can concentrate on his cricket and we can continue to have 100 per cent faith in him.

The questions turned to what the reporters here are calling 'the last frontier'. This is how many perceive this India tour from our perspective, because we Australians have won Test series all over the world in the past decade, except in India. No Australian Test team has won here since 1969. Despite some prodding from journos, I preferred to call this upcoming Test series 'a great challenge', even if I firmly believe that if we want to be put up with the finest teams in cricket history we do need to prevail here. What I didn't like was the way some reporters had drawn a very black line — if we did win we'd be a great side, but if we lost we'd be ordinary.

I know that we are an outstanding team, we've proved that, and that it will take a fine performance by the Indians to beat us. But when you look at their team, with the great Tendulkar their undoubted star, there's no doubt that they are capable of playing excellent cricket. Certainly, here at home they will be much tougher than the dispirited outfit we crushed in Australia in 1999–2000.

Forgetting what Ganguly might or might not have suggested, to the media and to the groundsmen, I still expect the pitches here to be flat and slow. Not that it'll matter much, because we feel we have a balanced side capable of handling whatever conditions are put in front of us. At the media conference, there were questions about some players' lack of experience in India. The fact that we've played in Pakistan and Sri Lanka recently is not an issue. The conditions are different and the teams are different. Despite the fact we've only played four Tests in India since 1986, most of the guys have played some form of cricket over here, so they've experienced the wickets, the conditions and the fanatical crowd support. This said, there will still be some adjusting to do because these tracks are so much slower and less bouncy than what we've been playing on back home, so we're treating the two 'warm-up' games before the first Test (which starts in Mumbai on February 27) as being very important.

One of the final questions concerned a fact that could prove crucial in deciding who will win this Test series. 'What impact will the absence of Anil Kumble have on the outcome?' I was asked. Kumble, an excellent, quicker-than-usual leg-spinner with 276 Test wickets to his name, has been ruled out of the entire series with a shoulder injury.

'There's no doubt it's a big blow for India,' I replied. 'We would have liked to play against the best. But remember, we don't have Brett Lee.'

I came away from the media conference convinced that we're going to be in for a tough series. You could tell by the way the local scribes fired the questions at me and vice-captain Adam Gilchrist that they are convinced that Ganguly is going to have the home team fired up. It'll be a contest, a confrontation, real Test cricket. By this, I don't mean you'll see two teams having the occasional petty verbal stoush. Instead, it'll be a stirring contest between two committed sides giving it their best shot.

I have found in the past that India become a very confident side when they get on a roll. The crowd gets behind them, and they get motivated by that support. We've got to stay calm and relaxed in pressure situations. The last time we were here for a Test series (when we lost 2–1 in 1998) we were too often dragged along with the emotion of the crowd, rushed our game and started playing at the Indians' pace. Though I can guarantee that we'll always play aggressively and to win, I honestly don't care if we win 1–0 or 2–1. I'm not fussed with trying to keep our winning streak going forever. But I want to see the team keep improving and I'm desperately keen to win.

One at a time, fellas! Mark Waugh tries his best to sign as many autographs as possible before the team bus gets into top gear.

February 20 *Nagpur*

**At Nagpur,
February 17–19**

Australians 291 (ML Hayden 49,
RT Ponting 56, JN Gillespie 57,
MS Kasprowicz 92) and 9–365
(JL Langer 115, RT Ponting 68, DR
Martyn 53) drew with India A 368
(S Ramesh 101, VVS Laxman 94,
NR Mongia 71*; CR Miller 6–90)

IF THE FIRST MATCH OF our tour is any indication, there's going to be plenty of emotion on display during the upcoming Test series. There was a fair amount of chat on the field from the young India A players during our match, which ended yesterday in a draw. I can't imagine that the Tests will be any different.

The most public on-field spat came on the final day, after the leg-spinner Balaji Rao gave me a 'send off' after he dismissed me for 17. Justin Langer, who was batting at the other end, didn't appreciate the bowler's exuberance one bit, and suggested to Rao that he show a little more respect. As an even more effective counter, Lang then launched a batting assault against Rao, the spinner going for more than 10 runs an over.

I truly didn't mind Rao's outburst, and told the media that after the match ended in a draw. To be honest, I was actually encouraged by the prospect of some passionate cricket ahead. My attitude is simple: if someone wants to have a go on the field then let them have a go, but remember . . . every dog has its day. I've seen it many times — top-grade cricket has a habit of sorting out the blokes who can give it but can't take it.

Balaji Rao sends me on my way on the final day of our match against India A in Nagpur.

They're All Starting

Mark Waugh is known as something of a lover of the punt, particularly the horses, so it came as little surprise that he jumped at the first opportunity to view some live action at the Mumbai Turf Club.

But even an experienced punter can occasionally come unstuck, and in Mumbai Junior was stung by a peculiar local rule. He plunged on one of the fancied runners, but was disappointed when it broke through the starting barrier just before the jump, and careered at breakneck speed right around the course. It was obviously out, a late scratching.

Or was it? Junior was already on his way back to the window to collect his refund when he noticed that the attendants were putting the exhausted horse back into the barrier. And then it was off, and actually led into the straight before compounding to beat only three horses home. Considering it had run an extra lap, it was a very brave effort.

Needless to say, Junior was dumbfounded, left searching for answers and a lost wad of rupees.

Already, I have been misquoted a few times in the press over here, which seems to have created a perception that we are a little too sure of ourselves. Let me make one thing very clear: I have the greatest respect for all the sides we play, but at the same time I have great confidence in my team. Sometimes people misinterpret this confidence as arrogance, which is unfair. I never lose sight of the fact that if you don't respect the opposition, you will pay the price for it.

I have had the benefit of going through tough years, knowing what it feels like to lose and being a part of a set-up that isn't working as it should. I've learnt a lot from those experiences. You need tough times to appreciate good times. I'm glad that I was part of the team from 1985 through to the 1989 Ashes tour, when it was tough being in the Australian side.

When we have lost Test matches on past tours of India, we have done so mainly because we've collapsed in one session. This time, we have to recognise when India gets on top and quickly stem the flow. If we have a bad session, we must come back strongly in the next session. We have to play tough Test-match cricket.

Are we unbeatable, as some Indian commentators are saying? It's better to have nice things written about us than bad things, so we will take the tag even if it is unrealistic. What we are is very competitive.

This match proved a good warm-up for us, even if we were slow out of the blocks. I was as unproductive as anyone on the first day, caught behind for a duck as we stumbled to 3–25. We actually crashed to 7–133 before Jason Gillespie and Michael Kasprowicz steadied the ship, adding 155 for the eighth wicket. Most touring teams struggle in their first game on tour, simply because it takes a little while to get over the jetlag and to adjust to the new environment, the light and the atmosphere. I reckon it can take as long as a week before you're truly ready to perform. So this was a good hitout. Batting was difficult on the turning track, and overall I thought we handled ourselves pretty well.

Apart from Kasper, who hit a career-high 92 in our first innings, the pick of our players was probably the newly crowned Australian Test cricketer of the year, he of the occasional 'Federation blue' hair, Colin Miller. 'Funky' finished the match with 6–90, and looked to be in excellent form. However, I must confess that I'm not sure if that will be enough to get him into the Test XI. Whether he gets picked for any or all the Tests will depend on the pitches served up to us. I've always felt that unless the tracks are slow turners our best chance of defeating the Indian batsmen is through our pace attack. Ganguly, Dravid and Laxman (except for one phenomenal innings in Sydney) all struggled to some degree against McGrath and Co. in Australia last season and could easily do so again here. But if the tracks are slow we won't lose anything, because then we'll just change tack and go with Funky alongside Warney.

That's one of the joys of leading this Australian side. We're a long, long way from being a one-man band.

Our second match of the tour, against Mumbai at the Brabourne Stadium, begins on Thursday. It appears that Sachin Tendulkar will not be playing, which means that the opening episode in his clash with Glenn McGrath will have to wait until the first Test. We'll be hoping for a better all-round performance than we managed here in Nagpur, and on a personal level I am very keen to have a long stay in the middle before the Test series begins.

Off the field, we've already been given a lesson in the changing attitudes of the media towards high-profile sportspeople. Back in Mumbai, four of our lads went down to the bar for a quiet beer in the bar of the Orchid Hotel. As a friendly gesture to welcome the lads to India, one of the locals bought four beers of a local variety, but unfortunately, because of a sponsorship agreement the team has with Foster's, the guys had to decline. The offending drinks were simply placed on the bar, but to satisfy the bloke who'd bought them the boys happily posed for a photograph, not knowing that they'd be appearing, complete with an extensive story about enjoying the local drop, on the back page of a newspaper the following morning. A very nice stitch-up indeed.

Sadly, we have to keep our wits about us and trust only those people we really know.

Michael Kasprowicz, the unlikely batting hero of our first innings of the tour, hits a cover drive on his way to 92.

February 26 *Mumbai*

I KNEW SIR DONALD BRADMAN was ill and there was a possibility he could pass away in the near future, but it was still a great shock when my wife Lynette rang at 2.15 this morning with the news. I'm sure the whole of Australia is mourning his death.

It has always been my cricketing fantasy to bat with Sir Donald, to stand there and observe how he went about his business, how he played his shots. He was ahead of his generation in the way he played the game, such as in the way he ran between the wickets, and from my reading of his career and life there seems no doubt that his thinking was also ahead of his time, too.

His statistics are mind-blowing. Of all the batsmen to complete 20 Test innings he has the highest average, 99.94. Next best is South Africa's Graeme Pollock with 60.97, two more men average in the sixties, more than 20 have averages in the fifties. Averages don't prove everything, but this one — that he was half as good again as any of the game's greatest players — is so unbelievably conclusive. And to think that after he retired he went to become arguably our most important cricket administrator and the author of the best cricket coaching book ever published.

One of the most touching memories of my life will always be my private meeting with Sir Donald in August 1999. I remember that, with his typical modesty, he told me he played with more talented batsmen than himself. The difference, he reckoned, was that he was more hungry for success.

He even went as far as to say he felt he was an ordinary captain — striking humility from a man who achieved so much as a leader.

That meeting went too quickly for me. It lasted about 90 minutes, but I could have listened forever. And there were a million things I wanted to ask him, but I didn't get the chance — things such as what happened when he met with the American baseball legend, Babe Ruth, in 1932.

Everyone loved Sir Donald Bradman in Australia. We should never forget his efforts in trying to unite the country in times of need after World War II. During our meeting, he explained that the main reason he made the 1948 tour to England was to give people hope after the War. He knew he was past his best but he also knew his country — and cricket — needed him.

Away from cricket, Sir Donald would have loved to lead a normal life, but it just wasn't possible. He told me he had little privacy, and I'm sure that in many ways his was a difficult life to lead. As unfair as that was, he was loved so much it was never going to be any other way. People loved him so much they hung on his every word.

That's the price of fame. Everyone wants a piece of your time.

Sir Donald told me he quite enjoyed the modern game, a refreshing attitude that contrasts with some former champions who seem obsessed with the belief that they

Having heard the sad news of Sir Donald Bradman's death during the night, I spoke briefly to the media the following morning.

don't make them like they used to. He enjoyed the one-day game, and thought cricket was going well.

Sir Donald is revered throughout India and his death led all morning television news bulletins. These reports featured heartfelt tributes from many of the greats of Indian cricket, including some generous words from a clearly moved Sachin Tendulkar. Sachin enjoyed a private meeting with Sir Donald recently, and clearly cherishes the memory of that experience.

There have been some suggestions here that perhaps the upcoming Test match should be delayed, as a tribute to all Sir Donald meant to cricket, but I don't think this should happen. What we need to do is from this day forward play the game in the right spirit, as he did, and use this sad event as a reminder that each of us has a responsibility to try to enhance the sport's reputation every time we take the field. The fact that some selfish people have not done this is the thing that has tarnished the game's image over the past couple of years.

We can all take so much inspiration from Sir Donald. He always tried to be one step ahead of the others and in doing so he set standards that mere mortals will never be able to reach. But we should try. He was a once-in-a-lifetime cricketer, and a once-in-a-lifetime man.

March 1 *Mumbai*

TODAY'S WIN WAS AN EXCELLENT start to the series — it was our self-belief and commitment as a team that ensured we came out on top. Despite the fact that we eventually prevailed by 10 wickets and the Test finished in three days, the match was for most of its duration a tight and absorbing contest. An hour after the game, my teammates and I were still sitting in the dressing-room, physically and mentally drained by the whole experience.

There were moments right through the Test when the game was in the balance; even as late as the luncheon interval on the third day, after Sachin Tendulkar and Rahul Dravid had got through the morning session to leave India just 57 runs behind with eight second-innings wickets still in hand. But after Sachin was dismissed, to make it 3–154 (a deficit of 19), we ran through the rest of the local batting line-up, taking 8–65, and the Test was ours.

Sachin seemed ready to play a major innings. Sure, his dismissal was somewhat fortunate for us but I'll always believe that you make your own luck. As he walked slowly back off the field, I knew we'd suddenly won an advantage, but I did not expect the rest of the dismissals to come quite so easily.

ALLSPORT

Before the series began, we stopped to observe a minute's silence as a tribute to the life and achievements of Sir Donald Bradman. Pictured to my left here are Adam Gilchrist, Shane Warne, Colin Miller and Damien Fleming.

Ricky Ponting and keeper Adam Gilchrist (above left) celebrate the crucial dismissal of a bemused Sachin Tendulkar (above right) on the final day of the first Test.

What I consider to have been the most significant moment of the entire Test was not seen by anyone but our players and support staff. After giving everything we had in the morning session but having nothing in the wickets column to show for it, it would have been easy to go into the luncheon interval in a downcast frame of mind. In fact, the opposite was true, with every player in an upbeat mood, and everyone in our dressing-room noting how well we had been executing our game plan and praising the effort and commitment everyone on the field had shown. The message for the lunch-to-tea session was 'hang in there, keep doing your job and the chances would come, just make sure you're ready for them'. This attitude had stood us in good stead during some testy moments in the past, and we believed it would see us through again if we persevered.

Back on the field, our resolve was tested still further when Tendulkar smashed Glenn McGrath's first ball after lunch through the covers for four. The roar of the capacity crowd after that shot was the loudest and most unified sound I have ever heard or felt. It shot right through my body, trying, it seemed, to take our hearts with it.

Thankfully, Tendulkar was out shortly after, when he smashed a pull shot, but instead of the ball racing to the boundary it crashed into Justin Langer at short leg and then ballooned towards square-leg. The Indian champion should have been okay, but Ricky Ponting at mid-wicket reacted quickly, raced to his right and caught the ball while flying parallel to the ground.

At the moment that ball, and the Test, hung in the air, Ricky still had plenty to do to make his memorable catch. If his concentration hadn't been 100 per cent sharp, if he hadn't kept his cool, if he wasn't the supreme fieldsman that he is, then Sachin might still be batting now.

Back to day one. Putting India in to bat was a gamble, but as a captain you have to trust your instincts. I felt that, because the Indians had not played any tough Test cricket in the previous six months, they would be a little unprepared to face our attack on a pitch offering some assistance to pace bowling. Moreover, we wanted to try to reopen some mental scars dating back to the series in Australia in 1999–2000. There's no doubt the decision did work, as the four wickets we got in the Test's opening session set the whole game up nicely for us.

Even though we have won the Test, I am hearing some muttering that we did so despite making an error in going in with only one spinner. I don't agree. Damien Fleming did his job by picking up the vital wicket of Rahul Dravid in the first innings, and there were times in the second innings when I thought he was the most likely bowler to get a breakthrough. There's no doubt, though, that we were helped by Mark Waugh's off-breaks. Junior is an underrated bowler; I'm sure he doesn't realise how useful he can be as a bowler. But after missing out with the bat he was eager to contribute; he even mentioned to me that he was keen for a bowl, something he rarely does.

That's what makes this side so special — everybody puts their hand up to make a positive contribution in any way they can, especially when the team needs it.

Of course, lunch on day three was not the only time when this Test was in the balance. When we slumped to 5–99 in our first innings, in reply to India's first-day 176, I imagine people were assuming the atmosphere was a little panicky in the visitors' dressing-room, but that was not the case. Matthew Hayden and Adam Gilchrist each had a plan and stuck to it, and they weren't separated until the score had reached 296, when Matty was out for 119.

Haydos' innings was something special. When you consider the nature of the pitch, the extreme pressure he faced as wickets fell around him and the fact that he is trying to secure his spot in the side, it really was a superb effort. It will probably be remembered less than Gilly's masterpiece, but from a team point of view it may in time be recognised as his best ever.

Gilly's innings of 122 from 112 balls was one of the best I have seen, a knock of 'Bradmanesque' proportions. As a match-winning tribute to the Great Man, it was perfect.

To hit against the spin is recognised by many as being a form of batting suicide. On a savagely turning track on which the ball often bounced as if the pitch was a trampoline, such a strategy was beyond comprehension. But Gilly backed himself to play this way, and proceeded to smash every ball right in the middle of his bat. This was surely one of the greatest counter-attacking knocks in Test history, and the Indians couldn't believe it, and had no answer to it.

Gilly is the perfect No. 7, a batsman capable of taking the game away from the opposition at any time. Adding to the merit of his performance was the ordinary standard of the wicket, which wasn't ideal, below Test-match standard. It didn't suit the quicks as much as we had hoped, but what was of real concern was the sight of the ball firing over the wicketkeeper's head when the spinners were bowling. Test-match tracks really should be more reliable, and this one didn't really help either team, though it did ensure that a close encounter would unfold.

Throughout the Test, I was proud of the way we never let the frenetic atmosphere put us off stride. Instead of rushing, we pulled back, relaxed, took a deep breath and focused on the next ball. Never was this better illustrated than when Gilly and Haydos launched their great partnership.

I can't help but think that we've built up a significant psychological advantage over India by winning this match. Their body language when they went out for the seven overs of our second innings was awful; they were clearly very down. And their morale wouldn't have been helped by the fact that their captain, Sourav Ganguly, was booed at the after-match on-field presentation, or by the incessant criticisms coming out of the local press.

Overall, though, the crowd was tremendous, fervent but fair. They supported their team passionately but were able to acknowledge our good cricket as well.

I think it is unfair to judge any team on the basis of one performance. We certainly won't be taking the Indians lightly in the next two Tests. In my view, the fans should support their team through these tough times and they should also not forget that their players are up against a pretty good team.

Above left: Matthew Hayden (in helmet) congratulates Adam Gilchrist on reaching one of Test cricket's finest hundreds. Above right: Michael Slater remonstrates with umpire Venkat after the third umpire gave Rahul Dravid the benefit of the doubt over what Slats firmly believed was a fair catch.

Some moves by Ganguly, such as his bringing on Tendulkar to bowl not long after Gilly and Haydos came together, have come in for flak. But I think a captain should go with his instincts on the field. If Tendulkar had taken a wicket, the same move would now be being hailed as a masterful piece of strategy. Similarly, if we had lost this Test, I would have been crucified for my decision to bowl first. Captains are put in charge to make decisions and many times it is unfair to criticise them just because their plans don't work.

One of the major talking points to come out of today's final day was Michael Slater's right-out-of-character reaction to not getting a decision in his favour when it seemed he'd caught Dravid in the tense first session. In my view, Slats' behaviour was over the top and wrong, and after the game he was censured by the match referee, Cammie Smith from the West Indies.

The incident came about when Dravid refused to walk after Slats claimed to have made a fair catch, millimetres off the grass. As the umps have been doing in recent months, this decision went to the third umpire and an inconclusive video meant that the doubt had to go the way of the batsman.

Slats couldn't believe it, which was one thing. Quite another was for him to stride up to the batsman and umpire Venkat and tell them at close quarters that they were wrong. What made Slats' reaction look even worse was that we had a couple such decisions go our way during the Australian summer, and we hadn't complained then.

I am aware there has been some criticism of my role, or lack thereof, in the incident. After watching the replay I can see why I was criticised, but I'm not sure the replay showed the full story. As is always the case in video umpire decisions, you are focused on the red and green lights that deliver the verdict (red for out, green for not out), hoping for a favourable decision. Unfortunately for Slats, the combination of the heat of the moment and a green light sparked his uncharacteristic display, which caught me off guard. By the time he had confronted Venkat and Dravid, all I could do was yell out from a distance, 'Get out of there, Slats.' Unfortunately, Slats either didn't hear me, or my message didn't sink in.

What's the Score?

The most amazing aspect of Matthew Hayden's spectacular Test century in the first Test was the fact that he didn't even know that he'd reached three figures until Adam Gilchrist offered his congratulations when their paths crossed mid-wicket after a boundary had been signalled. Haydos, or 'Unit' as we occasionally call him, never looks at his own score, only ever peeking at the team's progressive total.

Brother Mark and I are the exact opposite, but for good reason. During our under-age cricket days the team's scorers would regularly get our scores wrong, claiming they couldn't tell us apart. I'm sure the mistakes evened themselves out over the years but just to make sure we both began keeping our own tallies in our heads as we batted. Even today, I still have my own scoreboard ticking over in my mind and don't need to look at the official scoreboard to know how many I am.

Shane Warne (far left) sprays the boys with some of our team sponsor's product in the dressing-room after we'd sealed a 10-wicket win in the first Test.

There was also criticism that the match referee didn't bring down a harsher penalty. The important thing here is that there is a consistency in these penalties, and that players' previous records are taken into account. It would be great if there were set penalties for various indiscretions, rather than each case being judged independently by different people with different opinions.

This said, I'm sure that if Slats could have that dramatic moment over again, he'd do things differently.

I do think administrators should also be smarter in the way they use the video replay. I remember back to 1995 when I caught Brian Lara in Barbados. He was given out, and I remain certain he was out, but the video replays suggested the ball might have flicked the ground. If that dismissal had occurred in 2001, the umps would have referred the matter to the third umpire, who would have been obliged to give Lara the benefit of the doubt.

It seems to me that the third umpire can get these sorts of dismissals wrong as often as the officials on the field, so let's leave the decisions to the officials on the field. The video is great for run outs and stumpings, and perhaps some other unusual circumstances as well, but maybe that's as far as we need to go.

I just hope Slats' bad press doesn't detract too much attention from the fact that we've won one of our best Test victories of recent times. One lesson we've absorbed, if we weren't fully aware of it before, is that we're up against a fine, competitive opposition. However, despite their best efforts, throughout the past three days we backed ourselves and fought through the tough times. I am really proud of the guys.

Tomorrow, we have the day off, then a training session here at Wankhede Stadium on Saturday before a flight to Delhi on Sunday to prepare for a three-dayer against a Board XI.

March 3 *Mumbai*

ONE THING THAT IS GUARANTEED for any touring cricketer in India is that he'll receive countless requests to help out any number of worthwhile charities. A request that stood out to me came from a former hockey star who is based here in Mumbai. He has embarked on a mission to save street kids from their awful existences as children of sex slaves from Mumbai's notorious red-light area. He counsels and even houses many kids at a church and in the process has saved many children.

Yesterday, along with Justin Langer and John Buchanan, I entered the filthy alleyways that make up this terrible part of the city. We soon found ourselves being introduced to a collection of kids that quickly doubled in number, from around 40 to 80, when word got about that we were in town. The three of us chatted to the children for around 10 minutes, about the value of education and chasing dreams, trying to reinforce the messages their hockey champion has offered them. The setting, however, was not exactly comforting, as we were gathered outside the barbaric 'cages' where these kids' mothers seek their income to survive another day before the ravages of AIDS catch up with them.

Broad Horizons

Before we embarked on this tour, I'd hoped we had a squad prepared to accept and embrace the traditions and cultures of this unique country. Thankfully, this has been the case. Every player has enjoyed the tour enormously, and never before in my time have we experienced and appreciated touring life more than now. A happy and contented group will come from a busy and inquisitive mindset, while a negative, downbeat group emanates from idle minds.

India has a lot to offer if one bothers to open one's senses, with smell, touch, sight and hearing being bombarded every second of the day.

Take Justin Langer, who is always keen for adventure or a chance to broaden his horizons. Each day, at the CCI ground in Mumbai, on his way home, he distributes cakes, biscuits, drinks and fruit to the street kids, who, of course, now adore him. They were there again this evening, eagerly awaiting their precious cargo. In return, Lang got his smiles and even flowers as a show of thanks.

Colin Miller probably went further away from the norm of touring life when he took up an offer to spend half a day in a fishing village, not too far from our base in Mumbai, the opulent Taj Hotel. Funky met many people from that village, and learnt, for example, that each fisherman must pay 30,000 rupees for a plot of water 30 metres by 30 metres. This is very expensive when you consider they receive 250 rupees per kilo of fish caught.

But despite their terribly difficult way of life, Funky could not help but be moved by the friendliness and love in that community.

Right: The beggar at the bottom of this photograph was sitting in this exact same spot when I visited the Washing Sheds during my last visit to Mumbai.

Left: Meeting the street children of the red light district in Mumbai. Sadly, most, if not all, of these kids are heading for a life of trouble, suffering and exploitation. I was grateful to have the chance to speak to them.

The amazing thing with these kids is that they are the same as kids anywhere — short on concentration, mischievous, desperate for attention and craving affection. They all want a chance. I lost count of the number of boys who told me how desperate they were to play cricket for their country, while most of the girls, it seems, dream of nursing. One wants to be a doctor. By the time we'd finished our short talk, a crowd of 200 or more had congregated, all wanting autographs of Mr Langer and Mr Wog.

They were a terrific group, but it was in many ways a hollow experience to witness how excited they were to see us, yet hear how unexciting and grim their lives and prospects actually are. It was gratifying to be told that we'd made a positive impact, but we knew too that as soon as we walked away it was back to reality for them. In all probability, they and their families were already being treated like trash by a pimp while we were returning to the luxury of the Taj Hotel.

There are so many children in this country who will never get the chance to discover how good life can be.

I was still thinking about the plight of those kids in the evening, when I attended a function at the Cricket Club of India. I was pleasantly surprised, during the evening, to be informed that they were granting me an honorary life membership, and stunned to learn that the only other Australian to have been granted such status within the CCI was Sir Donald Bradman.

This honour means that I can continue my association with India after my playing days are over, and that there is always a place for me to return to in this cricket-loving country. The evening was marked by tributes to Sir Donald from the cricket writers, Mike Coward and Peter Roebuck, and the CCI President Raj Singh Dungarpur.

Apart from this function it was a day off for the Australians, and I took the opportunity to walk the streets and alleys of Mumbai. You cannot appreciate the extent of interest in cricket here unless you go out among the people. Everybody knew the result of the first Test and seemed happy to see us. Cricket is popular in Australia, but I don't think it is followed as closely as it is here. We went to a couple of markets, before heading for the Dhobi Talla. This was the first time I had seen a wash area here and as usual it was great to meet a few of the children who work there. Children are the same the world over; I love the way they smile even though they were being asked to work very hard.

We're now on our way to Delhi, to play a three-day match against an Indian Board President's XI, before heading to Calcutta for the second Test. Newspaper reports suggest that Sourav Ganguly will be playing in Delhi, which I think is a smart move because he did not make many in Mumbai. His confidence must be down and a good knock in Delhi ahead of the Calcutta Test would do him a world of good. For our part, we'll be trying to reduce his confidence still further.

RAY PHILLIPS

The next Test will be crucial for the Indian captain. Among other things, he will be playing in front of his home crowd, which should help him, though it might actually add to his headaches if things don't go his way. Ganguly is a good player, however, and I'm sure he knows how to rectify the mistakes he made in the first Test.

We thought we were pretty special when we established a new world record with consecutive Test win No. 16, but that was before we were confronted with this amazing if grotesque sight. According to the Guinness Book of World Records *these are the world's longest fingernails, cultivated through 50 years of love and attention. Here again was proof that India is a place where anything goes and anything is possible.*

The sweet innocence of youth. An eight-year-old girl with dreams of a bright future. Life is tough at the moment, though, as she works each day at Mumbai's washing sheds.

She works with a smile, even though there are plenty of chemicals in the water and many long hours ahead. It's a job and a way she can help her family.

Above: Time off. *The workers find an alleyway where they can relax for a moment. The colours and smells certainly liven up the senses when you walk around these washing sheds.*
Below: Other than these brief breaks, it's just about non-stop work. Little wonder that every person I saw was thin but muscular. The bleach and the dirt have combined to turn the water that shade of grey.

Right: Many generations of the same family live and work together at the washing sheds.

Left: As well as washing there is also ironing to be done. These antique instruments are filled with coal and heated to extremely high temperatures before they are used. I reckon these lads deserve a lunch break, especially considering the dungeon-like conditions in which they work.

Right: The view looking down on the sheds shows a hive of activity.

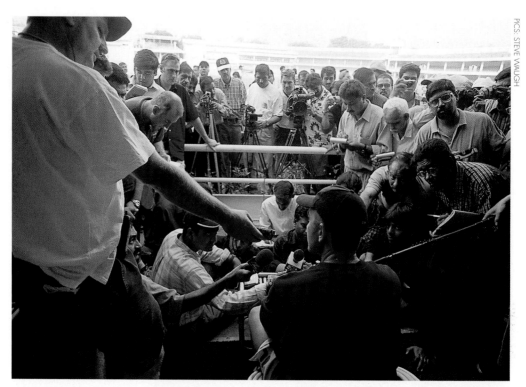

Above: Media coverage of our time in India was unrelenting. Players want to be open and helpful, but there is always a fear that a response might be twisted or misinterpreted if it is not expressed perfectly. Below: Matthew Hayden chills out in the Mumbai change-rooms soon after he was dismissed for 119 in the first Test.

Above: From my hotel window in Mumbai, I could see the Gateway to India (left) and part of the luxurious Taj Hotel.

Below: Elsewhere at the Taj, a little renovating was going on. I'm not sure I'd be as keen as this bloke to rely on the bamboo scaffolding.

Above: The infamous 'cages' in the red-light area of Mumbai, seen from my vantage point in the back seat of our car.

Below: Soon after, we stepped out to meet some of the children of the street prostitutes. The media cameras were an intrusion on our time there, but the smiles and optimism of the kids made the excursion worthwhile.

Celebrations on day one of the Test series, after Indian opener SS Das was caught Hayden bowled Gillespie. The excited Aussies are (left to right): Ricky Ponting, Michael Slater, Matthew Hayden, me (with my back to the camera), Justin Langer, Adam Gilchrist, Jason Gillespie and Shane Warne (obscured behind Dizzy).

Above left: Australia has just won the first Test by 10 wickets, to the immense joy of Matty Hayden.
Above right: Adam Gilchrist sweeps successfully against the spin during his fantastic, match-winning 122 on the second day of the first Test.

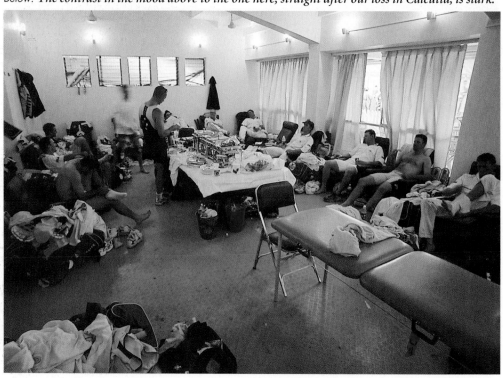

Above: John Wright, the former New Zealand Test opener and now India coach (standing near the television, to Matthew Hayden's right), was a welcome visitor to our dressing-room after our emphatic win in the first Test.
Below: The contrast in the mood above to the one here, straight after our loss in Calcutta, is stark.

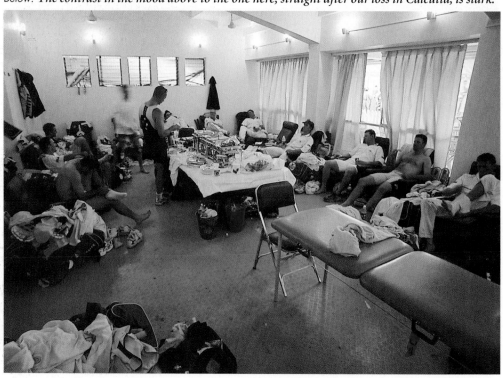

March 10 *Calcutta*

At Delhi, March 6–8

Australians 451 (SR Waugh 109, RT Ponting 102, ME Waugh 62) and 7–461 (ME Waugh 164, RT Ponting 102*, DR Martyn 54; Sarandeep Singh 5–114, ND Hirwani 5–168) drew with Indian Board President's XI 221 (D Mongia 66; MS Kasprowicz 3–68)

FOR ME, THERE IS ALWAYS something special about coming back to Calcutta, for it is here that the Udayan children's home that I have the good fortune to be heavily involved in is based. Udayan is a charity that sets out to support the children of leprosy sufferers and kids who carry disease. After successfully raising funds in the past three years that enabled Udayan to add a 'wing' that accommodated 50 girls at an existing rehabilitation centre, on this trip we are to announce plans to develop a separate rehabilitation centre for 200 more youngsters.

The impact we've made to date was amply demonstrated by the fact that we made the front page of the *Asian Age* newspaper.

When I first became involved, Udayan was concentrating its efforts on boys, so I took a different tack and tried to give girls a chance. There were 250 boys in the Udayan home then. The new centre will be for girls aged between six and 18 whose lives are affected by leprosy. The intention is to offer these kids rehabilitation, education and a chance to make something of their lives. My role is threefold — to assist in fundraising, to promote the existence of Udayan and also to publicise the message that leprosy is not a contagious disease and can be cured. There is no need to shun leprosy sufferers, nor is there any reason for the disease to carry the stigma it has worn for too long.

On my first journey to the decrepit colony in Calcutta where leprosy sufferers are confined, in 1998 after we'd been thrashed by an innings and plenty in the second Test, I had gone on my own. This time I was joined by Mark Waugh (who sponsors a child at the home), Justin Langer, reserve keeper Brad Haddin and coach John Buchanan, who all looked over the existing facilities at the rehab centre and learnt a little of our plans for the future.

The Bodyguards

A tour to the Subcontinent wouldn't be the same without the team being accompanied by the enormous entourage of security, carrying weapons ranging from hand weapons to machine guns. While in Calcutta, we have been escorted around by the elite Black Cat commandos, who are the same as the SAS back home, and carry quite a bit of clout around the place.

On top of this, the Calcutta Police have designated two bodyguards for me. These guys have looked after me before on my trips back here for Udayan. They certainly mean well, but it all becomes a bit too much when they follow you back to your room, and wait for you to tell them it's okay and that you can manage to turn the lights on by yourself. It's like being Whitney Houston with two Kevin Costners by your side the whole time.

Lang was in his element, in among it and chatting with the kids, holding hands, always smiling, showing them their photographs on his digital camera.

The development of the kids and their surrounds in the year since I have last been here has been remarkable. Not so long ago they were growing up in leper colonies with no direction and awful living standards. Today, they are well behaved and developing their talents in a number of fields, including music. You should have seen and heard some of the girls on the violin! It was remarkable, especially considering they had only started learning a few months ago.

The first time I came here I didn't know what sort of difference I was going to make, but I did know that I wanted to try. Today, it's enormously satisfying to see that something tangible has grown from our efforts and that better still is yet to come. On a personal level, I have certainly benefited from being involved. Seeing children's lives improve and knowing you played a small part in that improvement is a wonderful thing. Cricket is one of my priorities, family another; this is a third.

Cricket-wise, I've come to Calcutta with mixed memories of my past games at Eden Gardens, the Lord's of the Indian Subcontinent. The foremost among these recollections is our World Cup victory in 1987. Almost 14 years have gone by since then, but I will never forget how 95,000 people cheered us on in the final against England. We had been experiencing a lean time in the mid-eighties and had come to the tournament as underdogs, so inevitably the victory instilled enormous confidence and self-belief in the side and represented a significant moment for Australian cricket. That was terrific, but in contrast, in 1998 we were completely outplayed.

There are a few changes in the personnel in the team between then and now (though with Glenn McGrath here this time and Shane Warne fully fit we have a more potent attack), but there has been a significant change in attitude. As a group, we have decided to enjoy our trip to India by adopting a broad-minded approach. We have tried to move out of our hotel rooms and embrace the culture and meet the people at various venues.

While we are one up in the series, the pitch here looks flat and seems ideally suited to the Indians' style of batting. My feeling is that

STEVE WAUGH

John Buchanan sits beneath a recently unveiled photograph of The Don in the dressing-room in New Delhi, but at this moment Buck's main concern is the amount of food on his plate.

STEVE WAUGH

Cricketers are well known for their superstitious minds, but Lang and I probably have the strangest of the lot. Before the one-off Test against Zimbabwe in Harare in 1999 we visited an animal orphanage and were unceremoniously urinated on by the only lion on show. Looking to turn this rather embarrassing incident into something resembling a positive, we decided to agree that this was a good-luck charm rather than the worst smelling aftershave ever worn. Believe it or not, quite a few of the lads took a journey to Calcutta Zoo two days before the Test and yes, you guessed it, we were again in the firing line. Not as thoroughly as before, but enough to put us in the same class as Pepe le Peu. But again, it worked, as Lang bagged a fifty and I secured the double with another century. As fate would have it, I scored an unbeaten 151 in the Test and Lang made 44, but more importantly for him it was the start of a wonderful summer of run-scoring.

the game will go into the fifth day, and while the pitch will progressively take spin, it will be a good batting wicket throughout.

Questions have been raised about the form of one or two of our batsmen, most specifically Ricky Ponting and Michael Slater, but I think people can worry too much just because a player has failed once or twice. Punter certainly put his critics on the back foot by hitting a hundred in each innings of our drawn match in Delhi, where Mark Waugh also batted superbly. Slats, who scored only 19 and 26 in that match, did have one frustratingly bad outing in the first innings of the Test at Mumbai, but I have full faith in his ability. I firmly believe that once you choose a player, you should continue to believe he is the best until someone better comes along. Some teams complicate things by constantly chopping and changing. I don't think there is any point in altering a side unless you are sure that you are improving the side. One of the reasons for Australia's successes is the amount of faith we put in our players. If a player constantly feels that he could be playing his last game, there is no way he can relax and play at his best.

March 15 *Calcutta*

Australia 445 (ML Hayden 97, MJ
Slater 42, JL Langer 58, SR Waugh
110, JN Gillespie 46; Harbhajan
Singh 7–123) and 212 (ML Hayden
67, MJ Slater 43; Harbhajan Singh
6–73, SR Tendulkar 3–31) lost to
India 171 (VVS Laxman 59;
GD McGrath 4–18) and 7–657
(declared; VVS Laxman 281,
SC Ganguly 48, R Dravid 180;
GD McGrath 3–103) by 171 runs

WHAT THE CROWDS AT EDEN Gardens just saw was a fantastic game of cricket. In the history of Test cricket prior to this match, only two teams had come back after being forced to follow on to win a Test. Now there are three. I've been involved in a few fluctuating Tests, such as the remarkable one in Barbados in 1999, but there's no doubt that the turnaround in this match was the most extraordinary of them all.

And it wasn't just a game of one reversal in fortune. Take day one — after we won the toss, Michael Slater, Matthew Hayden and Justin Langer took us to 1–193, when Haydos was caught in the deep for a superb 97. It seemed we were set for a huge total, but 25 overs later we were 8–269. In one deadly 25-minute spell Harbhajan Singh spun out Mark Waugh, Ricky Ponting, Adam Gilchrist and Shane Warne. The latter two fell for first-ball ducks, as Harbhajan became the first Indian to take a Test-match hat-trick. The crowd, which had been vibrant and involved at the start but quiet as our early batsmen dominated, went home loud and happy.

On the second day, which started with the Indians keen to quickly snare the last two wickets, Jason Gillespie and I managed to add 133 for the ninth wicket, I went past three figures for the first time in a Test in India, Glenn McGrath hit a polished 21 not out (guiding me through the 90s once again!) and we took our first innings total past 400. And then Pigeon and Dizzy spearheaded an assault on the Indian batting that reduced them to 8–128 by stumps. The fans fell from delighted to despairing in a few short hours; I've rarely heard silence quite so silent as when Tendulkar was given out lbw McGrath for 10.

For us, it was almost the perfect day of Test-match cricket. Our collective will and hunger for victory reached a new level. We were 'on fire', nothing seemed out of reach, blinding catches were taken, bowling changes and field placements came off at the right time and the togetherness of the team was breathtaking.

On day three, which started with us eager to wrap up the innings, VVS Laxman kept the Indian innings going for 12 more overs and 43 more runs before we were finally able to enforce the follow on. Of course, it will be Laxman's second innings that is remembered forever, but he played extremely well in the first innings as well. After that knock, he was moved up the order to No. 3 and responded with one of cricket's great innings, a stirring 281 that covered a fair part of day three, all of day four, and a bit of day five for good measure. His innings was exceptional, the highest score by an Indian in Test cricket, and succinctly demonstrated how Test cricket can inspire incredible personal performances. This was a knock that compares favourably with the classic, unbeaten, match-winning 153 that Brian Lara made against us in that Test two years back in Bridgetown. Of all the special ingredients that made up Laxman's masterpiece, the one that stood out most for me was the way he scored his runs so rapidly, despite the fact his team was following on

Top: The Indian players have just received the news from the third umpire that Shane Warne is out, which means Harbhajan Singh (third from left) has become the first Indian to complete a Test-match hat-trick.

Right: Jason Gillespie has a batting technique that wouldn't be out of place much higher up the batting order.

Below: The wicket of Sourav Ganguly was always cause for celebration. Here Michael Kasprowicz (third from left) has dismissed the Indian captain, caught by yours truly for 23.

The fact that I made this hundred in Calcutta, where I've had the good fortune to work with the people at Udayan and where the fans are so knowledgeable and supportive of good cricket, made this a special occasion.

and he was under some pressure to make a decent score.

Laxman received strong support from Rahul Dravid, who batted with him throughout the fourth day and into the fifth, adding 376 for the fifth wicket. Dravid was finally out for 180. In a sense, the importance of Laxman's knock was reflected in the way Dravid batted. Laxman showed his colleagues that you can only succeed at the highest level if you believe in your ability. Dravid was smart enough to learn this lesson, and was a much more fluent and effective batsman once he did.

I know that many observers are now questioning the wisdom of our decision to make the Indians follow on, but I have no regrets on that score. Ninety-nine times out of 100 I would have done the same thing. We were 274 runs ahead, and India had failed in their last nine innings against us. Our bowlers had sent down only 58.1 overs in India's first innings. It was the aggressive move, in keeping with the way we've played our cricket over the past two years. And when their key batsman, Sachin Tendulkar, was out to reduce the home team to 3–115 in the second innings, I thought we were in with more than a reasonable chance. But we didn't count on the heroics of Laxman and Dravid. By the time Sourav Ganguly declared, we needed 384 to win and the chance to add to our 16-Test winning streak was gone. Rather than condemning the follow-on decision, I think the critics should be acclaiming the skill and gallantry of Laxman and Dravid.

Teams rarely make over 300 in the fourth innings to win a Test match. Once the Indian advantage went over that mark I knew our chances of winning had all but disappeared, which is why I deliberately tried to slow the Indian run-rate down late on the fourth day, in order to delay Ganguly's declaration and leave us less time to have to bat the final day and earn a draw.

Along with the questioning of the follow-on decision, we are also now being criticised for going into the Test with a third quick, Michael Kasprowicz, instead of a second spinner, Colin Miller. Hindsight is a wonderful thing. We included Kasper because we believe that in most circumstances the best way to break down the Indian batting line-up is to let our pace bowlers have a go at them. Here in Calcutta, we had a feeling that Kasper's ability to swing the ball in these conditions would prove useful, which is exactly what happened in the first innings. Kasper also has the ability to get the ball to go 'Irish', and this pitch, with its dryness and lack of grass, appeared certain to aid this ability. Our faith in pace worked to our advantage in Mumbai and again in the first innings here. It was finally thwarted by Dravid and especially Laxman.

Moreover, I'm not convinced the extra spinner would have had the impact many are suggesting. The only spinner who did really well on this pitch was Harbhajan Singh, who performed magnificently and did major damage in both innings. None of the others got much from the wicket until Tendulkar turned a few dramatically near the end. I thought the pitch was fine, typical of the wickets you get in this part of the world.

Harbhajan's hat-trick, which I witnessed from the non-striker's end, was more than a little bizarre. Ricky Ponting, his first victim, was as plumb in front as you're ever likely to see, but the next two dismissals were dubious to say the least. First, Gilly went from the penthouse to the outhouse thanks to a ball that not only pitched outside leg stump but collected a bit of bat on the way through to striking his pad. He was adjudged lbw.

Then Shane Warne lasted just as long, and was probably even more unfortunate to be a part of history.

There was uncertainty out of the field as to whether Warney had been caught at short leg from a bump ball. The ump on the field called for the third umpire, which was against the rules, because the video umpire cannot make a call on bump balls, only on whether a catch has or has not been taken. In this instance the catch had clearly been taken, so the official on the field was required to make a call. He, clearly, was in doubt (otherwise he wouldn't have gone to the third umpire), which meant he had to give the benefit of that doubt to the batsman. Instead, he explained to me why he called for the replay: 'I couldn't see the short leg fielder because you were in the way.' Suddenly, I had become massive in stature, because that

VVS Laxman hits another boundary during his extraordinary 281.

was the only way I could have blocked his view! So Warney was gone, as the third umpire quickly ruled that the catch had been completed.

We knew that our victory streak would have to come to an end sooner or later. Now, having suffered a defeat, we need to learn from our mistakes and gain some positives out of the match. This said, I don't think there is much point in over-analysing the play. It's not as if we were unprepared for Laxman; we knew he was an outstanding talent and we thought we knew where to bowl to him. However, to his great credit, he countered our game plan so now we have to go back to the drawing board. And we've only got a couple of days to do so.

Of course, losing is not a good thing. Never is. But at the same time, it's not the end of the world. Cricket does not always fulfil your aspirations. And life goes on. We cannot expect to save a Test match when we bat as poorly as we did today. Our worst failing, I thought, was our inability to adjust to the conditions that confronted us. There was a great challenge out there, facing Harbhajan on a turning wicket with the crowd baying for blood and the fieldsmen crowding eagerly around the bat, but on the day we weren't up to it. Why this was so, I'm not sure. If you look at some of the results during our 16-match winning streak, we've handled the pressure of chasing a total pretty well, most notably in Hobart against Pakistan and then twice versus New Zealand, in Wellington and Hamilton, but this 17th Test did not go well for us. One setback, however, does not mean that the guys have stopped talking to one another, and we remain positive we can win this series.

Sign Language

Not only have Jason Gillespie and Glenn McGrath been exceptional on this tour with their heroic efforts on the field, they have also managed to further enhance their *Dumb and Dumber* status. Straight out of the Harry Dunn (Dizzy) and Lloyd Christmas (Pigeon) characters, or at least something they would have been proud of, comes the following story . . .

Before the Calcutta Test, it was practice as usual for the boys, with McGrath keen to enhance his growing reputation with the willow. As he waited to go into his net, Pigeon looked down and noticed that Dizzy had kindly decorated his pads and gloves with a couple of sizeable and strategically placed autographs. Worse still, Pigeon was doubly shocked to find his one and only bat sporting a lovely new hand-engraved signature on the back, to complete the set.

Glenn McGrath is never outdone in these schoolyard battles, and he quickly caught his buddy out in the Test match. Many times during the partnership I shared with Jason on the second day, our gloves became slippery and needed changing. Dizzy always concentrates fiercely when he's at the crease, but this time he lost not only his focus but nearly his wicket as well when he peered down to see two lovely and not insignificant Glenn McGrath signatures on each glove.

Once Dizzy settled down, the incident probably helped both of us, as we had a good chuckle in between the overs during what was an intense period of cricket.

Laxman and Dravid leave the Eden Gardens arena, having batted throughout the fourth day's play.

I'd have liked my century to have contributed to a victory, but it was not to be. But at least I achieved my personal ambition to score a ton in India. If I had to choose a city to manage this feat it would definitely have been Calcutta, a city I love, and if I had to choose a ground it would have been the Eden Gardens, one of the game's most hallowed grounds. You have to earn the support of the crowd at the Eden. When you walk out to bat as an opposition player the atmosphere is hostile, but as you move towards three figures that animosity gradually evolves into a genuine appreciation for your play. And, to make the innings even more important to me, there are the little children in Udayan who live here and make this city a special place for me. I was pretty animated when I reached three figures, which reflected how satisfied I was with my effort and how I thought the knock had put us in a position to dominate the Test.

When I went out to bat, we were travelling along well, and I didn't feel much pressure. But then wickets started to fall and the grind began. Someone in the press conference after my hundred called me a 'crisis man', but I'm not sure if that's right — I've failed in pressure situations often enough. Take the second innings here, for example! However, I do think that, as I've become more experienced, a crisis often brings out the best in me.

Dizzy batted brilliantly for his 46 in the first innings. I've been criticised once or twice for giving tailenders too much of the strike in these situations, but I have faith in them, and Dizzy and Pigeon both came through today. I've seen our lower-order batsmen in the nets, working on their batting, preparing for these types of circumstances, and know that they deserve my support and confidence. Mind you, as we went out to bat, it was Dizzy who was encouraging me. 'Don't worry about me, Tugga,' he said, 'just play your normal game.'

It's funny when I think back to that second day. As I said, it was a day when we batted well, bowled very well on a docile track and, above all, we took some exceptional catches. There was a not a single aspect of the game where we failed to deliver. That was a day of cricket which I had been waiting for. Yet here we are, three days later, bemoaning our fate.

If there is one thing I regret about the match it is that I did not reinforce how we should bat to draw the match. On the last morning, during our get-together before warm-ups, I told the lads, 'If we are forced into fighting for a draw, let's do everything we can to do it. If that means not scoring or letting a long hop go through to the keeper then we must do it.'

We had lost only three wickets at tea on that final day, but needed an impossible 223 to win. I should have gone over this plan again during the interval, to make sure that everyone was clear as to what we needed to do. Obviously it wasn't clear to at least some of us, because four guys got out sweeping, and in the end it was only some discipline from Kasper and Pigeon that nearly saved us. Hindsight can be such a frustrating thing, but next time we are in a similar situation I guarantee no one will be under any illusions as to how we are going to play.

In all likelihood, this was my last game at the Eden Gardens — almost certainly my last Test — and while I would like to have signed off on a winning note, I'll always cherish the experience of scoring a Test century here. The memory of it would have been much sweeter, however, if we had gone on to win the Test, and the series.

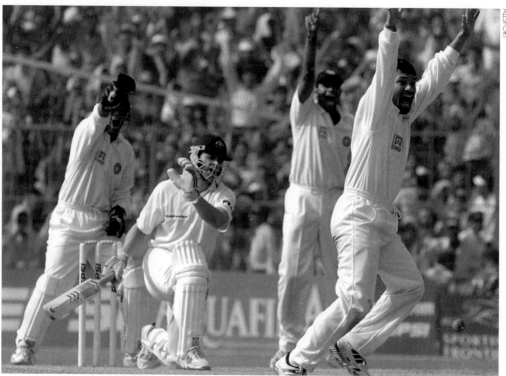

Sachin Tendulkar traps Adam Gilchrist lbw on the final afternoon, as we slide to our first loss in 19 Tests.

March 17 *Chennai*

ONE UNFORTUNATE SEQUEL TO OUR second Test defeat was the minor storm our coach John Buchanan created with his public comments about Shane Warne, and most specifically about Warney's fitness, his ability to handle the oppressive conditions in India and his future in the team. Just because we've lost one Test, I don't think there's any need to panic, but I guess some people reading Buck's remarks could have come to the conclusion that we are planning some major changes to our line-up, even that there are rifts in the camp.

As I explained to the media, Warney has been affected by the coach's remarks. He's a bit down, having read opinions in the paper that he would rather have had kept within the confines of the team set-up. It couldn't have done Shane any good and it hasn't, but I'm sure he'll bounce back. As for Buck, we all learn by our mistakes and I'm sure he'll learn from this experience. I have no problems with him having strong opinions and I recognise absolutely his right to express them, but this wasn't the right forum.

Shane Warne (left) and John Buchanan at training in Chennai.

Something we tend to forget is that Buck is a relative newcomer to international cricket. Statements made about superstars such as Warney have a completely different impact from a rev-up of a player in domestic cricket. Buck has found out the tough way and will be better for having gone through this episode. We also shouldn't forget that he's human. This is Buck's first mistake in what has been a truly outstanding first 18 months as the national coach, and as such we should all be man enough to move on. I got the three of us to talk the issue through, which — to both guys' credit — went well. The job of winning the third Test is again our main focus.

Having seen the pitch, I can tell you that it is hard, dry and has no grass, which is not unexpected. It will be a good pitch to bat on for at least the first two days, and has us leaning very strongly towards playing Colin Miller as a second spinner, instead of just one spinner and three quicks as we've done in the first two Tests. I think Warney will enjoy the chance to bowl in tandem with Funky, and I reckon we'll also benefit from the fact that the Indians have not faced the offie before in this series. Funky could easily end up having a major influence on this Test.

Colin Miller, who came into the Australian XI for the third Test, receives some advice from a famous name in Indian cricket — Bishan Bedi, the great left-arm spinner of the 1960s and '70s.

Despite our batting struggles in Calcutta, I'm sure we'll go in with the same top six. As good as Damien Martyn is, I think it would be very hard on him to bring him into the side now when he hasn't played much cricket on turning wickets in recent weeks. I believe now is a time to show faith in the men who have made the team so successful in the past 18 months. They deserve that.

The Test series is still up for grabs and we still think we're good enough to win it, but it's going to take a huge effort. I'm sure we'll learn a lot about ourselves from our performance over the next five days.

Third Test, at Chennai, March 18–22, 2001

Australia 391 (ML Hayden 203, ME Waugh 70, SR Waugh 47; Harbhajan Singh 7–133) and 264 (ME Waugh 57, MJ Slater 48, SR Waugh 47; Harbhajan Singh 8–84) lost to India 501 (SR Tendulkar 126, SS Das 84, S Ramesh 61, VVS Laxman 65, R Dravid 81; GD McGrath 3–75, CR Miller 3–160) and 8–155 (VVS Laxman 66; CR Miller 3–41, GD McGrath 2–21, JN Gillespie 2–49) by two wickets

March 23 *Chennai*

IT HAS BEEN AN INCREDIBLE two weeks of cricket, and sadly at the end of that time we have nothing to show for it, bar the knowledge that we've been a part of something special. All of us are physically and mentally drained after the twists, turns and turning pitches of the past two Tests — back-to-back five-day matches that involved some extraordinarily tough, competitive, passionate cricket. I am obviously very disappointed that we didn't win, but I'm certainly not unhappy with the side. I'm proud of the fact that we kept going until the very end and put 100 per cent into our pursuit of victory. The total and utter commitment of the players was outstanding.

At the end of the second day of the third Test, when India were 1–211 in reply to our first-innings 391, I commented to the lads during our warm-up that we would still be in with a chance if we could set our hosts a victory target of around 150 on the last day. When day five did come, and India needed 155 to win, I did think we could win, but I wished we had another 20 or 30 runs at our disposal so we could have attacked the Indian batsmen a little more. As it turned out, thanks to the stirring efforts of McGrath, Gillespie and Miller, 155 was almost enough.

The atmosphere on that final day was as tense as anything I've witnessed during my career. The fans so wanted their team to prevail, while we were determined to make it as hard for the Indian batsmen as possible. It seemed, during that thrilling climax, that most of the Indians were thinking more about victory than scoring. This is why we kept getting wickets at regular intervals. VVS Laxman was the only exception, looking nice and relaxed throughout his innings, and in the end he was responsible for India's successful run-chase, when the more illustrious players around him felt the pressure of victory too much.

Of course, India would have been chasing plenty more had it not been for the amazing exploits of Harbhajan Singh. His figures through this series are astonishing, and right from the moment he took that hat-trick back in Calcutta he has been a key figure in this series. His variety and guile had our batsmen guessing every time we faced him, and it was remarkable the way he found turn and bounce from pitches that refused to help the other spinners in anything like the same way.

A lot has been said about how the Australians were unable to read Harbhajan's straighter ball, but I think it was his subtle changes in line and pace that made things difficult for us. Here in Chennai he made us play out of the rough consistently, which proved decisive. In contrast, Shane Warne wasn't as effective. Things did not go Warney's way as the Indians, especially Laxman, attacked him whenever he came on to bowl. These guys don't overly worry about spin bowling, probably because they've been raised on it. Not only do they seem comfortable facing Warney, they are happy to attack him like no other team ever has. Hitting against the turning ball when it pitches in the rough outside leg stump is normally not a safe way to play Shane, but these guys showed enormous skill and courage to do just that. Once they'd established that they could counter the turning ball in this way, Warney had lost one of his major strike weapons and the Indians had broken a huge psychological barrier. It was now a level playing field and the Indians sensed this, thus ensuring a mentally and physically demanding couple of Test matches for Shane.

Throughout the series, even when they lost in Mumbai, the Indians had a tougher edge to them than they have when they play away from home. There is certainly a great difference between Ganguly's current team and the side that toured Australia a little over a year ago. This Indian combination is prepared to back themselves, and seem better organised than any of the Indian teams I have played against in the past. Their new steeliness helped them overcome difficult circumstances during this Test series and, crucially, they made a habit of winning the vital moments in the series. This is why they won.

Positives have emerged for both sides during the series and none more so for us than Matthew Hayden's imposing form. He had been on the bench for quite some time, so his success is proof that, if you want something badly enough and you're prepared to work hard enough, then you can achieve your ambition. He was our most successful player by far and never failed right through the series. Bowling-wise, I was thrilled with the brave efforts of Jason Gillespie and the continued excellence of Glenn McGrath.

On the Indian side, it's hard to work out whether the stunning rise of Laxman or Harbhajan is their biggest plus. Both were superstars in the final two Tests. Laxman's epic innings in Calcutta lifted the rest of his side and showed them that they could play positively against our team. I can't stress this point too much: until Laxman took us on, I don't think India believed that they could get runs against us. In their previous nine innings against Australia they never put up a big total and they were in trouble again in that second innings in Calcutta at 3–115, 159 runs behind after following on. Had Laxman wilted at that moment, I have no doubt we would have won the series 3–0. Intriguingly, our batsmen always scored off Harbhajan when he first came on to bowl, but then he'd come back to produce some lethal spells. He took an enormous number of wickets, significantly in batches, and in a way made the absence of Anil Kumble seem like a blessing in disguise. Who knows, if Kumble had been fit, Harbhajan may not have even played. Instead, he bowled beautifully, with an excellent line, always on a length and always getting bounce through his unusual, high delivery.

There is no doubt that India deserved to win this series, especially after the way they fought back in Calcutta. It was a wonderful achievement, as was their effort to bounce back here after we reached 3–326 by the end of the first day's play.

I was proud of the spirit and persistence we showed on the dramatic final day of the third Test, as we strove to dismiss the Indians for less than 155 to win the series. When I caught Rahul Dravid off the bowling of Colin Miller (above), I really thought we had a chance.

If it wasn't enough for Harbhajan Singh to take 32 wickets in the three-Test series, he also hit the winning runs in the third Test. Here Harbhajan (centre) and Sameer Dighe go back for the second run, off the magnificent Glenn McGrath's bowling, to win the match by two wickets and the series 2–1.

When I'd first approached our dressing-room here in Chennai, I couldn't help but turn the clock back to the famous Tied Test of 1986 and recall Dean Jones' legendary double hundred. Walking into the rooms I tested the memory bank and visualised where Jonesy had sat in the breaks in play during his epic innings.

Not surprisingly, many images flashed back, such as having to change his clothes for him during a tea interval. Cricketers can be a superstitious lot, and I'm no different, so before anyone else could grab it I dashed for his spot, hoping there might be some magic left in it for me. And there certainly was some history still remaining, but not the kind I'd had in mind when I plonked my gear down where the Jones boy once had . . .

There were a few defining moments in the series, and I think my handling the ball on the second morning here was one of them. Only five batsmen before me had been dismissed in this manner in a Test match. It was a peculiar incident: I went to sweep, but missed, the ball flew out of my sight and, as I looked up at the umpire to see his reaction to an lbw appeal, the ball suddenly reappeared in my vision, spinning back towards the stumps. Matty Hayden yelled down the pitch to 'look out' and I instinctively palmed the ball away before I had a chance to think. It was as if everything was in slow motion. As soon as I'd laid a glove on the ball I wanted to retract what had happened. I knew I was gone. And then, suddenly, everything was happening in very fast motion, with excited fieldsmen running towards me from all directions, the umpire's hand raised and me ruefully walking off. I was desperately unhappy with myself for being so unprofessional and so dumb to have got out that way.

I don't think there's a lot for me to learn from the dismissal; it was a freak incident akin to what happened to Sachin Tendulkar in Mumbai, when Ricky Ponting caught him after Sachin slammed a pull shot into Justin Langer at short leg.

The mood of the camp at the end of the Test was one of enormous disappointment. We're feeling pretty hollow, after coming so close to our dream. Most of all, we're exhausted, utterly knackered. But there's a feeling of contentment, too, because we know we gave it everything. We were in a position to win all three Tests. That might not have happened, but we did get a lot closer to a series win than most Australian sides touring India have done. So now we're reflecting on the fact that there is often only a very fine, cruel line between victory and defeat.

The stark contrast in the faces of keeper and batsman confirm that I'm about to become the sixth batsman to be given out handled the ball in a Test match.

Left: Lang faces up to the children of Udayan on their treacherous pitch, with plenty of close-in catchers ready to enjoy their moment of fame.

Below: I'm lucky to be able to help residents of Nivedita House, Udayan, such as this young girl, and so proud to be backing such a worthy project.

Above: After Lang, I had my turn at the wicket, and had no alternative but to go over the top.

Right: Our visit to Udayan coincided with the traditional day of Holi, and I was happy to join in the festivities.

PICS: ALLSPORT

Left: An off-drive during my century in Calcutta, one of the most satisfying knocks I've ever played.

Right: After stumps on day two of the second Test, the press photographers were keen for some happy snaps of the new holders of the ninth-wicket partnership record for Australia v India Tests.

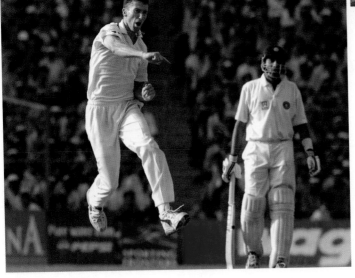

Left: Glenn McGrath has just taken the wicket of Sourav Ganguly on day three of the second Test. No one could have imagined that we wouldn't take another wicket until the fifth morning.

Above: The big scoreboard in Calcutta tells the story. The previous record was 236, made by the great Sunil Gavaskar against the West Indies in Madras in December 1983.
Below: Harbhajan Singh traps Glenn McGrath lbw to end the second Test, setting off huge celebrations across the country. India have levelled the series!

PICS: ALLSPORT

Above: Matthew Hayden, the one dominant Australian batsman of the India Tests, hits a six during his third-Test double century.

Right: Sachin Tendulkar gets Shane Warne away very fine during his crucial century in Chennai.

Below: A scene that was repeated time and again in the second and third Tests. Harbhajan Singh celebrates the fall of an Australian wicket off his bowling, this time Ricky Ponting during the third Test.

Above: Fanatical crowds congregate around the team bus, all hoping for an autograph, a wave or any acknowledgement at all. Note the helmet being worn by the bloke near the front, a bit left of centre. Below: A secret weapon unveiled. Errol Alcott helps Glenn McGrath with his ice vest, which our bowlers used during the lunch and tea intervals to cool their body temperatures.

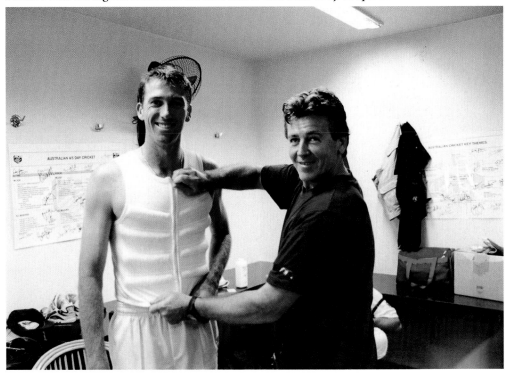

These photographs were taken at fishing village near Vizakhapatnam, or 'Vizag' as most know it, on the Indian east coast.

Left: The local fishermen are out to sea in search of a living for their families and the village, working in an old wooden vessel that is just about seaworthy.

Right: The elder gents of the village still play a part in the day's activities, passing on knowledge to their sons and grandsons.

Left: Would-be buyers at Vizag's fish markets haggle over the value of the morning's catch.

Four key members of the Australian one-day squad. Top left: *Nathan Bracken has Sachin Tendulkar caught behind in Margao.* Top right: *Ricky Ponting rediscovers his best form with a century in Vizag.* Bottom: *Ian Harvey (left) and Michael Bevan during their series-winning unbeaten partnership in Margao.*

Above: **Glenn McGrath, Justin Langer, Matthew Hayden, Colin Miller and Michael Slater at the extraordinary Taj Mahal in Agra.**

Left: Team fitness co-ordinator Jock Campbell points out the obvious.

March 30 *Indore*

THERE'S NO GETTING AWAY FROM the fact that it has been very difficult to get motivated for this one-day tournament, coming as it has so soon after such a draining Test series. You must remember that the last two Tests, both played in hot, enervating conditions in Calcutta and then Chennai, were played back-to-back, 10 days of cricket in 12 days (March 11 to March 22). Two days rest and we're playing the first one-dayer in Bangalore. We probably needed at least a week off after the Test series, and I'm only just starting to feel refreshed enough to want to go out there and play some tough international cricket. In today's cricket world, there's an enormous workload put on the players, and I'm not just talking about the physical side of things. More so these days it's the mental wear and tear that needs the most attention.

This is one of the reasons I'm so committed to the rotation system we are applying to our one-day squad. I have no qualms about making a number of changes to a team that won its last game by eight wickets, because we want all the guys to remain as sharp as possible for as long as possible. Of course, we can only do this and remain competitive in every match we play if all the members of our squad are up to international standard, and in my view this is the case with this Australian side. The past 18 months have demonstrated this. Such a

First One-Day International, at Bangalore, March 25

India 315 (49.5 overs: R Dravid 80, V Shewag 58, V Dahiya 51) defeated Australia 255 (43.3 overs: ML Hayden 99, MG Bevan 49; J Srinath 3–49, V Shewag 3–59) by 60 runs

Second One-Day International, at Pune, March 28

India 9–248 (50 overs: HK Badani 100, VVS Laxman 51) lost to Australia 2–249 (45.1 overs: ME Waugh 133*, ML Hayden 57) by eight wickets

---

The Best Medicine

Two guys who kept their spirits high throughout the Test-match leg of the tour were Matt Hayden and Justin Langer. Not only did they get and enjoy all that India has to offer in the way of culture, sights and people, they also stumbled across a very different way to start the day.

One early morning in Mumbai, Lang was woken by the sound of hysterical laughter coming from a park near the Gateway to India, not too far away from our hotel. He peered out the window to see a group of locals in a neat circle, all 'losing the plot', pointing at each other, doubled over in agony, giggling at absolutely nothing. Lang soon related this story to Haydos, and the pair had to find out what this was all about. They discovered that these people were in fact members of 'The Laughter Club'.

From that point on, my two ever-curious teammates became regular observers of this 6am phenomenon. And it certainly didn't hurt their demeanour for the testing times ahead.

Mark Waugh (centre) isn't impressed by Sourav Ganguly's argument that Mark, and not Darren Lehmann, should have been given out, run out, after a mid-pitch mix-up in the second one-day international, in Pune.

selection strategy might, in the eyes of some people, cost us the odd game from time to time, but in the long run I'm sure we'll benefit as a team. Consequently, the four players who missed the last game in Pune — Ian Harvey, Shane Lee, Ricky Ponting and Shane Warne — will definitely play here, while guys who contributed to that victory, including Glenn McGrath and Matthew Hayden, will have a game off.

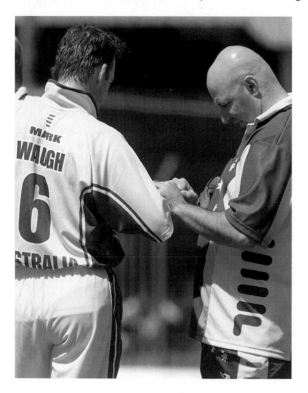

The first two one-day games ended in comfortable victories, the first to India, the second to Australia. As I said, many of us were not at our sharpest, though Matty Hayden carried on his Test-match form, scoring 99 in Bangalore and then 57 in Pune, while Mark Waugh scored a superb unbeaten 133 at nearly a run a ball to lead us to an eight-wicket success in game two. No one has bowled badly, but no one has dominated either.

Team physio Patrick Farhart examines Mark Waugh's injured finger during the second one-dayer. X-rays later confirmed a bone was broken, though most of the local doctors who examined the damaged digit were not so sure.

An issue that raised its increasingly ugly head again was the use of the video umpire. During our innings in Pune, Junior and Darren Lehmann got themselves in a tangle, which led to the two being in mid-pitch when the ball was returned to the keeper. Boof immediately walked off, but the Indians complained that because the batsmen had crossed it should have been Mark who was out. Sourav Ganguly was particularly agitated, and his mood wasn't helped when it became clear that the video replays weren't going to shed any light on the subject.

I've reached the point where I think that unless the authorities are going to put in technology that is up to the task, and able to cover every angle, then maybe we shouldn't be using the third umpire at all. At the moment, it seems to be creating more dilemmas than it's solving. At the very least, there should be more thought put into the use of the third umpire than is currently happening.

A more pressing problem for the sport is the overall standard of umpiring. In my view, it is too often not up to the required standard, such as in Game One of this one-day series, where the umpires' decisions had a major influence on the final result.

March 31 *Indore*

THE HUGE DEFEAT INDIA INFLICTED on us today at Indore had more to do with poor batting than us missing the presence of Matthew Hayden. Some commentators had questioned our decision to leave our form batsmen out of

Third One-Day International, at Indore, March 31

India 8–299 (50 overs: SR Tendulkar 139, VVS Laxman 83; GD McGrath 3–52) defeated Australia 181 (35.5 overs: AC Gilchrist 63; AB Agarkar 3–38, Harbhajan Singh 3–37) by 118 runs

Bad Timing

During previous tours to the subcontinent many players have been caught short when forgetful receptionists fail to make pre-ordered wake-up calls. To counteract the possibility of this happening, each player must now provide himself with an additional reminder via an alarm clock, phone or watch.

The only problem with the watch is that if you don't adjust it to the local time or if you have two times locked into the watch's memory, things can go very wrong.

At one point of this tour, Ricky Ponting got the shock of his life when his alarm startled him out of his slumber. A quick, dazed look at the watchface told him, to his great shock, that it was 10am. This was not good, because the team bus left for training at nine. After cursing the boys for not giving him a call, Punter raced to the bathroom, splashed cold water on his face, cleaned his teeth, gathered his clothes in a mad rush and then raced across to open the curtains to allow some light in. To his amazement, it was pitch black outside. A total eclipse of the sun was the only explanation. Or was until he rang the hotel operator and was told that it was actually 4.30 in the morning.

the starting line-up, but we were simply staying solid with our policy of rotating our squad. I know that the guys who started for us today are capable of delivering — they've showed that in the past. In the case of Damien Martyn (who moved up to open the innings with Haydos on the sidelines), many times in the past. But we fell short as a team today.

Flexibility is a word that we as a team want to be associated with. It goes hand in hand with the rotation system. While Haydos didn't play today, he wouldn't have even been on the tour if we weren't flexible — remember that he wasn't picked in the original squad of 14 for this one-day tournament.

All in all, it was a very disappointing day, right from the toss. Sourav Ganguly was late again, which didn't amuse either me or match referee Cammie Smith, and then, after the coin landed, there was a short dispute as to who had won. We were using a new two-rupee coin, and obviously it is a little difficult to distinguish between heads and tails. I was sure I'd won, but Ganguly seemed to think he'd won as well, and it took a brief chat before the matter was cleared up. All I could do was shake my head; it all seemed so unnecessary. We decided to bowl first, and the Indians strode out and belted us all over the park.

Sachin Tendulkar's century was fantastic. His clash with McGrath (who played because Nathan Bracken has the flu) was a classic, and his shot-making seemed effortless on a pitch that was not all that easy to bat on. Pigeon, for his part, was not completely outdone, taking three wickets including Sachin. But if you wanted to sum up this game in one sentence you could simply say that Sachin batted superbly while we batted poorly. Complementing the little master's performance, Harbhajan Singh once again made a significant contribution with the ball, though it did not help that a couple of our batsmen have not played him too much and were a bit unsure against him.

Adam Gilchrist takes in the unusual welcoming party at our digs in Indore.

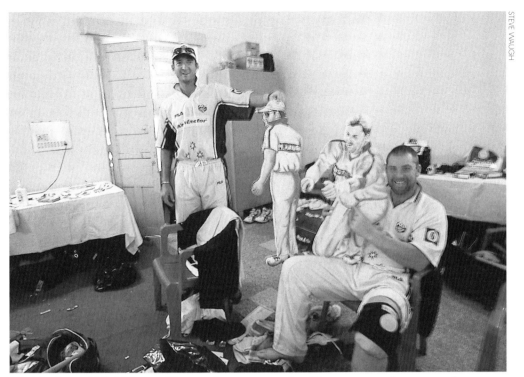

Mini-Junior and Mini-Warney. These are just two examples of foam cut-outs that were made up to resemble the Aussie players. I must admit there were times on this tour when the cut-outs might have been more useful than the real thing.

We'd lost in Bangalore after the Indians had batted excellently to score 315 from their 50 overs, and we've done pretty much the same thing here. In both cases, we put ourselves in with a chance to pull off a successful run-chase, but when you're after such a big total you need to bat well throughout the innings, not just for part of them. In that first loss, we got to 4–212 in the 36th over before falling away, and here we were 1–102 in the 20th over, with Gilly and Punter going well, before things went awry. In one ugly period we lost six wickets in eight overs, with many of the batsmen fatally going for one shot too many.

Adding to our disappointment at the loss, we've learned that Junior will be returning home early because of a fractured finger. I was most surprised, because originally I thought it was only a minor problem that would only cost him one game. But the X-ray said differently, though not at the doctors' first glance. Thankfully our physiotherapist for the one-dayers, Patrick Farhart, can read an X-ray better than the seven local medicos who had decided that there was no serious damage to or break of Mark's little finger. This was quite an astonishing assessment, as you could actually see a stray piece of bone in the X-ray, floating around where it shouldn't have been.

We'll obviously miss a player of his quality and experience, but we have players in the squad who I know will step up and take the opportunity to show off their talents. Besides, as I've said before, I believe that we can win with any team built from the players in our squad.

THE AUSTRALIANS IN INDIA 2001 **69**

April 5 *Goa*

THERE MIGHT HAVE BEEN A point, immediately after the Test series, when the idea of playing five one-dayers in a short space of time looked to be almost too big an ask. But now I'm very keen to end it with a win. This is the last game in what has been pretty much a continuous six-month run of international cricket, from the first Test against the West Indies last November to here, so it would be nice to add a loud and positive exclamation mark to that long, hard road. I've been thrilled by the way the guys have fought hard and worked hard throughout the days since the disappointing end to the Test series against India, and like all the lads, I want to take at least one series victory away from this tour. A win here, after all the psychological highs and lows we've been through, will show just how tough and professional this side is.

We will use the rotation system again for this last match, despite the continuing criticism from sections of the media. I must admit to being amazed by this debate. After all, we always pick a side we think can win the game, and surely the critics can see there are benefits to be had by giving guys a break from the constant stream of cricket. In English football, the big clubs such as Manchester United, Liverpool, Arsenal and Chelsea have responded to their ever-increasing program by doing the same thing for the last couple of years. They each play about 70 games a year. The Australian cricket teams play around 100 days of cricket, so why shouldn't we rotate?

Prized Catches

The cricket has seemed so relentless here that we have always grabbed whatever personal time might be available. Take our time in the east-coast seaside city of Vizag, when we managed to sneak in an early-morning visit to the fish markets, where, albeit very briefly, we saw the morning catch being brought in and the frenzied business transactions that followed. The first thing that hit me was the smell — with not a hint of refrigeration or block of ice in sight, the blazing sun was obviously not doing the piles of fish lying on the ground any good at all.

This was quite a sight, and it was fascinating to see the fishermen ply their trade, women haggling with great animation over prices, while others carried fish away in baskets perched upon their heads. Within 30 seconds, however, a massive crowd had gathered around us. We had suddenly become the prize catch, as the circling masses swarmed in, desperate for an autograph or a photo, and we were forced to scurry back to the seclusion of the team bus. It's nice to be recognised, but the adulation we are held in over here can lead to a total lack of privacy, to the point where you feel as if you have to escape from the constant attention.

I can guarantee you that in 12 to 18 months every other cricket team will be doing it. The sooner people successfully get their heads around the concept and realise that it is based on common sense the better.

In my view, two examples bear out the virtue of our approach. First there's the success of Nathan Bracken, who in the most recent fourth one-dayer, in Vizag, dismissed the key Indian openers, Sachin Tendulkar and Sourav Ganguly, and bothered all the right-handers with his 'angle' and bounce. He's definitely one for the future, and the selectors deserve great credit for making such an inspired choice.

And then there's Matthew Hayden. When we left him out of the third game here, there was uproar in some circles, but in Vizag, to prove that the rest hadn't done him any harm, he peeled off another glorious century. I heard Matthew himself telling reporters how grateful he was for the break, during

The toss before the fourth one-dayer, in Vizag. Why the Indian captain was dressed this way, and not in his playing attire, remains a mystery.

which he did very little. He and Ricky Ponting added 219 for the second wicket in 35 overs to set the platform for our huge total of 4–338, which proved too much for the Indians.

After the match in Vizag, it was like being part of a ticker-tape parade as thousands of people lined the streets all the way back to our hotel, which was seven or eight kilometres from the ground. Similarly, the scenes around the grounds before a game can be chaotic, as long queues battle to get in, while some fans struggle desperately to find someone who will sell them a ticket. Often adding to the confusion are the ticketing arrangements, which have seen some genuine people who've paid their money unable to get into matches while others with counterfeit tickets are able to swindle their way through the turnstiles.

The words 'fanatical', 'obsessed' and 'infatuated' are not enough to describe the passion all Indians have for the game of cricket. Some fans go to the extent of booking rooms in the team hotels, so they can catch a glimpse of their favourite players or achieve the Holy Grail, a signature. It is both a humbling and frustrating experience, because you can feel their genuine love of the game in everything they do, but their lack of regard for privacy can be very demanding. It is nothing for a cricket fan over here to walk into your room, interrupt breakfast or try to grab you through the bus window.

I was very pleased to see Punter back among the runs. In international cricket every player has good and bad days, but the good ones always come back eventually, so long as they work hard and their teammates keep faith in them. Ricky has worked diligently in the nets for the last couple of weeks, especially in the last couple of days, and although he was a bit scratchy early doors today, once he had time in the middle he played very well. He remains a class player, and a key part of both our Test and one-day teams.

One of the criticisms we've copped is that we're too inflexible, that having decided we want to rotate players in and out, we're not prepared to admit it's not working. But if we weren't flexible in our approach, Matthew Hayden wouldn't even be here playing in the one-dayers. He wasn't originally selected in the one-day squad, but after having such a prolific time in the Tests we asked him to stay on and he's responded magnificently.

As for the cynics who reckon the rotation system isn't working, let's just wait and see. Win or lose here, I think the real benefit of the strategy won't be seen until the World Cup in 2003. We don't want to go into that tournament — easily the biggest event in the one-day game — having totally relied on the same 12 or 13 players in the previous three years. If two or three of our main players were suddenly injured just prior to the World Cup and we didn't have a worthwhile base of around 16 players then we'd be struggling.

April 6 *Goa*

Fifth One-day International, at Margao, April 6

India 6–265 (50 overs: VVS Laxman 101, SC Ganguly 74) lost to Australia 6–269 (48 overs: AC Gilchrist 76, MG Bevan 87*; J Srinath 3–62, SR Tendulkar 3–35) by four wickets

AFTER THE INDORE ONE-DAYER, WHERE we were thrashed to go 1–2 down in the five-match series, as a unit we made a commitment to give the next two games our absolute best shot. We decided to try hard, remain upbeat (which was pretty tough after the amount of travelling and playing we had done) and improve our batting, which had let us down in the first and third games. I told the lads that we are world champions for a reason, and that every time we walk onto the field to play we are defending our No. 1 status.

For game four, in Vizag, we decided to concentrate on building partnerships and putting pressure on their bowling — two things we had failed to do well during the earlier matches. The confidence we gained from our batting performance in that game stood us in good stead during the decider here in Goa, when Matthew Hayden, Adam Gilchrist and Michael Bevan all batted superbly.

The ground at Goa was fantastic and the facilities were pretty good, too. However, the wicket was a little soft and not as batsman-friendly as the ones we batted on earlier in the tournament. This was not necessarily a bad thing, since giving the bowlers a chance usually makes a one-day game more interesting, and under these circumstances VVS Laxman's century was a brilliant effort. Similarly, the unpredictability of the deck magnified the quality of Michael Bevan's match-winning effort, as he once again proved that he is the best one-day batsman in the world. Others, especially openers, may score more runs, but Bevo is invariably obliged to craft his runs towards the end of the innings when the pressure is on.

The partnership that secured us this very impressive win was the unconquered seventh-wicket stand of 67 in 8.5 overs between Bevo and Ian Harvey. This was a major breakthrough for Harvs, as he withstood enormous pressure to see us home to victory. It's a lot easier to blast a quick 20 or 30 when your team is in control than it is when your team needs seven an over to win from the final seven or eight overs. I've got a feeling this match may represent a defining moment in Harvs' career, because he'll gain a stack of self-belief from his performance here.

Now, of course, is a time for reflection. It's been a wonderful cricket tour, even if we didn't get the Test result we were looking for. We've learnt from our mistakes, on the field and off, and now I'd like to concentrate on the positives that have come out of the adventure. Foremost among these, I believe, is that Test cricket in India has been given an enormous boost. The full houses at the matches and the colossal media coverage confirmed just how much the locals were involved in the matches. I'll never forget the noise as the Indians fought their way back into the Test series and then won that famous victory in Chennai; nor will I forget the ardent cricket fans who followed us everywhere we went, often impinging on our privacy but always making us feel very important and very lucky to be where we were.

One amazing statistic to come out of the tour was the fact that 70 per cent of people with access to a television set in India tuned into the Test matches. That's 70 million cricket watchers. Who said Test cricket was dead?

On the field, there's no doubt that our biggest plus has been the prolific run-getting of Matthew Hayden. His efforts over the last two months must rank with the greatest performances by an Australian batsman on tour, especially when you consider that there were some critics who wanted to write him off beforehand because they reckoned he couldn't handle high-class spin bowling. On top of his efforts in the Test matches, Matty has also put his name forward as a one-day player of the highest class. He always had visions of being an effective one-day opener and finally made it into the squad last year, but only as a replacement for an injured Ricky Ponting. But so dominating was he in the Tests over here that we had to keep him on for the one-dayers, and he responded with a continuation of his Test-match form. All he's been doing on this tour is proving that things will happen if you work hard enough. In the past, Darren Lehmann and Damien Martyn have performed quite well at the top of our one-day batting order, so Matty's emergence now means we have five genuine alternatives at the top of the batting order. This is the kind of flexibility the team is striving for.

One of the major talking points of this tour has been the Australian team's relationship with the Indian captain Sourav Ganguly, and specifically the relationship between Ganguly and me. This has been the subject of much media conjecture since before the tour began, and there's no denying that we've found him to be an unusual, often niggly opponent. But while there have been some unnecessary flare-ups on the field, with both sides at fault at different times, the bottom line for me is that the cricket has been tough, passionate and competitive. And enjoyable, too.

I must admit that I didn't get on with my opposite number on this tour. It was interesting to see Ganguly in our dressing-room after the series ended, sharing a drink with a number of our guys. I couldn't help thinking that it was a great pity that we hadn't made a move in this direction much earlier. Perhaps he thought that by being provocative he was helping his team, putting his opponents off their game, and that if he had socialised with us he would have been relinquishing this perceived 'advantage'. Maybe he is just a victim of his own inexperience as a captain at the top level. There is no doubt that he is a very competitive cricketer and knows what he wants to get out of the game. But frankly, there were times where we thought he was just being childish. The reality, of course, is that the Indians won the Test series because VVS Laxman, Rahul Dravid, Sachin Tendulkar and Harbhajan Singh were magnificent, not because of their captain's shenanigans.

There's also no doubt that the media got plenty of headlines out of the story of our relationship with Ganguly. Hopefully, next time we meet, there won't be so many negative stories.

What can't be denied is that there were certain protocols that weren't followed on the field — simple things such as the two captains walking to toss together, and the captains being on time for the toss — and for a while Ganguly was something of a serial offender in these areas. We were also annoyed by the way he became something of a 'protected species' when it came to his on-field behaviour, because he often seemed to be putting unnecessary pressure on the local officials. A classic example came in the game yesterday, when he batted very well to score 74 off 83 balls but then, after being caught by Ricky Ponting off a short ball from Glenn McGrath, stayed to argue that it was a no-ball, because he felt the delivery had climbed above shoulder height. We had a couple of blokes fined earlier in the series for disputing decisions, yet Ganguly got away with a warning here, just as he had back in Pune when he had an on-field argument with the umps over whether they should have gone to the third umpire over the Lehmann/Mark Waugh run out decision.

Things had got so ridiculous before this last one-dayer that ICC referee Cammie Smith organised a meeting between the captains, coaches and team managers to discuss the situation. Ganguly then strode out five minutes early for the toss, dressed in his training attire, which seemed a pretty juvenile response to the complaints about his habitual tardiness. His gesture in coming into our rooms after the game was much more encouraging.

While the rights and wrongs of our relationship with Ganguly will soon be forgotten, the quality and drama of the cricket played on this tour will be remembered forever. Our win in the one-day series does not make up for the defeat in the Tests, but while the Test series disappointment remains, it certainly is nice to end the tour on a winning note. In my view it was an outstanding and inspiring achievement on the part of the players who joined us for the one-day games to get acclimatised in such a short time and then play a critical part in our victory. And it took character on the part of the guys who played in both series to straightaway put the disappointments of the Test matches behind us.

A couple of people have asked me if I'm concerned that this Australian side might be past its peak. I do concede that a period of transition is looming, as some of the key members of this team near the end of their distinguished careers, but despite the loss of the Test series here I believe we are still a very good side. On the question of ageing, statistics are being produced that show that this is one of Australia's oldest ever sides, but I think that stat is simply a reflection of the fact that star players are remaining in the game longer because there are plenty of incentives for them to stay. In the 'old' days, international cricketers often retired at the peak of their careers, simply because they couldn't afford to keep playing. Bob Simpson, who retired in 1968 when aged just 32 but came back nearly a decade later to score two more Test centuries, is a classic example of this.

We are looking for some younger guys to stake a claim for a place in the side, but in the meantime, so long as the established guys remain competitive, fit and ambitious, then I don't believe we have a problem. This said, there's no doubt that everyone in the current team needs to keep performing if they want to stay around. Anyone who has a below-par Ashes tour will be struggling to keep his place for the start of the 2001–02 Australian season. However, because we're all professional players, this type of pressure won't be a negative thing; in fact I'm sure it will act as a spur. At this level, you need players on edge, wanting to be consistent and excellent.

Overall, I'm reasonably happy with the way we've played over the past few weeks. We certainly gave it our best shot, and were so close to coming away with a really successful tour. While I probably won't be back as a player, I just hope that future Australian teams that tour India will learn from our experiences, and get the historic victory that we couldn't quite manage.

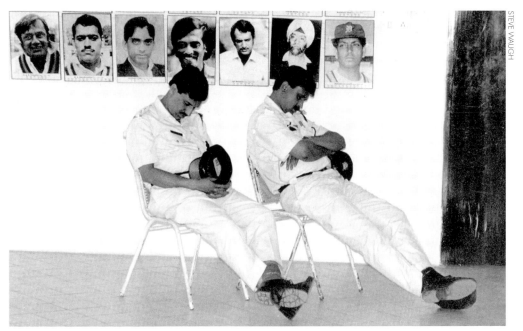

By the end of this tough tour, even the security guards were looking for a place to lie down.

THE ASHES
2001

Gallipoli — What it meant to us

Soon after we drove away from Anzac Cove, I asked each of the guys for their brief reflections on their Anzac experience. The responses came from a variety of angles, some relating to the team, some personal, some philosophical, some just single words that summed up what the bloke was thinking at that moment . . .

Glenn McGrath: Gave me an understanding as to why we march on Anzac Day . . . Why were we at war with Turkey? Why did we land in the wrong spot? . . . Guys didn't know what they were in for . . . Turks and Anzacs didn't hate each other . . . Love to go back . . .

Ricky Ponting: Made me feel proud to be an Australian.

Matthew Hayden: An ironic experience . . . beautiful place, terrible tragedies . . . very confusing. It's hard to comprehend how courageous they were . . .

Pat Farhart: Selflessness of those who fought . . . I'm grateful to have been there . . . Feel more Australian, 100 per cent for the first time . . .

Damien Martyn: A wake-up call . . . sobering experience . . . felt proud and emotional. Courage . . . standing next to your mate, knowing you are going to die . . .

Adam Gilchrist: Very emotional, but not sure why . . . confused, sadness, pride, reflective . . . Words to sum up the place: commitment, loyalty, trust . . . Ultimate need for leadership, trust, teamwork . . . Our time together at Shell Green was special . . .

Steve Bernard: Privileged to go . . . Money can't buy the experience . . .

Wade Seccombe: Admiration for the Diggers . . . Historical value from an Australian point of view . . . forged our identity . . . Special to be there as part of an Australian representative group . . .

Damien Fleming: Courage . . . Sacrifice . . . They gained respect from the world . . .

Mark Waugh: We underestimated the Turks . . . Plan to know your opposition and what they do . . .

Jock Campbell: What a waste . . . so young . . . Need for teamwork . . . adapt to anything . . .

Jason Gillespie: Tried to imagine what it was like to spend 240 days in the trenches . . . Made me feel proud . . . have admiration for the Anzacs . . .

Mike Walsh: I now appreciate Anzac Day even more. . . . Proud . . . My father was involved in war . . .

Michael Bevan: Such a waste . . . needless deaths . . . Why did it happen and why did they (Anzacs) put their trust in someone else?

Shane Warne: Sacrifice of people . . . commitment . . .

Brian Murgatroyd: You can read as many books as you want, but until you go there it doesn't seem real . . . More respect for the Turks . . . Atatürk's word's are profound . . .

Andrew Symonds: How lucky are we? . . . Draw on it for inspiration and strength . . . Something forever to remember . . .

Ian Harvey: A learning experience . . . Started to think about my own life, my complaining . . . we've got it easy . . . Their age, so young . . . Feel proud . . .

John Buchanan: Wore my father's medals, but I didn't know why . . . Felt compelled to ring my son Mike (18 years old) and tell him how much I loved him, as you never know what might happen tomorrow. We don't spend time telling our family how much we love them . . .

May 28 *Gallipoli*

GAZING IN ADORATION AT CATHY Freeman as she sat motionless on the track after winning Olympic gold in Sydney, willing the Aussies to take away the America's Cup from the Yanks or screaming with the masses as Thorpey mowed down Gary Hall jnr to snatch a thrilling win in the men's 4 x 100 metres freestyle relay at Sydney — these were all famous sporting moments that made us proud to be Australian. I didn't think I could ever feel more content or honoured to have been born in this great land of ours than when I saw these famous sporting moments ... until today, when I was able to take in the meaning of the small portion of the Gallipoli Peninsula known as Anzac Cove.

It was a moment in my life that is hard to describe, yet it is something I'll never forget. The irony of this place is almost too hard to comprehend. Today, the sky was a beautiful shade of pale blue, the waters crystal clear and turquoise while the landscape is strikingly ragged but not in an untidy way. It defies the secrets and hidden battles that permeate the whole area. It is now a peaceful, beautiful part of the world that has a story to tell and a calming influence on those who come to pay their respects to the courageous, dedicated men who lost their lives building their respective nations' culture, character and soul.

This was a real learning experience. Beforehand, I knew little of the detail of Gallipoli's battles beyond the story told in the movie that starred Mel Gibson, but I desperately wanted to learn more. The idea of this stopover came out of a conversation I had with Lt Gen Peter Cosgrove, head of our Army, over dinner in Sydney last year. We were comparing cricket and the army, especially things that are important in both endeavours — such as camaraderie, discipline, commitment and the importance of following a plan — and things evolved from there.

With a swarm of media surrounding us, initially things were somewhat artificial and an appreciation of what was around us wasn't really possible. Things were happening too quickly. It wasn't until brother Mark and I laid wreaths at Anzac Cove that I was able to get a sense of the sadness at the massive loss of life that had occurred in the surrounding landscape. Looking up into the hills, I tried to comprehend the mindset of the soldiers as they valiantly tried to get a toehold on the Turkish land, and the fear and apprehension they must have felt at the thought of never going back home to loved ones. These were real heroes. I'm sure the whole team has received a very clear perspective as to the superlatives and tags we are often given for just playing a sport we love.

It's hard to comprehend their heroism. This morning, when the shower started playing up, I starting cursing, but then I pondered the fate of those who died and those who froze in the trenches, fighting for eight months. I didn't have much to complain about.

There were many images of our day that will be forever etched in my memory. The sight of John Buchanan, proudly wearing his father's service medals from the Second World War, and Matthew Hayden, scaling a section of hills opposite Anzac Cove to get an inkling of how hard it would have been to climb it with the 42 kilos of additional gear that many of the Anzacs carried, are two. Another was standing in the trenches at The Nek with all the lads while our tour guide described what actually happened in the moments leading up to the soldiers' deaths. It was a humbling time and also a proud moment to think that these Australians stayed as one as they went over the top despite knowing they weren't coming back. They believed they were helping the Allies by sacrificing themselves in order for a bigger plan to work.

Visiting Lone Pine was an occasion that put one's life into perspective. Here, horrific hand-to-hand battles took place and over 6000 men perished on a battlefield the size of two tennis courts. I left that place with a heavy heart, especially after reading the ages of the men and boys who lost their lives. The images of Simpson and his donkey were described to us; how he rescued critically injured soldiers — and not just Anzacs but also two Turks who had been wounded on the hills near Beach Cemetery. I tried to conjure up in my mind the heroism that kept him going, but his selflessness and gallantry are almost too difficult to imagine.

As a tribute to the Anzacs, we decided to try to recreate the famous cricket game that involved eight soldiers playing on Shell Green during the evacuation from Gallipoli. The idea of the original game was to distract the Turks into believing everything was as normal, when in fact men were being quietly shifted back to the ships. That no one died in the process suggests that the subterfuge worked (although Turkish historians reckon it was more a case of the locals not wanting to shoot brave opponents in the back).

A historic photograph of the match was taken by the celebrated Australian war correspondent and historian, CEW Bean, and the idea for a re-enactment came from one of our guides here, Colonel Don Murray, an army adviser to the Australian High Commission in London. So we clambered through the knee-high grass to the spot where that famous game was played, to recreate the image that was preserved for all time in that original photograph. Glenn McGrath played the bowler, Adam Gilchrist, the keeper, I was the batsman, while the rest of the guys took up positions on the area's only flat piece of ground.

Everyone talks about the Anzac spirit. To me, it means being together, fighting together and looking after your mates. These are Australian values, which I want the Australian cricket team to always carry. I'd like to see all Ashes sides stopover at Gallipoli on the way to England. If that's a tradition that began here in 2001, then it will be a very, very good thing.

This was a daunting but wonderful experience. The camaraderie of our team was clearly evident as we learnt and appreciated the lessons learnt together. We will all grow as individuals because of the insights and knowledge we have gained and we now admire and respect even more these true heroes who helped forge and shape our nation. The epitaph of one 19-year-old soldier from the Lone Pine battle somehow struck me more than any other. On his headstone were the words:

Duty Done.

May 30 *Worcester*

IT'S OBVIOUS TO ALL THAT England have had a tremendous past 12 to 18 months. It appears that they are now a side who can be a match for any adversary, ourselves included. However, it is more than this feeling that has we Aussies licking our lips in anticipation at the upcoming Test series. On the previous couple of tours, upon arriving at Heathrow, we have been bombarded with statements such as, 'Good luck, but not too much,' or, 'Take it easy on our boys.' Not this time; in fact, far from it. We've been greeted with, 'Look out, we're gonna get the Ashes back this time.'

It is this new-found self-belief that has led England back to the forefront of international cricket. The vision and planning of coach Duncan Fletcher and captain Nasser Hussain have clearly inspired the team to not only back themselves but also to fight every centimetre of the way, no matter what the circumstances they are confronted with. Fast men Darren Gough and Andy Caddick appear to have got something special happening with the bowling and Graham Thorpe is batting as well as he's ever done. The others seem to be moulding around that trio, and the result is that they have a good team spirit and are all pulling in the same direction. You don't win two series on the Indian subcontinent unless you're a 'together' team; any series win in these countries requires a steeliness of not only the body but also the mind. They're going to be a lot tougher than they have been in the recent past. But we see ourselves as worthy opponents.

The Cast and Crew

Steve Waugh (captain) — Tugga
Adam Gilchrist (vice-captain) — Gilly
Nathan Bracken — Bracks
Damien Fleming — Flem or Flemo
Jason Gillespie — Dizzy
Matthew Hayden — Haydos
Simon Katich* — Kat or Kato
Justin Langer* — Lang
Brett Lee — Bing or Binga
Glenn McGrath — Pigeon
Damien Martyn — Marto
Colin Miller* — Funky
Ricky Ponting — Punter
Wade Seccombe — Chuck
Michael Slater* — Slats
Shane Warne — Warney

Mark Waugh — Junior
Michael Bevan# — Bevo
Ian Harvey# — Harvs
Andrew Symonds# — Symmo or Roy

Manager: Steve Bernard
Physiotherapists: Errol Alcott and
                  Pat Farhart
Fitness Co-ordinator: Jock Campbell
Cricket Analyst: Mike Walsh
Media Manager: Brian Murgatroyd
Masseur: Rebecca Lauder

* Will join the tour for the Ashes Test series
# Will play only on the early tour and in the one-day NatWest series

England are probably ranked around No. 3 or No. 4 in the world, and if they do beat us, they'll be entitled to be ranked as high as No. 2, maybe even No. 1. They're playing as well as anyone at the moment, they've won a lot of Test matches and if they beat Pakistan in the series they're involved in at the moment that will mean they've won five series in a row. That, in anyone's eyes, is a significant achievement.

There have been many debating points in the weeks between the end of the India tour and now. For us, the loss in the Tests to Ganguly's team is yesterday's news and our quest for cricket's most traditional and sought-after prize, the Ashes urn, is our No. 1 priority. Some critics have argued that our average age, which is over 30, may be our downfall, either here or in the near future. I must say I totally disagree, as youth does not inevitably mean intensity, hunger, desire and skill. All of these traits may be missing from a 20-year-old. As long as your fitness levels are acceptable, to me it makes no sense to drop someone simply because of their age, especially as they have spent many years working on their techniques, practising their skills, knowing their own game and becoming stronger mentally. Why automatically discard them for someone who is yet to go through that process?

This said, I think one of young guns, Brett Lee, will make an enormous impact on this tour. Unfortunately for us he isn't part of the one-day team, due to his continuing rehabilitation from his elbow surgery, but he will join up with the boys in about a week's time to begin his quest for a successful comeback. Brett will not only excite and

Welcome to Heathrow. There is no way through the media scrum, so the only option is to oblige their requests and be as positive as possible.

ignite the cricket-loving folk of the United Kingdom, he will make a huge impact on the events on the field, for he has the killer instinct to match a phenomenal talent. His pace will get pulses racing, his looks will get the females watching, and his deeds will get the record books rewritten in time.

One of the stranger things to occur during our break was the decision by the Australian Cricket Board that selections on this Ashes tour would be made by a trio of me, as captain, Adam Gilchrist, as vice-captain, and Trevor Hohns, the chairman of the regular Australian selection committee. John Buchanan, the coach, who has been a part of this process on previous tours to New Zealand, South Africa and India, won't be involved.

I would have liked to see Buck remain in this role. I heard Malcolm Speed, the ACB Chief Executive, explain that the decision would mean that players could now go to the coach if they are concerned about an aspect of their game, without fear that such problems would then be raised at the next selection meeting. 'If a player comes and says, "I'm struggling with fast bowling" or "I can't play Harbhajan Singh or whatever," ... they need to be able to do that in a full, frank, open way without feeling that that may be something that ends up at the selection table and works to their detriment,' he was quoted as saying.

Apparently this is also the view of the selectors, but I don't agree with it. It hasn't been a problem in the past, and shouldn't be in the future. If it's true, then players won't be talking to me if they've got a problem. I want players to come to me, if they need to talk about relevant issues. I found that Buck brought a different perspective to the selection table, and it's a shame he won't be doing so directly on this tour.

The one-day internationals section of the tour, which will also involves England and Pakistan, begins in 10 days time. The English usually play good limited-overs cricket in front of their home crowds, while Pakistan, as they always seem to be, are running hot and cold. As such, they are a dangerous foe, never to be underestimated, for they invariably strike when you least expect them to.

As the leaders in both forms of the game at present we must always strive to be one step ahead of our opposition, particularly as they always seem to lift against us to try to take away our claims to the No. 1 spots. We've already experienced this from India and their mighty come-from-behind Test series win. To be the best requires vision, a sometimes radical way of thinking, and the commitment of everyone involved to not only follow the vision and plans but to put the team's best interests ahead of personal glory.

May 31 *Worcester*

I ENJOYED THE FIRST PRESS conference of the tour, which took place yesterday here in Worcester. The press guys had a bit of fun at my expense, but I managed to laugh with them and make a couple of points as well.

One of the first questions posed concerned my future. Is this my last Ashes tour? A fair question, as I'm just three days short of my 36th birthday.

'The time will come when the squad will change pretty dramatically in the next couple of years,' I responded. 'You'd have to look at this squad and say not many of the guys — probably more than half — will make it back next time.

'I'm not absolutely sure about myself. I don't know when it's going to end — it could be in six months' time, it could be the end of this tour. I've got to have that competitive will to be out there, the selectors have got to want me to be out there and my body has got to be willing to go on.

'A lot of aspects come into it. I'd like to go to another World Cup (2003) and try and retain that trophy. But I may go beyond that. I love playing cricket for Australia, wearing that baggy green and the canary yellow — and their something special — so I want to soak that up for as long as I can.'

I truthfully don't know when I'll give it away. Money isn't an issue; if the desire isn't there, I'll get out straightaway. I reckon it would be impossible to hide the fact that you weren't 100 per cent committed. You couldn't hide it from your teammates, the selectors or the coach. At the moment, however, while I'm still enjoying the challenge and discovering new things about the game and myself, I see no specific end in sight. Age is irrelevant to me. However, I am really missing my kids and family now, and I could see that becoming a major factor as I plan for the future. Apart from that, whether I'm good enough to keep my place and whether I can retain my fitness also have to be considered.

I really don't know if I'm going to be able to recognise exactly when is the right time to retire. If I believe I can't improve any more, I reckon that might be when I should give someone else a go. I know it's not going to last forever, but for the moment all I want to do is perform to the best of my ability, and prepare for each contest as if it's going to be my last. That way I won't have any regrets whenever my career does come to a halt.

This was one of the most relaxed press conferences I've been to. The traditionally tough and testing pommy press were quite friendly, while the responses Gilly and I gave them were open and honest, for which they seemed grateful.

As I said, they don't look like Aussie prawns!

MirrorSport WELCOMES THE AUSSIES

Let's throw a few prawns on the barbie ..and watch England clean up The Ashes

SIZZLER: Will it be a long, hot, uncomfortable English summer for Steve Waugh, Glenn McGrath and Shane Warne?

By MARTIN ROGERS

SIGNING IN: Aussie skipper Steve Waugh is greeted by fans at Heathrow last night

STEVE WAUGH'S Australian cricket team touched down at Heathrow last night and immediately told England: "You haven't earned our respect."

The confident Aussies head the world rankings and have won six straight Ashes series – and Waugh believes they are on course for another resounding triumph this summer.

He said: "We are the number one team in the world. We have worked hard for it and we are very

TURN TO PAGE 43

9 MONTHS FREE 50 FREE TEXTS PER MONTH EXTRA 30 FREE TEXTS PER MTH FOR 3 MTHS

ONLY £11.99

One somewhat humorous moment came when a journo from the *Mirror* pulled out a copy of yesterday's edition of his paper, which had the melons of Glenn McGrath, Shane Warne and me replacing the heads of three sizzling prawns on a barbecue underneath a back-page headline which read, 'Let's throw a few prawns on the barbie ... and watch England clean up the Ashes.'

What did I reckon? 'They don't look like Aussie prawns, they're not big enough,' I laughed. 'It's a nice look, thanks very much — something to show the kids when I get back home.'

It was interesting that, despite the fact that the first England–Australia Test series is still more than a month away, England are currently in the middle of a two-Test series with Pakistan and there's a one-day tournament to be staged before we play a Test, it was the Ashes that all the media guys wanted to talk about. Of our upcoming Tests, I said simply what I have been saying for a month now: 'I've got a gut feeling this series is going to be very competitive. We're here to play aggressive and positive cricket and win every Test match.

'Getting that urn at the end of the series is very important to all Australians. We've won six in a row and we'd like to make it another one. I'm the only player here who has played in a losing Ashes series and I'd like to keep it that way.'

June 1 *Worcester*

IT'S NICE TO KNOW THAT cricketers and coaches around the place sometimes use my tour diaries for motivation. During the first match of our tour, a one-dayer against Worcestershire, the coach of their second XI and development squads told me that he'd been using my last two books, *No Regrets* and *Never Satisfied*, as a

At Worcester
June 1–3

Australians 351 (DR Martyn 108, SK Warne 68, SR Waugh 30; DA Leatherdale 0-46 from five overs) and 8–360 (declared: ML Hayden 65, RT Ponting 65) defeated Worcestershire 163 and 188 (DA Leatherdale 72; GD McGrath 4–31) by 360 runs reference guide for his young charges, to help them plan, train and go about their cricket in a professional way.

However, another player at the county used my last Ashes tour diary in a quite different manner. During the 1997 match at Worcester, a part-time bowler named David Leatherdale cut us to pieces with his innocuous looking medium pacers, claiming 5–10 to force a victory for his side. Writing about his exploits, I commented that despite his wickets he 'wouldn't even get a bowl in a Chinese restaurant'.

Of course, he and his teammates got wind of this appraisal and, sure enough, when I came out to bat I was immediately confronted by his deadly little swingers and dippers. Before facing up to his first ball, I had the slip cordon and various others having a good-natured chirp at my expense. Trying to get your head down and concentrating when the boys are encouraging the bowler with lines such as 'How about some sweet and sour,' and, 'Would you like some fried rice with that order?' isn't easy. Naturally enough, I went from being totally relaxed to extremely keen not to get out to this guy, but nearly perished first ball when I was rapped on the pads, which brought a chorus of very healthy appeals. Thankfully the verdict went in my favour, and I survived to hear many more orders being placed.

June 4 *London*

IT WAS NICE OF THE lads to give Mark and me a birthday present each two nights back, but I was a little disappointed by their gift selection: a walking stick. I'm not quite sure what they're getting at.

I'm also not exactly sure how many birthdays I've spent in England, but I think it would be around seven. Like most of the others, this was a low-key event, with a cake in the dressing-room and a barbecue after the match.

The three-dayer at Worcester was a good one for us, and not just because we were able to come away with a victory. Most of the guys had a good hit-out, especially the bowlers, who knocked our hosts over for 163 in the first innings after we'd made 351. The fact that Glenn McGrath (3–31), Nathan Bracken (3–29), Damien Fleming (2–47) and Shane Warne (2–38) shared the spoils in that innings was encouraging, and Pigeon then followed up with another excellent display on the final day. After I decided not to enforce the follow-on, Matthew Hayden, Ricky Ponting, Mark Waugh and Michael Bevan all took advantage, while earlier, on day one, Damien Martyn had scored an impressive century. Marto's knock reinforced what we've all known for a while — that he a genuine Test batsman crying out for an opportunity. I reckon he's at the peak of his career right now.

From Worcester we travelled back to London, and soon found ourselves at the Home of Cricket. It's always special to come back to Lord's. And for many reasons. Firstly, the change-rooms are the best in world cricket. They're roomy, comfortable and relaxing, with an excellent viewing area and honour boards on the walls that feature the names of all players who have scored Test centuries or taken five wickets in a Test innings at the ground. The food on offer is restaurant quality and smorgasbord quantity, with options ranging from baked cod, rack of lamb, salmon, baked pies and a mass of vegetables and salads. If you can still move there are plenty of dessert options, ranging from mousses, ice creams and English delicacies such as bread and butter pudding to finish you off. During Test matches, it's dangerous to dine here when you're bowling, because you don't really want to be running around on a full stomach in the field or bowling 10 overs straight with a couple of chocolate mousses swirling around inside you.

Cricket-wise, it's a special place, with its tradition, uniqueness and history. The memories last forever. Having to walk past the applauding members in the Long Room as you make your way onto the field is both strange and stimulating, while playing on a surface that slopes alarmingly from one side to the other is rather ridiculous yet curiously intoxicating. Striding out to training with Wade Seccombe took me back to my first visit to Lord's, when I was playing for Somerset in a one-day game back in 1987. I was so overcome with the emotion of playing at Lord's that I entered the playing field via the wrong gate, much to the amusement of the 'eggs and bacon' brigade (so named after the peculiar colour scheme of the MCC ties).

Chuck was blown away by the history and ambience of the ground. It was very humbling to be back here and to be able to watch someone such as our reserve keeper take it all in for the first time. For me it was extremely valuable to observe that look on his face, because it ensures that I'll never ever take this place for granted.

You know you're getting long in the tooth when your mates give you a walking stick for your birthday. Our 36th was also celebrated with a bottle of aftershave for Mark and a bottle of Southern for me.

Old and new at the Home of Cricket. A well-used pitch roller heads off in the direction of the state-of-the-art media centre, while we prepare for a team photograph.

At Lord's June 5

Australians 232 (44.2 overs: RT Ponting 57, IJ Harvey 84) lost to Middlesex 4–233 (47.1 overs: BL Hutton 73, OA Shah 50) by six wickets

At Northampton June 7

Australians 3–234 (50 overs: DR Martyn 101*, ME Waugh 88*) tied with Northamptonshire 234 (50 overs: ME Hussey 73)

At Edgbaston NatWest Series Game 1 — June 7

Pakistan 6–273 (50 overs: Saeed Anwar 77, Inzamam-ul-Haq 79) defeated England 165 (47.2 overs: NV Knight 59*; Shahid Afridi 3–15) by 108 runs

June 8 *Cardiff*

Having lost to Middlesex and then tied with Northamptonshire in our two preparatory one-dayers, I've got to be honest and say I can't be sure how we'll go against Pakistan in our opening match of the competition. What I do know is that we certainly haven't had the same tough lead-up as our opponents, who are coming off a two-Test series and then two limited-overs victories over England.

We had to have some time off after the India tour, to get right away from the game, but the downside of that is that when we arrived here we didn't have much time to get back in the groove. We'll be relying on our know-how, experience and skill, but whether that can make up for the lack of time we've spent in the middle, tomorrow will tell.

Our lead-up games have shown that Mark Waugh, Ricky Ponting, Ian Harvey and Damien Martyn are all in good form, but countering this are the niggling injuries to players such as Nathan Bracken (shoulder), Damien Fleming (calf) and Ponting (hip). One impressive effort was Harvs' final over against Northants, which featured three wickets (two of them run outs) and precisely no runs. He is a player who is on the verge of star billing, which — once he reaches his full potential — will see him as a regular matchwinner.

We need to improve our spark in the field, and our enthusiasm, hunger and desire. But that comes with the big games. We'll also be continuing with our 'rotation' system, or whatever you want to call it. I know some critics don't like it, but have a look, just as one example, at the opening batsmen. We've got four or five guys who can open the innings, including our two highly-successful regulars, Mark Waugh and Adam Gilchrist, plus Damien Martyn, who has scored hundreds in both our warm-up matches on this tour and who averages well over 200 as an opener in one-day internationals, and also Matthew Hayden, the star of our recent tour of India.

I'd say just about everyone will miss a game. But we've got a lot of matches coming up in a short space of time, including back-to-back games this weekend, so perhaps niggling injuries might ease our selection dilemmas.

June 9 *Bristol*

LAST NIGHT IN CARDIFF WAS one of those nights you dread as a professional sportsperson on tour — when you don't get any sleep because of things that are out of your control. The roar of a fire alarm at 11.30pm, when you're fast asleep, has the same effect as a red-hot dagger being prodded into you. It invades your body and leaves you stunned, unaware of your surroundings. Eventually, you have to gather your thoughts and work out what's happening. Unfortunately for all of those on floors seven and eight, the maddening sound of that ear-piercing noise continued to make its presence felt every 20 minutes until sanity prevailed sometime after 2am. My agitated state wasn't helped by the refusal of anyone to answer my calls to reception or the operator to find out what the problem was. I finally made contact with a staff employee, but what number I dialled I wasn't sure of, given that I was pushing numbers in the dark.

'What's going on?' I asked testily. 'Why hasn't the problem been solved?'

And then, before I could get a response, I muttered impatiently: 'This'd better get fixed shortly or else you'll be missing at least one alarm bell off the hotel walls.'

'I'm terribly sorry, Sir,' a somewhat shocked fellow replied, 'but I can't really solve anything for you ...

'I'm just the hotel chef!'

How could I respond, except with a rather timid, 'Sorry, mate.' It was later revealed that the problem was caused by vandals, who had broken into the leisure centre and kept setting off the alarm to satisfy their warped sense of humour.

Needless to say, the boys weren't all that happy or all that rested when we gathered for our breakfast before leaving for the ground at 9am. Further bad news came my way as I was downing my Crunchy Nut Flakes, when team physio Pat Farhart sidled up to me with a concerned expression on his distinct looking melon. Another quick had bitten the

At Cardiff
NatWest Series
Game 2 — June 9

Pakistan 257 (49.5 overs: Yousuf Youhana 91*, Rashid Latif 66; SK Warne 3–52) lost to Australia 3–258 (45.4 overs: ME Waugh 47, RT Ponting 70, MG Bevan 56*, SR Waugh 54*) by seven wickets dust, leaving us with only Glenn McGrath in the pace stakes. Dizzy has pulled up sore in his hamstring and the consensus was that it was too big a risk, with the rest of the tour in mind, to play him on the weekend. Immediately, I found team manager Steve Bernard and asked him to call the Australian Cricket Board and the selectors to find out whether Brett Lee could play. Bing is here, of course, but not, technically, in the squad. At this point, he is with us purely to work with our support staff to hasten his rehabilitation from his elbow surgery. The decision was eventually made by ACB chief executive, Malcolm Speed, after chairman of selectors Trevor Hohns couldn't be contacted in time, and Brett was rushed into our starting XI. I don't see any problem, as in a couple of days time he was due to make his comeback in a game of league cricket at Durham.

These injury problems added up to less than an ideal preparation for the opening game of an important one-day tournament. However, I've been saying for the last couple of years that I want a team that's flexible, one where any batsmen can bat in any position, where bowlers can come on at any time and fielders are capable in all positions. We need to be able to overcome hurdles that might hamper a lesser team, such as injuries, retirements or loss of form by some team members.

This squad is about creating opportunities for every member to improve his game and his self-belief. It is a squad that doesn't want to rely on a few players to do the 'hard yards', but rather one that wants to be the strongest, tightest unit, with everyone capable of winning a match for their country more often than not. We're committed to improvement and improvisation. I expect us to be able put any combination from our squad on the park and not be weakened, and I want our side to be able to cope with adversity and change with a minimum of fuss. This is the essence of the so-called rotation system.

I THINK WE'VE MANAGED to get close to that objective in recent times, so while most would have been surprised by the quality of our play today, I wasn't. It was inspirational and committed. Leading up to the game, we had copped our fair share of criticism because of our sluggish form and ordinary results, and rightly so. Deep down, we knew we could lift, but form isn't something that can always be turned on like a tap. Our attitude was summed up with my answer to the BBC commentator, Jonathon Agnew, after I had lost the toss.

'Many are questioning your form this week — have you lost your belief?' he asked.

'You may be questioning us but we are certainly not doubting ourselves, we are ready to go,' I replied.

The pre-match plan to blunt Pakistan with our discipline, consistency and a relentless attitude worked well. We played with hunger, intensity and desire. Shane Warne's bowling was very encouraging, and he evoked memories of the 1993 tour when he again took a wicket with his first ball. He certainly looks pumped up for a big tour, and when his confidence is up he can do anything.

Our batting was simply professional, with the tempo being maintained throughout. Ricky Ponting was 'in the zone' and looks set for a big tour after the disappointment of India. He has been totally dedicated from the moment he stepped off the plane, and

Under the Microscope

In the lead-up to the one-day competition, Buck split us into pairs and then gave every duo two players each from England and Pakistan to analyse, after which we were to report our findings back to a team meeting. My partner was Ian Harvey, and the four opponents we were allocated were Paul Collingwood, Dominic Cork, Abdur Razzaq and Yousuf Youhana. This is how we rated them:

Paul Collingwood (England)

TECHNICAL: Correct technique, doesn't like being tied down, tries to take spinners over mid-on.

MENTAL/CURRENT FORM: In good form, but hasn't played for England yet.

Dominic Cork (England)

TECHNICAL: Batting — Unorthodox. Stay patient. Looks like getting out. Not comfortable against spin. Bowling — Can swing it away. Play in the V. Wait for balls on your legs. Likes to be aggressive, takes wickets.

MENTAL/CURRENT FORM: Fragile. Talks a good game. Gets distracted from the job at hand.

Abdur Razzaq (Pakistan) KEY PLAYER!!

TECHNICAL: Batting — Likes to hit quicks over mid-off/mid-on. Very versatile, can play sedate role or pinch hitter. Short of a length to him, so he's hitting on the up. Bowling — Quicker than he looks, hits the seam. Comes on between 10 to 20 overs to keep it tight. Can be driven, and is hot and cold. May be able to pick him off your legs.

MENTAL/CURRENT FORM: Good temperament. Doesn't get flustered. Leave alone.

Yousuf Youhana (Pakistan)

TECHNICAL: Good all-round player. When bowling to him, stick to basics, line and length. Good nicker of the ball, can be caught in cordon perhaps by 'floating' slip.

MENTAL/CURRENT FORM: Poor Test series. Out of form, under pressure.

---

finished with 70 from 68 deliveries. Mark Waugh looked in excellent touch, particularly against the express pace of Shoaib Akhtar; while Michael Bevan and myself completed the job with a breezy, unbeaten 116-run partnership to start our tour in the best possible fashion.

The crowd invasion at game's end was unpleasant. A number of kids got beaten up in the melee as the officials tried to manage proceedings but were hampered because adequate precautions had not been taken. A seven-year-old boy was set upon by an ugly group draped in Pakistan flags, in an attack that was an indictment of modern society. We duly signed an autograph sheet to sooth the poor kid's wounded pride and body, which was the least we could do for the lad. It was a sickening end to a tumultuous day.

My duties as captain require me to attend the match presentation ceremony, then a media conference and various other interviews, and finally I'm obliged to fill out a report on the umpires. A quick feed of pasta followed before we all boarded our

Ricky Ponting's early-tour form was sensational.

coach, bound for Bristol, an hour-long journey, in preparation for tomorrow's much-anticipated clash with the old enemy. One tough part about back-to-back, day-night, one-day internationals at different venues is the travel, which comes on top of the physical strain and lack of recovery time. Accentuating that lack of recovery time is the fact that, with so much adrenalin still running through your body, it can be hard to get to sleep, despite the fact that sleep is what you desperately need. Action replays and thoughts of games ahead continually race around your head. It was 1.30am before I hit the sheets, and much later still before I finally dozed off, somewhat ready for tomorrow's action.

June 10 *Bristol*

At Bristol
NatWest Series
Game 3 — June 10

England 4–268 (50 overs: ME Trescothick 69, NV Knight 84) lost to Australia 5–272 (49.3 overs: ME Waugh 46, RT Ponting 102, DR Martyn 46) by five wickets

A SWIM, STRETCH AND SPA with our fitness man, Jock Campbell, was of immense value in trying to loosen up the tight hamstrings and aching joints before catching up with the lads for breakfast and a team meeting. Briefly discussing England's players individually proved useful, but I was more concerned about our guys sticking to our plans and improving in each outing.

Buck, meanwhile, seemed to have other things on his mind when he asked our bowlers to analyse the English batting tail and how we were going to bowl to them. 'Can anyone sum up their tailenders in one word or less?' he asked.

Andy Bichel, here on standby in case Brett Lee wasn't able to play in two games in two days, exclaimed, 'I guess the meeting's over now!'

We arrived at the ground with only an hour remaining before the game was due to start. The old way of thinking is that you need at least one-and-a-half hours to stretch, practice and prepare yourself, but we've begun to experiment by using less time. The logic is that we'll be fresher for the game from having less of a workload before the toss.

Losing the toss isn't such a big deal in one-dayers, because the pitch doesn't alter much in the course of a single day and I always believe the best team will show itself over the course of 100 overs. The one thing that did surprise me was the gist of the comments by England's stand-in captain, Alec Stewart, at the toss. I'm not sure whether he was playing on the underdog tag, much in the way the Kiwis always seem to, or perhaps he genuinely didn't expect his team to do well. But when asked how he thought his team would go, his words were to the effect of, 'We're playing the world champions and I would be very happy if we can compete, and if we do that, then you never know what might happen.'

To me that sends out the wrong message to his team. Even if he believed what he said, he could have kept it to himself and given a more positive response for his team to feed off.

England's innings was clearly divided into quarters, with Australia winning the first and third and England the other two. Our best bowler was Mark Waugh, who only got a bowl when his captain decided that sometimes you've got to follow your instincts and not regimentally do what's expected of you. Junior tied down Stewart with his deceptively flighted offies at a crucial time of the innings and prevented a total of around 300 being achieved. Even so, chasing 268 was a tough ask but we knew the ground was small and extremely quick and the English attack inexperienced. Our run-chase was again superbly orchestrated by Ricky Ponting (102 runs from 116 balls) and Junior, and finished off by Damien Martyn, Andrew Symonds, Ian Harvey and me in another polished, professional batting effort.

For Punter, that makes two man-of-the-match awards from our first two games. Roy hit 23 from 15 balls and Harvs 19 from 13. The defining shot came from 'The Freak', as Harvs is known in some parts, who slammed the last ball of the penultimate over, bowled by Ben Hollioake, over the cover fence to leave us requiring just five to win, which I managed to get with three balls to spare.

Harvs, of course, has become a legend here at Bristol, helping Gloucestershire to numerous titles in the past couple of years, and this match-winning shot will only add to his reputation. This was an outstanding team win and the feeling among the lads in the change-rooms was of genuine joy. There was a real camaraderie here. This is not always the case with wins in one-day internationals, which, for me at least, suggests I am leading a special group capable of achieving great things. Often, early on in a tour, you can sense what lies ahead. With the Gallipoli experience fresh in our minds, many players in all likelihood on their last Ashes tour and our status as the world's No. 1 team under threat, we have plenty to play for.

We will often have masseurs in for the day, working on the players to freshen them up or to rehabilitate niggling injuries, and this was the case today. Warney came up with the quote of the day when he said to Paul, our Welsh masseur, 'I don't know what you've done, Paul, but my legs feel like a gazelle's.'

Overhearing this, Pigeon chipped in with, 'Warney, I wouldn't mind being a lion in your park!'

A superb day's cricket was capped off by an equally enjoyable night spent with younger brother Danny, who is over here sampling London life and cricket for five months. It was terrific to have a decent chat because life at home doesn't allow such luxuries, as we never seem to cross paths owing to my incredibly busy lifestyle. Top-level cricket is a great way to earn a living, but such are the demands on one's time, family often has to be sacrificed to make all the glory possible.

June 11 *Manchester*

OUR FIRST TWO ONE-DAY INTERNATIONALS have been tremendous results for us considering our limited preparation and the fact that so many of our quicks are carrying injuries. That injury toll reflects an unavoidable difficulty with modern cricket itineraries. Our fast men have had to endure an enormous workload in the past 12 to 18 months, and as a consequence desperately needed the six-week layoff before this Ashes adventure to physically and mentally recuperate. But when we get back into a long tour such as this one, it's almost like a pre-season for the quicks, as they struggle to readjust to what has quickly become unaccustomed muscle use. On top of this, our early-tour preparation is very intense and there are endless trips on planes and buses. It is little wonder that the quicks, in trying to get match fit, succumb to various niggles and tears. The answer is not an easy one, but I'm sure once we've had a close look at what is happening here we'll be better prepared next time.

It might be that the quick bowlers have to stay bowling at least twice a week during the 'off' times, to keep their bodies in tune with the ever-increasing demands of international cricket.

If our fast bowling stocks are something of a concern, we have fewer worries with the form of Ricky Ponting, which to date has been extraordinary, especially if you compare it with his meagre returns from much of the recent India tour. This shows again how uncertain one's fate can be in this great game of cricket, and also demonstrates how mentally tough the Tassie boy is. He has been focused from day one of this tour and like all very good players has moved on from his disappointments but not totally forgotten them. His duel with Shoaib Akhtar, who clocked over 97mph, in game one was a classic and brought the best out of him, in terms of courage and skill. Better was to follow at Bristol, where Punter kept the tempo and flow of the game in our grasp while adjusting superbly to what was a slow, low wicket. Few players can better adapt to changes in pitch conditions. It is an example for all of us who temporarily find a pothole in the road that you must be proactive and do the hard work if you want to get back on the path you wish to take.

Shane Warne is another looking to bounce back after a frustrating tour to India, and he has started in fine style, claiming wickets with his customary deception of flight and variation, scoring runs freely and catching brilliantly. He clearly wants to excel on this tour, not only for his own satisfaction but to remind those who have written him off that he is still a champion.

This is the keenest I've seen Shane for three or four years. You can see it in the way he's batting in the nets, the way he's concentrating and is so keen to do well. He's had a lot of serious injuries, which have taken their toll, and maybe opponents have become more used to him. In India, guys such as VVS Laxman were more aggressive against him, and he took a while to come to grips with that. But he's still got a lot of tricks up his sleeve. He's incredible, the way he's constantly working on different deliveries all the time. To see him at practice, thinking up a new idea and then working on it, is always fantastic. He's got a very active and inventive mind, which keeps him very competitive.

As for Glenn McGrath, what can I say? He is just a great bowler. I can't decide whether he or Warney is the best bowler I've played with. That's how good Pigeon is. Critics reckon that Shane is a genius and one of the five cricketers of the century, and as far as that ranking goes they might be right, but in my view McGrath is just as good a bowler. And he's actually getting better. He doesn't seem to bowl a bad ball any more. Even in the nets, he never gives you a half-volley.

While Punter and Warney, being Tasmanian and Victorian respectively, might not have been too concerned with what was on the television during our three-and-a-half hour trip to Manchester this morning, Pigeon and I were certainly excited by the magnificent sight of the Blues steamrolling the Maroons in game two of the rugby league State of Origin. Into the second half, and Symmo was trying to hide down the back of the bus, while I celebrated the fact that our £50 wager was coming my way.

After the bus reached our new hotel, this afternoon represented our first chance since we left Sydney some two weeks ago to actually have time to ourselves. I'm sure everyone was not only grateful but also very much in need of some privacy. Haydos and I went into town to check out a space documentary at the Imax Cinema, while some other lads took to shopping or golf courses. Also on my mind were thoughts of my family being mid-air on their way over here for a seven-week stay. I can't wait to see them and their imminent arrival certainly kept my mind occupied with many pleasant thoughts.

June 12 *Manchester*

LIFE ON TOUR THESE DAYS is very hectic, with continuous commitments, ranging from playing, travelling, media obligations and planning sessions, to keep us extremely busy. In order to get some perspective in our lives and some semblance of normality we try to get away from cricket when the opportunity arises. One such occasion will be the Bon Jovi concert which all of the squad are going to in Huddersfield tomorrow night. It will be a great way to unwind, relax and still be together as a group.

At Lord's
NatWest Series
Game 4 — June 12

Pakistan 8–242 (50 overs: Yousuf Youhana 81) defeated England 240 (50 overs: ME Trescothick 137, OA Shah 62) by 2 runs

We've already had the benefit of being exposed to all the band's hits, thanks to Slats, who enthusiastically takes control of the team's music machine at every opportunity and transforms himself into an imperfect mimic of Jon Bon Jovi. In fact, we have quite a cross-section of musical interests in our side, with Flemo being somewhat left of centre with bands such as Grinspoon and Limp Bizkit among his preferred options, while Pat Farhart prefers various albums from the legendary Beatles. To me, this is one of the better things about being in a team environment — you get the opportunity to sample your colleagues' interests and likes, which couldn't happen if you were involved in an individual sport.

To help break the routine of net sessions at training, sometimes we will dedicate a whole session to fielding or fitness. Today we got a double whammy, back-to-back.

The morning session was run by Gary Palmer, a former teammate during my two years at Somerset, 1987–88. Back then, Gary was a prodigy about to follow in the footsteps of Ian Botham, but life rarely follows the envisaged path and he faded quickly from the playing scene. As far as cricket was concerned, his talents lay elsewhere, through his inventive way of thinking and willingness to try the unusual option.

Buck is often portrayed as a left-of-centre thinker, but he is relatively run-of-the-mill compared with Gary, who is way off the map with his excellent ideas. Today he took us for one-and-a-half hours of fielding drills, most of which were highly entertaining and original. While many looked a little strange, with witches hats, cones and pads strapped to stationary objects as props, all had that essential element to them in that they simulated match conditions and made us concentrate and strive hard to make them work. It was gruelling, but satisfying, and will no doubt leave us all a little stiff and sore tomorrow.

Jock Campbell then took control. He had planned a workout at the gym that was supposed to be 10 minutes away, but in fact took 30 minutes to get to. One piece of advice, Jock: don't make this mistake again. If you do, you'll again cop an almighty barrage of abuse and obscenities for 29 of the 30 minutes. Maybe this sledging was the reason why we were given a tougher than usual session, but though we didn't like it we respect Jock and the reasons why we put ourselves through this regime. We're all aware that being fit and healthy will aid our recovery from games and injuries and increase the length of our careers.

Shortly after, it was back to the hotel to give the Australian media contingent a quick press conference about the upcoming match and how the tour is shaping up. By the time I finally reached my room it was 3.30pm, which gave me a chance to call my family, who had arrived this morning after their 23 hours in the sky. Not surprisingly, they seemed zonked out and in need of some rest, but it's great to know they have arrived safely.

Three hours later, and we had another obligation to meet, a joint Australian Cricketers Association/Australian Cricket Board function that unfortunately wasn't as well organised as it could have been. This was one of those occasions when I felt like a commodity, being traded here and there, signing autographs, posing for pictures, endless small talk to please the guests. They say it's all part of the job, and I can agree in principle with that, but it can become very tiresome at times. I was interviewed for some 20 minutes, but the questions were boring, along the lines of: 'What is your favourite ground?'

Still, the night was going reasonably well until the auction, which failed to excite anyone's interest. Item No. 1 was a chance to bat against our bowlers at a practice session. First came a bid for £250, then another, grudgingly it seemed, for £275. And that appeared to be it, so I decided that unless someone in the audience was willing to make a serious bid then this little event wouldn't take place. 'Three hundred pounds,' I called. Quickly catching on, Warney raised his hand with an offer for £350. However, thinking this would liven things up was a mistake, as Shane and I found ourselves the only participants in a duel, until I walked away with the chance to train with the boys. Maybe I should have offered £500 not to train with the lads.

Now that would represent good value!

Right: I'm standing in a bunker at The Nek, scene of one of the grimmest battles in Australian military history. This is exactly where communications and instructions were sent and received.

Left: The view down to Anzac Cove.

Right: A headstone at the Lone Pine Cemetery, a place that stirred my emotions. I just felt these words summed up the Anzac spirit perfectly.

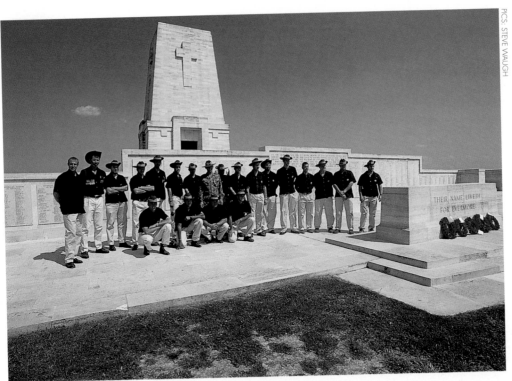

Above: *A team photograph of a different kind. Col. Don Murray, our guide and the man most responsible for the organisation behind our stopover, is in the centre.*

Below: *This is how we tried to re-enact the famous photo of the soldiers playing cricket while the Anzacs were evacuated.*

Above: *John Buchanan (in tracksuit) and Jock Campbell (with backpack) join in a dance that was part of our welcome to Gallipoli.*

Left and below: *The spectacular Blue Mosque in Istanbul.*

Media day at Lord's, during the first week in England.

Left: First up, we had to be available for a team shot and individual snaps for the assembled photographers and camera crews. In the foreground, Nathan Bracken is changing his one-day strip for a sponsor's shirt.

Right: As always, Warney was in big demand with the print journalists, the television and radio interviewers and the photographers.

Left: Getting serious for the official team shot. Back row (left to right): Campbell, Farhart, Seccombe, Fleming, Symonds, Bracken, Gillepsie, Hayden, Martyn, Harvey, Warne, Walsh. Front: Ponting, M Waugh, Buchanan, S Waugh, Gilchrist, Bernard, McGrath, Bevan.

Above: Wade Seccombe, Adam Gilchrist, Matthew Hayden, Simon Katich and Mark Waugh join me for a guided tour of Old Trafford, home of English football's most successful club of recent years, Manchester United.

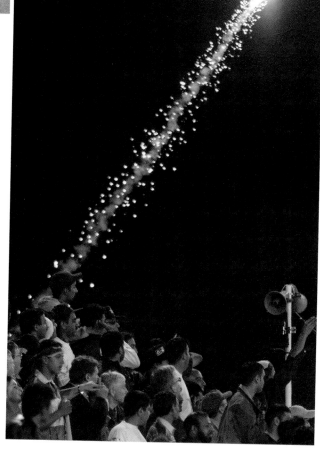

Right: A sight I hope I never see again at a day/night cricket game — an angry flare lights the evening sky above a crowded Trent Bridge during our controversial match against Pakistan.

Above: Three slips and two gullies is not the field you'd usually see in a one-day international, but that's what we used when we faced England at Old Trafford.

Below: Dizzy Gillespie is too quick for Michael Vaughan at Old Trafford, a valuable wicket not just in terms of this game but also for the psychological impact it would have on the entire English squad.

Above: Bing, Warney and Slats at Bon Jovi. Slats is in nirvana, with his idol magnificent in the background.

Below: Mark Waugh points out where the can came from, while Bevo (centre of photograph) begins to feel the pain from being struck in the face.

ALLSPORT

Left: A scene a million miles from the chaos of that one-day final at Lord's. Marto begins his outstanding Ashes tour in the relaxing and picturesque surroundings of Arundel.

Below: A group shot in the grounds of the beautifully maintained Arundel Castle. In the background are some of the original walls of the Castle, which date back to the 11th century.

STEVE WAUGH

June 13 *Manchester*

We began today with a rare morning off, which gave a few of us the chance to visit Manchester United Football Club and do the visitors' tour around the great club's Old Trafford stadium. It is certainly a very impressive operation — a business that incorporates sport, not vice versa.

It was interesting to check out the change-rooms, which aren't as opulent as I'd expected they would be. However, in other ways the United players are certainly pampered. On top of their amazing salaries, around £30,000 a week, they have their cars parked for them at the ground when they arrive on match days, and are then handed all their playing gear, including boots, in their section of the change-room. They don't have to bring anything with them. After the game, their dirty gear and boots are thrown in a heap and taken away for cleaning, to be ready for next week's game.

I'd hate to have that job with our team. However, if there was such a person, it might enhance my playing career because I simply detest packing and unpacking.

For me, the highlight of this guided tour, without a doubt, was watching an intellectually disabled group who were one step ahead of us the whole way through. Their enthusiasm was infectious. I'll never forget them as we waited in the players' tunnel under the grandstand, to walk out onto the pitch. This part of the tour involves visitors lining up, preparing, as champions such as Roy Keane and David Beckham do, to walk down the tunnel and out on to the ground, with the taped noise of the crowd on match day in the background to add to the realism. As the fans roared, off these guys went, charging down the runway, arms in the air, fists pumping, smiles beaming across their faces. One young lad dressed in the famous No. 7 shirt, with the name 'Beckham' emblazoned across his back, couldn't stop smiling, and to see him so happy reinforced for me how much sport can mean to people and the responsibility that we, as high-profile sports people, have.

David Beckham is, of course, now the captain of the England football team, and is a player who has been impressing me from afar for a number of years. One English batsman to impress me this season has been the 25-year-old opener Marcus Trescothick. We arrived in time to see him make a hundred in the second Test against Pakistan, and he's been impressive in the one-dayers as well. He appears to have the right temperament for big cricket; in fact, he reminds me a little of Mark Taylor in the way he can focus on the job at hand and not get too fazed by what is happening around him.

Whether he'll be successful in the Tests, only time will tell. We'll be studying him closely in the remaining one-dayers, though it's likely our methods in these games will be different from how we'll attack him in the longer matches. In the Tests, we'll have more options, different types of deliveries we can bowl and the opportunity to give our frontline bowlers longer spells at him, and all the other English batsmen.

As far as our injuries go, Dizzy might be right for our game against England tomorrow, Flem is still struggling with his calf strain, and while the long-term

At present this is easily the most crowded trophy cabinet in English football — in the last 10 years Manchester United have won a Champions League title, three FA Cups and seven Premier League championships.

prognosis on Nathan Bracken's shoulder is good, he's still not right at the moment. One positive has been the way Binga has pulled up after his first couple of games. My first thought was that it was amazing that he was going so well physically, but when you consider that he's been training for around five weeks while the rest of us have been on R&R, perhaps he's fitter than the rest of us. I'm sure he'd like to be bowling a little straighter, but it's hardly been a bowler's tournament to this point. A lot of guys from all three teams have been hit for plenty so far, and it could be that the team whose attack gets it all together first will prevail in the end. Given that we're the side who has had the shortest preparation leading into this competition, that could well be us. At the moment, I'd say we're at about 70 per cent of where we'd like to be.

With England still winless, a victory tomorrow — which would give us three wins and the hosts four losses — would seal a place in the final, though it would make no difference to the way we'd approach our later games. We will always try to win every major game we play.

Our training session this afternoon was again positive but we had something else on our minds — Bon Jovi. Sometimes the build-up to an event can be so hyped that the actual outcome is a real downer, but I'm here to tell you that in this case this wasn't so. In fact, the show was even better than we all expected. Perhaps the fact that we managed to get ourselves a guernsey on the stage platform for three songs, no more than three metres away from the man himself, may have swayed our judgement. As you'd expect, Michael Slater had the time of his life, wearing his idol's trademark singlet, newly acquired 'Bon Jovi — One Wild Night' bandanna and, crucially, a Superman tattoo on his left shoulder, just like the lead singer himself. At one point, Jon Bon Jovi came our way, to interact with we groupies, and even high-fived Slats, who held on for a few precious extra moments before the real star of the show could break the grip and continue the performance.

Watching Slats scream every word of the songs was just as riveting as the actual concert on stage. And I'll always remember feeling as if we were part of the band, looking out into a sea of 40,000 people, most of whom were totally and utterly in awe of the man and his music.

This was one of the most memorable nights on tour. If you weren't a fan before this night, then you would have been converted.

It's funny when you think of it — when I was a kid, dreaming about playing cricket for Australia, I often pictured myself batting at the SCG or Lord's . . . but I never thought about having the opportunity of being so close to one of the world's greatest bands in a stadium in the north of England. I'm forever grateful for the many fantastic opportunities away from cricket that being an Australian cricketer offers me.

Relentless, Nuisance, 'Genius'

The one word that describes Glenn McGrath just about perfectly is 'relentless', although some of his teammates might say nuisance would be more appropriate. Whatever, it wouldn't at all be surprising to see him settle down in his rocking-chair as the taker of the most Test wickets in the history of the game.

Pigeon is a man of many opposites; on one hand he appears to be a snarling, aggressive, and occasionally abusive, in-your-face fast bowler; in reality he is a quite well-spoken, soft-as-marshmallow country boy. While likely to offer his train seat to an elderly woman if required, he wouldn't blink an eyelid in the pursuit of gunning down with glee a bush pig or taking out a kangaroo at 50 metres with a .303. He spent time living in a dilapidated caravan when he first came to Sydney from his home town of Narromine; then became the proud owner of a flashy yellow convertible sports car some years later, much to everyone's shock and amusement. On the field he regularly gets his positions mixed up, yet when analysing batsmen and their weaknesses he has no peer.

To unlock the secrets to McGrath's success is quite easy: the guy wants to be the best, and will do everything in his power to make sure he is. He certainly trains as hard as anyone in the squad, maintaining weight sessions, gym routines and endurance work to ensure he has the physical demands of his trade under control when he needs to dig deep and produce when the going gets tough.

Of course, there are going to be times when he will suffer niggles and strains, as the art of fast bowling is a very unnatural succession of movements for the body. However, Pigeon seems to be able to work through these problems and bowl when others would prefer the luxury of the masseur's bench. Occasionally, to his own detriment, he has soldiered on and paid the price later. For example, during a Sydney Test against South Africa back in 1997–98, he continued bowling with a stomach complaint that required strapping, only later to find the true diagnosis was a tear, 1cm by 1cm, that put him out of cricket for the next couple of months.

His desire to be the best is matched by his love of bowling; he genuinely enjoys having the leather in his palm. As a captain he is a dream to have in the team, because he always wants to bowl, no matter the situation in the game or the type of pitch we are playing on. The sure way of knowing when Pigeon should hang up his boots is when he doesn't ask for one more over when you tell him to have a rest. Invariably, he believes he is on the verge of another wicket or just beginning to get his rhythm. Many times I will ask him how he's feeling after a long spell and he'll say, 'It feels like I haven't bowled a ball yet,' or, 'I'll be right to bowl through till the end of the session.'

As a batsman you are always under pressure. He gets you into his clutches, like a wrestler engaging his opponent into a sleeper hold, until he strangles the life out of you. His continual production of line and length, coupled with awkward bounce, leaves batsmen with very few scoring opportunities and even fewer deliveries that can be negotiated without cause for concern. It's a battle of attrition and with skill, guile, strength and body language harnessed, along with a mental toughness second to none, the end product is as good as it gets.

While his bowling is widely admired and applauded, his batting is ridiculed by many. However, to his enormous credit he has worked hard to improve his technique and can now be relied upon to contribute to partnerships on a regular basis. In fact, he's got me to about five or six Test hundreds . . . and then I've got out; more than once, he's claimed that I cost him his first Test fifty!

I've actually got a couple of theories on Pigeon's batting that may raise a few eyebrows. The first is that he may be a natural left-hander trapped in a body whose brain won't recognise this fact. Second, he may be a batting genius in disguise. One only has to watch him at net practice, where he often goes in before the session starts, and uses only a stump to repel the bowlers. He rarely misses, suggesting that the width of a mere willow is too wide for this craftsman, and that he obviously needs the stimulation of a real challenge to show his ability. Often he gets tangled up in his choice of shots out in the middle, but this can simply be put down to the fact that, as Glenn says sadly after being dismissed, 'I had too many options — I thought about four shots I could have played to that ball.'

Many things have been said about Glenn McGrath over the years, but the simple truth is, he is a great bowler, fantastic competitor and a thoroughly decent bloke.

Glenn McGrath and his son James at Edgbaston.

June 14 *Durham*

**At Manchester
NatWest Series
Game 5 — June 14**

Australia 7–208 (48 overs:
SR Waugh 64, DR Martyn 51*)
defeated England 86 (32.4 overs:
JN Gillespie 3–20) by 125 runs
(D/L method)

AFTER CONSULTING WITH JOHN BUCHANAN, we have decided to form a small group of players to develop some team plans on specific points that we have been unable to resolve in recent times. Often at team meetings we will discuss issues and end up confusing ourselves through a glut of input and varied information, rather than coming up with a firm solution. Having such debates is, of course, in no way a negative, as I want a team full of thinkers, always looking to improve and broaden horizons. But with a smaller group we can take an unresolved matter, use the information gleaned from the bigger discussion, and, hopefully, come to a conclusion.

One dilemma revolved around our inability to finish off the last 10 to 15 overs of our bowling in one-day games with any consistency. We haven't been able to settle on exactly what we should do, despite trying many variations, including different bowlers, various combinations and designated deliveries. After throwing the issue around with Warney, Pigeon, Gilly and Buck, we settled on a new, more precise way in which we want bowl these overs. Buck had come up with some interesting statistics, which revealed that the fate of most limited-overs games is actually determined by the 40 to 45-over mark of the team batting second. That suggests that you may as well use up your frontline bowlers early to set up the match, rather than hold off and let them try to stem a late run flow or finish strongly. With this in mind, we resolved to attack even more than we normally do, to try more decisively to win the game rather than let it unfold.

Of course, in order to implement this plan we need to have a strategy in place in case we bowl first and the opposition aren't all out by overs 40 to 45. Going down the 'road less travelled', we decided we'll buck conventional wisdom and use the so-called lesser lights, such as Junior and Symmo, to finish off the innings. Whenever they do, they'll be armed with a clear set of plans as to where they are to bowl and what fields they will be set.

I explained these new tactics to the entire team at the end of our usual team meeting to discuss the English team we'd be facing. Before I finished, I also asked for an increased effort and more intensity from the lads, for the whole match and not just part of it. Our key word would be . . .

ENERGY.

NOW, I FIND MYSELF sitting by myself down in the corner of the change-rooms, having completed two TV interviews, two separate radio interviews and a full press conference, and filled in the voting form for the Allan Border Medal and an umpires report. Not surprisingly, I feel extremely satisfied and proud of the way the team played today. It was a stunning performance, punctuated by brilliant individual efforts, most notably Jason Gillespie's outstanding exhibition of sustained pace bowling, complete with a radar-like control of the seam, that made batting look ridiculously difficult. The aura and intimidation we gave out was awesome tonight, and it allowed me to attack relentlessly with field settings usually seen in Test matches.

It's difficult to know how big an advantage we might have gained by the manner of our victory. We certainly won a few battles, such as when Dizzy knocked over Michael Vaughan first ball and also by the way he constantly beat Marcus Trescothick. Warney's effort, coming on and straightaway bowling one that was a little too good for Ben Hollioake, would have been noted, I'm sure. And with the bat, Damien Martyn and Michael Bevan were outstanding after we lost a few wickets early on.

For me, one of the most notable aspects of tonight's match was the way we enjoyed the cricket and the win. It was a real buzz to be out there. Anyone who dismisses one-day cricket as not the real thing . . . well, I wish I could give them a sample of what and how we felt out in the middle. There was a real sense of team and a genuine joy in seeing your mates do well. The 12th man duties were performed superbly by Wade Seccombe, whose attitude and demeanour have already made their presence felt within the team.

From a personal point of view, I was pleased to be able to provide a meaningful contribution with the bat when the team needed it. And I felt my captaincy was proactive and instinctive in the field tonight, which gave me even greater satisfaction.

The ice sessions on a bruised wrist, which came courtesy of a wayward throw when I was batting, meant I didn't get to bed until 1.45am.

June 15 *Durham*

I DECIDED TO MAKE A public statement in regards to player behaviour, giving a commitment that the Australian players would make every effort to avoid disputing umpires' decisions. I can't guarantee that there won't be any dissent — in the heat of battle sometimes things get said — but I can promise that we'll be trying to do the right thing.

This is in part a reaction to the flak we received following the incident involving Michael Slater during the first Test of our recent India tour. The feedback we received from our supporters, via letters, and from the Australian Cricket Board, confirmed what we already knew: that it wasn't pretty.

'We've made a conscious decision for this series that we'll endeavour to accept every decision,' I told reporters. 'Disputes never look good on TV and they replay it many times. Sometimes you don't realise how bad it looks. The Australian team will be trying to accept every decision in the best way possible. If we get into a similar situation [to the Slater incident] I'd like to think our guys will walk away. Whether that's being realistic or not, I'm not sure until it actually happens.

'We want to be remembered as a really good cricket side, not for the wrong reasons. And we've talked about that. That's important to us. You can judge us at the end of the tour as to whether we have improved in that regard.

'I don't see it as a big issue with the team. We've stepped out of line a couple of times. I don't think we've been worse than anyone else, but we want to be the best at what we're doing and that's all part of it.'

Player behaviour wasn't the hot topic in this morning's papers. They were more concerned with the fact that last night England recorded its lowest ever one-day score, seven short of the previous debacle. To be fair, they gave our boys an equal billing for their star-studded display, in particular praising Glenn McGrath and Jason Gillespie. I've no doubt that mentally we are damaging the English team; this humiliation won't help their state of mind. It's amazing to see how quickly everyone — not only the media but people in the streets — has lost confidence in this English team. This must be a source of frustration to the players, after their superb work of late, but here more than anywhere in the world you are only as good as your last performance.

The three-hour bus trip to Durham was made somewhat more enjoyable by a screening of *The Shawshank Redemption*, endless games of 500, newspaper scouring and novel reading. As soon as we arrived, in keeping with our quest to be the fittest side in international cricket, Jock Campbell ordered the lads down to the gym for a quick weights and stomach stabilising work, followed by a stretch and swim.

Ricky Ponting reflects on the first two weeks of our Ashes tour while walking along the banks of the River Wear in Durham.

The rest of the day was ours and the usual activities took place. All except one. The Queensland lads in the squad are renowned for their camaraderie and trust in each other, but Haydos and Chuck stretched the faith to the limit. Haydos, employing his own trusty hair-clipping tools, took to the head of his mate with great enthusiasm, giving him an army looking back and sides, all for the right price. Both seemed satisfied with the work done, but Chuck didn't have the benefit of seeing the back of his head which, to my untrained eye, it didn't look as if a level playing surface had been left.

June 16 *Durham*

At Chester-le-Street
NatWest Series
Game 6 — June 16

Australia v Pakistan: game abandoned due to rain without a ball being bowled

At Lord's
NatWest Series
Game 7 — June 17

England 156 (BC Hollioake 53; Waqar Younis 7–36) conceded the match to Pakistan 4–153 (39.5 overs: Abdur Razzaq 75) after spectators invaded the ground

IT WAS TERRIFIC TO HEAR from the family again. Rosie is very excited at the prospect of catching up with Daddy tomorrow. She's even kept a 'Milky Bar' she bought from Australia for me, confirming once again that she's a sweet little thing with a caring nature.

Austin won't be making the trip up north, instead remaining in London with Lynette's parents, Phil and Ethel. It's been both exciting and frustrating to hear Austin grow up via the phone. He now says words on the phone and interacts with me and I can't wait to hold him again and tell him he's such a champion. Lynette is now past 25 weeks with the pregnancy and coping well considering the difficulty in travelling in such an advanced state.

I miss all of them. The sacrifice of being apart has acted as a motivational tool over the years, ensuring that I focus on the job. Otherwise, I'm wasting my time and not seeing the kids grow up. By succeeding, it allows me to justify the time away.

We have a new member of our squad on the bus as from today. In a ground-breaking move, Bec Lauder has assumed the role of team masseur, a position we players have been pushing for quite a while. To illustrate how much better the players and Board interact these days, we joined forces recently to hold a debrief on the Indian tour and also to look ahead to the Ashes tour. The idea of a team masseur had been floated many times, but no decision had been made. This time, however, with the CEO, Cricket Operations Manager and Commercial Operations Manager in attendance, I put forward the concept again, which was backed by our support staff. The outcome was this appointment and the quality of choice first class. We have regularly used Bec in Adelaide over the years, and thus are fully aware of how good and valuable she is. As far as I know, she is the first female to be a part of an Australian Test touring team.

Brack's unfortunate run of late continued in a freakish manner. While preparing to receive some treatment from 'Jaws' Farhart, he got up to pull a sliding door shut,

Nathan Bracken at Chester-le-Street, waiting for our one-dayer against Pakistan to be abandoned. Why is it that fast bowlers always smile when it rains?

to negate the body-numbing cold and sleety rain that had engulfed the ground and delayed the start of play. In reefing the frame across he gashed his bowling hand, necessitating four stitches from the ground doctor.

Meanwhile, in the corner of the room, Roy assumed the role of a penned-in sheep, being shorn firstly by Chuck, who seemed to be looking for some form of revenge after yesterday's events. Binga, the team hairdresser (or so he says) took over the reins and conjured up a Mohawk looking fashion statement. Whether Roy liked it is irrelevant now, as the press 'snappers' (photographers) got the scoop and their shots were being sent around the world in a matter of minutes.

Wet weather has the same effect on the boys as a full moon — they go stir crazy in the cooped-up confines of a change-room. Dizzy took to trimming his beard, ending up with a pencil-thin look that semi-circles his melon. Haydos hogged the bench, working our jet-lagged newest member into a lather of sweat.

Thankfully, common sense prevailed in regard to the rain. With, very obviously, there being little chance of play both umpires came into the rooms and said simply, 'Let's have lunch early and then, if it's still raining, we'll probably call it off.' As soon as he heard this, Jock's ears pricked up and he pencilled in a gym session for the lads. Retribution, however, was swift: a torrent of abuse was hurled his way, and he'll soon learn that a thick skin is his best form of defence.

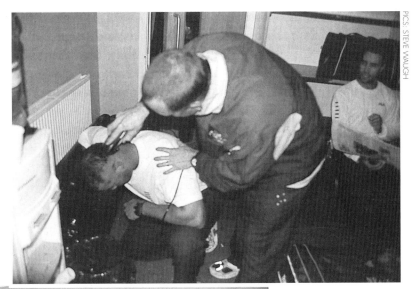

Right: Chuck takes to Roy's melon with the hair-clippers, but soon he would realise that he was way out of his depth . . .

Left: Bing takes control in front of a frenzy of photographers, all desperate for the shot of the day after our game against Pakistan was abandoned.

With the rain continuing, I was left to reflect on the appalling scenes at Headingley yesterday, when a mob stormed onto the ground with Pakistan still four runs from victory, and left a ground steward lying by the pitch being treated by paramedics. Apparently the poor bloke has broken ribs and a damaged spleen. Certain sections of the crowds seem to be out of control. The players were forced to run for their lives, and England captain Alec Stewart conceded the game. It was a very sad state of affairs, taking all the gloss away from a match that featured Waqar Younis taking 7–36, the second best figures ever recorded in one-day internationals.

This was too similar to the ugly scenes we witnessed at Cardiff a bit more than a week ago. Sadly, though, I still wonder whether the local authorities are getting fair dinkum in their approach to this serious problem. Judging by their comments, they seem to think they're powerless, but they have to do something before a very ugly, even tragic, incident occurs. Perhaps the time has come for the cricketers to make a statement, and refuse to perform until the problem is eradicated.

After the nasty events at Headingley, Alec Stewart was pretty blunt with his comments, and in my view he was right on the money. 'The fellow [the steward, Stephen Speight] was only trying to protect the players,' Alec said. 'That might have been a player lying out there, which might prove to the authorities here that something has to be done about player safety.

'It was obvious what was going to happen here,' he continued. 'The ECB [England and Wales Cricket Board] cannot guarantee the players' safety, so all I could do was concede the game in the interests of the England players, the two Pakistan batsmen and the umpires.

'Spectators who come on to the ground in Australia are fined heavily. I can count on the fingers of one hand the numbers who have done it in my three tours there.

'It's a very sad day for English cricket. We saw some brilliant bowling by Waqar Younis, but at the end we saw some disgraceful scenes.'

June 18 *Nottingham*

WHEN I WOKE THIS MORNING I knew a busy day lay ahead. First up was a photo shoot involving Nasser Hussain and me for a TV advertisement for the *Telegraph* newspaper. Again, like a commercial we did earlier for npower, the sponsors of the Test series, I was required to take the mickey out of the England captain, which I don't mind as long as we back it up on the field. If I were the England captain, however, I wouldn't be giving too many compliments to the scriptwriters, but the English tend to laugh at themselves by nature probably more than we do.

From there, I headed to an emergency meeting that had been hastily arranged at Trent Bridge by the Nottinghamshire CEO Dave Collier to brief us on the extra security measures they were going to put in place for tomorrow's match. I'm sure these measures are all well intentioned and admirable in intent, but trying to stop a crowd invading the ground with a wire mesh fence held in place by volunteers is surely a band-aid solution at best. At least they are trying and for that I give them full marks, but the solution needs to be more all encompassing and for that they need government legislation to change.

A press conference followed and it was here that I felt as if I was being set up as the fall guy. Every question was loaded, with the journos clearly wanting me to bag the officials, the spectators, anyone. The safety problem was one that I raised many years ago and ever since, whenever there is a problem, the journos come straight to me for a comment. It's about time other teams, boards and players put their hands up and have their say. I stopped the continuous, repetitive questions with one final statement: 'I'm not going to give you guys a headline, write the facts yourself.'

Practice was delayed until tonight, under the lights, though they didn't make a lot of difference because it doesn't get dark here during summer until around 10pm. Really, day/night cricket in England is a waste of time, because the lights don't play any part in the match (provided the weather stays fine) and at Trent Bridge at least the lights have a 'club oval' brightness. The practice pitches were fairly ordinary, but I was most impressed by Adam Gilchrist's attitude and willingness to make the most out of his session with the bat. Time will tell if the hard work pays off for him, and full marks to him if it does, because his form with the blade to date has been patchy. Gilly should always remember that form is temporary, class is permanent.

June 19 *Nottingham*

At Trent Bridge
NatWest Series
Game 8 — June 19
Pakistan 9–290 (50 overs: Saleem Elahi 79) defeated Australia 254 (46.3 overs: AC Gilchrist 70, SR Waugh 56; Waqar Younis 6–59) by 36 runs

AN EARLY-MORNING SWIM WITH ROSIE, followed by some stretching, had me in a relaxed frame of mind for today's match. As is the case for day/nighters in Australia, we had lunch at the ground before a brief team meeting where we outlined our plans and reinforced the style of play we expect to produce. It's amazing to look back on the losses we've had over the previous couple of years and find a common theme running through them. For me, the best gauge as to how we are going to perform is the mood of our warm-up routine and the alertness of the guys in our pre-game catching and preparation. Today, we were lacklustre and sloppy, traits we took out for our fielding through the entire 50 overs, particularly during the first 10 overs, when we dropped catches, missed run-out opportunities and consequently helped Pakistan take control of the match.

The crowd was extremely vocal in their support of Pakistan, with flags, banners and firecrackers all making their presence felt. I'm not talking nice little fizzy crackers here, but massive bungers accompanied by masses of smoke. By the time we got into the last 10 overs the crowd had whipped itself into a frenzy in certain sections of the ground. It got so noisy and dangerous that Brett Lee rushed in from the boundary, fearing for his safety after a massive firework lobbed directly past his face to land only a metre or two away. Michael Bevan had also endured many near misses and couldn't concentrate on the job at hand for fear of injury.

Binga told me he didn't feel safe and wouldn't go back down to the fence to field, which said to me that we should leave the field. In consultation with the umpires, we all agreed to walk off until the situation subsided to acceptable levels of safety. Our move was applauded by most people, especially the decent, genuine cricket fans who have to suffer these idiots all day long. Match referee Brian Hastings eventually agreed that we would go back on, but not until the crowd had settled down and the ground announcer had stated firmly that no more firecrackers would be tolerated. We did make it back onto the ground, to receive fireworks of a different variety — from our opponents' blades as they smashed their way to 9–290.

Gilly's response to the massive task of chasing this total was breathtaking, treating the all-time great opening duo of Wasim Akram and Waqar Younis as if they were net bowlers in a blitzkrieg assault that had us well ahead of the asking rate. My dig of 56 was very encouraging for the rest of the tour. I played with confidence and authority, moving my feet well and placing the ball into the gaps until the murky conditions, dubious lights and poor sightscreens made batting virtually impossible. It's amazing how, in what is now a multi-million dollar industry, a pitch can be prepared in a part of the square that doesn't allow for the sightscreens to be behind the bowlers' arms. Tonight we were looking into the crowd and an open door in search of the ball. I accept that it was the same for both teams, but I still can't understand why the powers-that-be overlook such a basic necessity. Don't they want to help produce the best game possible?

My night was spent icing a left big toe that had been smashed by a pacy Azhar Mahmood inswinger. It's amazing how these guys can 'reverse' swing the ball further, better and more consistently than any other side!

June 21 *London*

At The Oval
NatWest Series
Game 9 — June 21

England 176 (43.2 overs:
NV Knight 48; B Lee 3–63) lost to
Australia 2–177 (30.1 overs:
AC Gilchrist 80, RT Ponting 70*)
by eight wickets

THE NEWSPAPERS OF THE PAST couple of days have been littered with headlines and comment about our walk off at Trent Bridge, which was always going to make good print. Most respected our decision and approved of it, suggesting to me that people here have had enough of the 'soccer mob' mentality that has crept into one-day cricket like a virus that is spreading with no cure in sight.

Fortunately, there was none of that about in today's game against England at The Oval, which we won convincingly. This was just the tonic we needed before the final against Pakistan in two days time; more importantly, it must have put a psychological dint in the England squad in regard to what lies ahead for them over the next couple of months. I wasn't about to talk this fact up in the media, but deep down both teams know we have the upper hand.

Binga and Flem both looked impressive and the duel between them for a guernsey in the first Test is going to be closely fought. Again, our batting was outstanding and I hope has set the tone for the whole summer ahead.

Today saw the arrival of the Test boys in our change-rooms and it was terrific to see them around. Their keenness and a strong desire to start their tour were evident; the enthusiasm new players bring into a squad is always infectious. In some ways, it's been a little strange to know that the Test contingent have been in England for a number of

Above: *Australia v Pakistan at Trent Bridge. Attacking fields for our bowlers have evolved thanks to their quality and our self-belief.*

Left and below: *These letters were just two from a stackful that responded positively to our walk-off later in the game.*

days but have stayed at a different hotel and trained away from the one-day squad. It's a new way of doing things and I'm not sure it has worked, because it has tended to alienate the two groups when we pride ourselves on being one big happy squad. Buck has been putting in incredible hours at the nets, looking after both groups in back-to-back sessions, which means he has been at the nets for five to six hours at a time. By the end of the tour he'll need reconstruction surgery to his right shoulder because of the amount of throwdowns he's been doing.

June 22 *London*

THE WEEKLY SELECTION MEETING WITH Trevor Hohns and Adam Gilchrist obviously focused on our thoughts as to the make-up of the starting XI for the one-day final. The end result was a team that has yet to play together in this series, which demonstrates the depth and strength of the various line-ups that have played the preliminary rounds.

A media conference gave me the chance to announce our side, which generally never happens over here. Normally, it's cloak and dagger stuff with regard to naming a team and the press can't believe how relaxed we are with it. So much so that they think we're playing mind games with the opposition by being positive and not hiding anything. In reality, it's just my way of being up front about an issue — potential late changes — that I see as being overrated anyway. It's not as if you're going to change your whole game plan if someone does or doesn't play.

My family bid me farewell this afternoon as they headed off to EuroDisney by train for a six-day adventure. The kids are so excited at the thought of seeing Mickey Mouse ... I think I'm almost as keen to play in a one-day final at the home of cricket.

At Lord's
NatWest Series Final
June 23

Pakistan 152 (42.3 overs:
SK Warne 3–56) lost to Australia
1–156 (26.3 overs: AC Gilchrist
76*, ME Waugh 36; RT Ponting
35*) by nine wickets

June 23 *London*

MATTHEW HAYDEN SUMMED UP THE day ahead at breakfast when he said, 'Geez, I'm looking forward to today, it's going to be a great day.' Pretty impressive words, when you consider he was one of the reserves, missing out on the opportunity to play at cricket's holy grail in a final. This is the sort of spirit and character we need and want in the squad.

Buck's trusty home video recorder confronted the lads as they boarded the team bus in preparation for the 20-minute drive to 55 St John's Wood. We were a relaxed and confident team, knowing that our fate lay entirely in our hands, with one word meaning the difference between winning and losing — discipline.

As it turned out, the day was almost a carbon copy of the 1999 World Cup Final. Events began to unravel with an uncanny similarity to what transpired on that momentous day some two years ago. Pakistan again won the toss and batted, before losing their first wicket to McGrath after a 28-run partnership. This was what occurred in the World Cup. Again, Pakistan slumped to 4–60 and then 7–102 before making 20 more this time than they had in 1999.

In truth, today's score was probably a poorer effort, because the wicket was very easy paced and anyone not wanting to get out could safely prepare for a long innings. However, our bowling and ground fielding were superb. Consistent, persistent pressure strangled the life out of their line-up, which was exactly how we thought we could unsettle them. In a way, Pakistan's strength is their unpredictability, but this can turn into a weakness when put under the microscope by quality cricket, which translates into pressure.

Just like 1999, we strode off Lord's all reinforcing to each other the fact that the job was only half done, and that we could not relax until we had put together the consummate performance.

Adam Gilchrist and Mark Waugh got us off to a solid start, nullifying the danger men, Waqar and Wasim, and Ricky Ponting finished off proceedings with another gem of a short innings. This rounded off a thoroughly professional team win, made all the more special by the fact that it had come after much hard work and planning during the entire series.

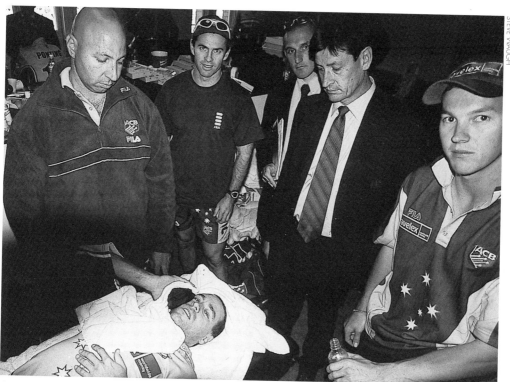

A concerned Pat Farhart applies ice to Michael Bevan minutes after Bevo wore a full can of VB in the face at the presentation ceremony that followed the one-day final.

And then, just when we least expected it, disappointment, controversy and upheaval reared their ugly heads. First, to somewhat taking the gloss off our excellent performance, we learnt that Bracks had failed to overcome his shoulder ailment and would no longer be a part of the squad. He needs to fly home to have the damage evaluated by a specialist. This was devastating news to a lad on his first Ashes tour, but he must now find a positive out of this negative. Perhaps it will be his chance to work on his overall fitness, maybe to get the shoulder stronger than it previously was, or even a chance to work on aspects of his life unrelated to cricket. Minutes later, during the presentation on the Lord's Pavilion balcony, our win was again soured when Michael Bevan was struck on the face by a full can of VB, thrown by a spectator some 30 metres away on the ground and two storeys below us. We were just about to receive our souvenir stumps and trophy, lined up behind the Pakistan side, when I heard this noise to my right, as if someone had copped an almighty slap. Two people along, I saw Bevo holding his face and a can of VB on the ground to his left. He seemed to almost be in shock, and said flatly, 'I've been hit in the face by a can of beer.'

Haydos confirmed it had come from the crowd and that was all the information I needed to say, 'Let's go, we're not going to put up with this!'

It was a cowardly act from a weak individual who knew when he threw it in the direction of the players on the balcony that he could seriously hurt someone if it hit them. And with such a congregation of people, he could hardly miss. Inzaman-ul-Haq

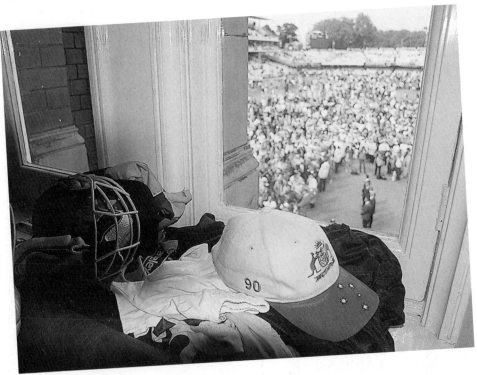

The view from my spot in the away dressing-room at Lord's. This photograph was taken shortly after the aborted presentation ceremony. The number 90 on my cap represents my place in the order of players who have worn the Australian one-day colours.

was extremely lucky, as it sailed not more than an inch above his head before making contact with Michael's face. Fortunately, Bevo was struck by the full side of the can and not the end or an edge, either of which would have caused serious damage.

The presentation ceremony was hastily rearranged indoors, while the head of the Marylebone Cricket Club (MCC), Roger Knight, apologised, on behalf of the club, to our whole squad. Not surprisingly, most of my post-match media conference was spent dealing with and discussing this unsavoury act. By the time I'd finished with the media, filled out my umpires report and Allan Border Medal voting form, met with the selectors to discuss a replacement for Bracks and had a meeting with one of the players, the winning atmosphere had all but subsided. This is one of the few downsides to being a captain — not being able to soak up the win until about an hour after the partying begins. On a happier note, all the wives and girlfriends of the team had the chance to celebrate with the team in the change-rooms, which was a break with the traditions of the past.

One tradition that didn't change was our team song, admirably led by Punter, who as usual whipped the boys and girl into a frenzy. Bec became the first female ever to join in the chorus of our team anthem and duly got drenched by the lads at its conclusion.

June 24 *Chichester*

IT'S HARD NOT TO READ the papers when we win. The important thing is not to get carried away with the praise that has been showered on us after our big win yesterday. It was a trifle overwhelming and very gushing, which is nice, but you must be able to know what the reality of the situation is. We played very, very well, but we need to keep moving forward and not get too carried away, because the game will get you the moment you think you've got it.

At today's team meeting we discussed 'what cheeses we like, what cheeses we don't like and what cheeses we would like to taste'. These questions related to a book we have all read and discussed before, called *Who Moved My Cheese!* and had been left under every player's door for him to consider before the meeting. The book is in part about the different directions life takes us and how we cope and embrace those changes. One person who, upon finding these questions, thought Buck had lost his marbles was Brett Lee. Binga didn't know anything about the book, because he had joined the tour party later than everyone else and thus hadn't read it, so to him the questions looked as if they'd come from an alien galaxy or a crazed man.

A few sore heads found solace at our next destination, the Marriott Hotel at Goodwood Park, where our Test-match tour begins against an MCC XI at Arundel. My spirits soared when the phone rang and my daughter Rosie informed me she was with the family underneath the Eiffel Tower in Paris. She explained quickly that she was so excited at being there and having seen Minnie Mouse the day before at EuroDisney and that Austin has apparently taken an instant liking to Chip & Dale having followed them around like a shadow.

Back at our hotel, a gym session took place, followed by a team meeting where I struggled to talk about Gallipoli, before presenting to each player a Digger's .303 bullet. Some of the team, of course, having not been a part of the one-day squad, had not gone to Gallipoli and I wanted to share what it meant to me. Which is plenty. I can't explain exactly why, but each time I talk about Gallipoli I become very emotional and find expressing my thoughts a tough assignment.

June 26 *Chichester*

At Arundel
June 25–27

Australians 390 (SM Katich 168*, SK Warne 69, SR Waugh 45; JH Dawes 4–74) and 8–294 (declared: SR Waugh 105, DR Martyn 80) defeated Marylebone Cricket Club 124 (MH Richardson 64*; CR Miller 4–41) and 280 (JC Adams 81*, DM Ward 57; CR Miller 3–87) by 280 runs

OUR MATCH AT THE EARL of Arundel's magnificent cricket ground is providing us with the perfect tonic after the turmoil of the post-match controversy at Lord's. Pimms and ginger ale, boater hats, egg-and-bacon ties, polite and rapturous (if that's possible at the same time) applause and eager autograph hunters of all ages were the order of the day. The only dampener on proceedings was the debilitating symptoms associated with hay fever that had struck many of the tour party, myself included. While Slats approached the *Guinness Book of World Records* mark for most sneezes in a day, my eyes itched to the point where the easiest option seemed to be to gouge them out to relieve the pain.

Just being at Arundel, in the tranquility of beautiful rolling green pastures with the historic castle dating back to 1067, nestled neatly behind clusters of impressive and imposing trees, was as close as you'd get to cricket being played in heaven. It was such a relief to escape the unwanted publicity that one idiot armed with a VB can and a strong arm created. Our time here has been both productive and cleansing, with some excellent cricket and hopefully a victory to go with a dash of culture and a spot of learning.

Yesterday, we had a team photo taken with the Earl of Arundel, a very amiable and down-to-earth chap. I mentioned to him that we wouldn't mind having a look at his castle if that was at all possible, and not only did he say yes, but he also took on the role of excursion leader and gave us a personal tour this morning. As far as castles go, this one is extraordinary, with a vast array of artefacts, antiques and family heirlooms in perfect condition and superbly presented. The in-house church is incredible, the most magnificent and tastefully designed I'd ever laid eyes on. It was built to serve a Catholic family, which even 100 years ago was very much the minority in England and looked down upon. Nowadays, the church is used occasionally for family weddings and christenings. Crossbows, knives and other weapons from hundreds of years ago adorn the walls, alongside suits of armour that had been worn into battle by the Earl's ancestors.

Lang was about the only one who could have fitted into the suits — the men of yesteryear were clearly much smaller than those of today. And after copping a full-blooded sweep from the bat of the West Indies' Jimmy Adams on the wrist during the match today, I bet Lang would have loved the mesh and metal safety barrier around him. The cost of maintaining the castle is around £300,000 per year and even Warney would have second thoughts about that one, but its beauty and presence were breathtaking.

Tonight we attended the traditional MCC welcoming dinner for the Australian team. Traditionally this is a bit of a stiff-upper-lip affair, where the players are split up, one per table. To add a little bit of humour and to relax the evening somewhat, I enlisted the help of Damien Fleming and Adam Gilchrist to spice my speech up a little and give some insights into our squad. After saying all the necessary thank yous I asked each player to stand up as I introduced them, and how I did so is listed on the following three pages. The jibes continued on until finally it was payback time for our manager, who is notorious for taking the mickey out of at least one player in every speech he makes. I'm not sure if he appreciated being described as a 'former NSW seam bowler who now doesn't seem to do too much', but I do know I'll be in serious trouble next time he graces the microphone.

Gilly and I explore the magnificent library at Arundel Castle.

The 2001 Australians

Matthew Hayden
Recently broke the all-time Australian record for runscoring in a three-match Test series. Proceeded to nickname himself 'The Don'. Also holds the record within the side as the only skipper of a fishing boat that was turned over by a wave and sunk. Rates himself as a bowler.

Michael Slater
Has now played 70-odd Tests for the impressive tally of 14 Test hundreds and a record-equalling nine 90s with someone else . . . can't remember who. Has a Superman tattoo on his left shoulder, like his idol Bon Jovi, and loves to kiss his Aussie helmet upon reaching a century.

Justin Langer
The leading runscorer in our 16-match Test winning streak and possibly our worst bowler. If he had to write his own player profile, would list his hobbies as 'throwdowns and abdominal work'. His favourite holiday destination would be the Lord's indoor nets.

Mark Waugh
Has scored over 7000 runs and is only six catches away from Mark Taylor's world record mark of 157. Has played in 111 Tests and reckons he got a dodgy decision in every one of them. His most prized possessions are a comb and a mirror.

Ricky Ponting
Has played in 42 Tests for seven hundreds. Is the only man to score three ducks in a row and then back it up with three consecutive hundreds. One of the best drivers in the game, which is interesting given that he has never secured his driver's licence.

Damien Martyn
Made his Test debut some nine years ago and averages 40-plus in his 11 Tests. Spends a lot of time doing bench weights in the gym for little or no result.

Simon Katich
On his second overseas tour. Scored six first-class centuries last Australian season to gain selection. Has a temperament and technique tailor-made for Test cricket. Also has the hairiest body and biggest appetite since Merv Hughes.

Adam Gilchrist
Began his Test career with 15 straight Test-match wins, then made sure he lost his first one in style by bagging a king pair in Calcutta. Averages in the high 40s with the bat and one suspects that it will stay there.

Shane Warne

One of *Wisden's* five cricketers of the century. Also picked in Australia's Test team of the century. But the prize he most wants is a Test-match 100.

Colin Miller

Oldest player in the side and probably in world cricket. Holds the Australian record for most first-class wickets in a domestic season. Has a testing tour ahead — may become the first man to bat behind Glenn McGrath in a Test match.

Wade Seccombe

On his first tour for Australia. Has been an integral part of Queensland's most successful era, winning four Sheffield Shield titles. Can match it with Ian Healy in the appealing stakes.

Glenn McGrath

Has taken 326 Tests wickets, behind only Warne and Lillee among Australian bowlers. Owns half of Australia, but it's the half no one else wants. Can remember all his wickets — who he dismissed, how he was out, etc — which constitutes an amazing memory. Unfortunately, he can't seem to remember where his wallet is when he's at the bar.

Brett Lee

Fastest bowler in the world. Averages 16 with the ball and has a strike rate in Tests of a wicket every six overs. Runner-up in *Cleo's* Bachelor of the Year competition, an achievement somewhat soured when it was revealed that David Boon had won it 17 years before.

Jason Gillespie

Has a strike rate and average up there with the greats. On the field, he is a pretty handy bowler as well. Fields well away from the captain.

Damien Fleming

Has taken 75 wickets in 20 Tests. Part of the Test hat-trick club, which he nearly joined twice. Favourite player as a youngster was Trevor Chappell, as we all saw in the 1999 World Cup semi-final.

Ashley Noffke

No one knows him.

John Buchanan (coach)

Dead ringer for Ned Flanders from *The Simpsons*. Enjoys giving throwdowns to the players and loves nothing more than to pin the lads in the ribs or crack the odd helmet.

Steve Bernard (manager)
Second year in charge. Former NSW seam bowler who now doesn't seem to do too much.

Jock Campbell (fitness)
Gym junkie, net bowler, hated by all.

Errol Alcott (physio)
Most experienced member of the tour party (17 years). Got his nickname of 'Hooter' when he asked, during his first day on tour, 'What time does the hooter go off?'

Mike Walsh (cricket analyst)
Formerly the team scorer. Is eyeing off the manager's job and loves getting in team photos.

Rebecca Lauder (team masseur)
We had 30 applicants, 29 were male, so Bec got the job. A valuable member who has worked part-time with the side before.

Dinner

to the

Australian Touring Team

at Arundel Park

Tuesday, 26th June, 2001

The autographs on my dinner program belong to the MCC President, Lord Alexander of Weedon, QC (Bob Alexander), and the guest speaker Richie Benaud.

June 27 *London*

UNFORTUNATELY, AND NOT FOR THE first time on a cricket tour, the size of the change-room at Arundel was insufficient for a squad of our number, and the ensuing chaos of cricket gear and clothing had only one way to go — downhill. And that it did, particular so in my close vicinity. A quartet of Fleming, Slater, S. Waugh and Hayden wasn't the best draw in terms of neatness and order, and within hours there were plenty of 'Is that your tracksuit top?' or 'Have you seen my training hat?' questions being asked.

The game proved to be an excellent workout, against opposition captained by Jimmy Adams and including six former or present Test players and five other first-class players. In fact, they gave us a tougher examination than most county sides could or will give us.

Unfortunately for Slats and Lang, the desired time in the middle to gain match practice and mental toughness didn't materialise, which means that our next match against Essex now assumes extra importance for both players. Matt Hayden is currently in about second gear but isn't far away from where he wants to be. All he has to do now is work hard in the next match and during training to fine tune his game, for he at present seems to be getting too far ahead of himself rather than letting the process determine the outcome as he did so magnificently in India.

The big plus for us from the game was Simon Katich's innings, which oozed class, temperament and technique, and had an air of authority and calmness, suggesting — as he's done in the past — that he is tailor-made for Test-match cricket. Kat came to the crease on the first day when we were struggling a bit at 4–64, and hit 168 not out from 167 deliveries, sharing a partnership of 190 with Shane Warne. At one stage the Queensland paceman Joe Dawes had bowling figures of 4–26. Six overs later, his figures were 4–74.

On a personal note, I couldn't be happier with my form. It wasn't so much the totals that gave me confidence, as the manner and composed state I found myself in. A small change in my grip and stance, which allowed me to get a touch more side-on and to swing through the line in an arc similar to rocking a baby, gave me the confidence to play in the 'V' between mid-on and mid-off with a great deal of confidence. My main danger, as always, will be my concentration during this series, and if I manage to master that then I believe I can have a very successful summer.

Others to impress were Damien Martyn, who continues to improve and push for a regular Test spot, and the pace duo of Damien Fleming and Jason Gillespie. Flem has responded well to the challenge of forcing his way back into the Test XI, training with intensity and purpose, and the results are showing. He may yet prove to be our trump card, as he is our only genuine swing bowler, perfectly suited to the English pitches and atmosphere, and also to the type of balls used here, which are Dukes. These locally-made balls have a wax-type finish on the outside of the leather, enabling them to last longer and to 'buff' up better, which leads to the ball swinging around more than in other countries.

Dizzy appears to be peaking at exactly the right moment, and for the first time in a long while is letting himself go without the thought in the back of his mind that there's a niggling injury lurking, waiting to happen. His pace and rhythm have been mesmerising to not only the spectators but also to his opponents, who are yet to get the better of him. I believe he will have a sensational series and wouldn't be at all surprised if he ends up being the leading wicket taker on either side. His place in cricket history will be assured if he manages to stay on the paddock. Jock Campbell has been pretty relentless in his campaign to keep us all fit and each player has been allocated gym, swimming and stabilising sessions to keep on top of this aspect of our game. His enthusiasm for and enjoyment of fitness work has been invigorating, and he has listed some of the oldies to unknown heights in front of the mirrors and dumbells

Nathan Bracken's replacement is now on his way. He is Ashley Noffke, a young Queenslander who instantly impressed me with a 10-over spell against us (New South Wales) in our domestic one-day competition during the last Australian season. He hits the wicket hard and has good control over his line and length, in the same way Glenn McGrath has. Stuart Law, the Queensland captain, has stated that he is like a 'mini McGrath', but we can only hope he is referring to his cricket. We don't want three pests in the one team; Pigeon and Buck are quite enough.

The great news for the team is that Brett Lee is okay, after scans in London cleared him of any back damage, much to the relief of everyone except the English batsmen. The only scare he had was during the trip down to Arundel late at night with the departing physio of our one-day team, Pat Farhart. They slammed into a deer that had bounded out of the bushes to meet the hire car's bonnet at good pace. The boys described the deer's tumble as being 'like watching a fieldsman slide into the fence to try and stop a boundary'. Fortunately, unlike Ricky Ponting in Sydney a year ago, the startled animal leapt straight to its feet and sauntered off into the mist to see another day.

Simon Katich at Arundel, where he scored 168 not out at slightly better than a run a ball.

June 30 *London*

The last three days have given me a break from the tour, to enjoy some time with my family at Disneyland in Paris. We went on all the kids' rides, including Dumbo, the Mad Hatter's Tea Party, Peter Pan Flight, It's a Small World boat ride, and so on and so on. I hope Rosie and Austin had as much fun as I did!

Seriously though, it was fantastic to get away for a couple of days from the relentless nature of touring life, and all that seems to engulf the team. I know it wouldn't have happened in the old days, but with so much time being asked of the players these days, I think it is a natural and common-sense approach to give the players some time to themselves and their loved ones. This is another example of how the Board and the players are working together for the overall benefit of the team and Australian cricket.

Our trip went very smoothly in every way until about 30 minutes from Waterloo Station, when Austin woke up, tried to stand up, then dropped down and cracked his head on the fold-up tray table on the back of the seat in front. He split his skin just below his eye. What followed was a mad rush to secure some ice, which was crushed into his sock and applied to the wound to control the bleeding until we reached Waterloo. From here it was off to St Thomas' Hospital, while Rosie, Phil and Ethel went back to the family apartments in Kensington. Rosie promptly added to the night's drama by vomiting in the cab on the way home, much to the driver's consternation. By the time we saw a nurse and a doctor, it was 1.30am. The diagnosis was that a butterfly bandage was needed for the cut, but otherwise, thankfully, there is no damage.

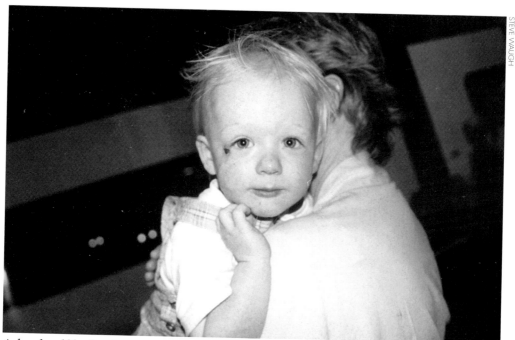

A dazed and bleeding Austin Waugh moments after cracking his head on the tray table of the train on which we were travelling from Paris back to London.

Left: A self-portrait taken on the flying dumbo ride. I was feeling more than a little nauseous at the time.

Below: Rosie and Austin introduced themselves to Minnie Mouse.

Above: This is a magic place, not only for children but for the whole family. Phil and Ethel Doughty — Lynette's parents and the kids' regular babysitters — enjoyed the experience as well.

Right: Rosie, straight after a wild ride on the Mad Hatter's Tea Party.

July 1 *Birmingham*

At Chelmsford
June 29–July 1

Australians 5–405 (declared: RT Ponting 63, DR Martyn 114*, AC Gilchrist 150*) and 9–569 (declared: ML Hayden 98, B Lee 79, RT Ponting 79, CR Miller 62; PM Such 5–131) drew with Essex 231 (JS Foster 74, GR Napier 59; JN Gillespie 5–37)

ON MY PREVIOUS THREE ASHES tours, we were lucky enough to be supported by a car sponsor, but this is not the case in 2001, which means that if you have a few days off and want to get away then you have to organise your own transport. Fortunately, the in-laws volunteered to drive me from London to Chelmsford, to enable me to catch up with the lads for today's day three of the game against Essex. However, an accident on one of the arterial roads that leads to the County Ground turned a one-hour journey into a three-and-a-half hour marathon, much to everyone's frustration.

Before I could even say hello, Haydos beamed a 'told you so' smile about the latest State of Origin scoreline, which was mind blowing to say the least. Queensland, having brought the legendary halfback Allan Langer back from playing at Warrington here in England, thrashed NSW by an unbelievable 40–14. It just goes to prove not only the greatness of 'Alfie' Langer, but also the genius and foresight of Maroons coach Wayne Bennett, who instigated Alf's return.

During the lunch break, I met briefly with Buck and Gilly who, of course, were running the show in my absence. To my surprise, they had opted to take some batting practice on this final day rather than attempt to bowl Essex out and in the process cause

Glenn McGrath attacks England captain Nasser Hussain during our tour match against Essex at Chelmsford.

Nasser Hussain some problems by hopefully dismissing him cheaply. The view of Buck and Gilly was that the quick bowlers had done enough and were ready for the Test match that lies ahead. They wanted to keep the lads fresh, an idea that obviously has merit, but I am a little concerned about Binga's lack of bowling. Some might say I should have stepped in, but responsibility must be shared in order for others to mature and expand their capabilities. Gilly has outstanding leadership qualities, and this type of decision is typical of what the top job is all about.

Predictably, everyone got bored with us batting all day and perhaps the spectators were right to complain. But they should remember that there was also an onus on their team to put out a side capable of taking 20 wickets to give themselves a chance of victory. It shouldn't have been totally about us being obliged to make a sporting declaration.

After a fitness session with Jock, in which we also involved the young kids who had been looking for autographs, we headed off down the motorway to Birmingham to finalise our preparation for the first Ashes Test.

July 2   *Birmingham*

THE TOUGHEST PART OF THE captaincy is being a tour selector. When I linked up today with Trevor Hohns, by phone, and Gilly we reluctantly agreed that Lang had to be left out of the first Test XI, to give Marto an opportunity at No. 6. Punter will bat at first wicket down. Recent form, tour scores and gut instincts all told us that we needed to make the change no matter how gut-wrenching a decision it was. Lang is an excellent team man and exactly the sort of guy you love to see standing next to you in battle, for he is courageous, committed and passionate about not only what he's doing but what the team is all about. He has always done the hard yards and given himself utterly to the team, factors that mean that statistics don't necessarily give a true indication of his worth. He would be the first to admit that he has not made the most of his recent opportunities, but would also feel somewhat singled out and unlucky to lose his spot. On the other hand, Marto's form, not only on this tour but throughout the past 18 months, has only been matched by his attitude, which has been first class. We owed him

ALLSPORT

Damien Martyn tries on his new Australian cap.

the chance to express himself on the international stage.

Telling a player that he's been dropped is certainly a tense and uncomfortable time. Knocking on Lang's door and seeing his expression when I said, 'Can I have a couple of minutes of your time?' wasn't easy. Even bearing in mind that we are really good mates, it is still a difficult task and the meeting was brief and to the point. We both realised that we need to get back to each other to talk the situation through, but emotionally it isn't the right time right now.

I must admit I was somewhat shattered by the experience. A hollow feeling in the pit of my stomach developed almost immediately, as I thought about what was going through Lang's mind right now and the utter confusion we selectors have just created for him. No doubt, he phoned home to relay the bad news and then he would have had hundreds of thoughts,

Talking the situation through with Justin Langer 24 hours after Lang's demotion from our starting XI.

mostly negative, racing through his head. Hopefully, with time, realistic, positive, upbeat thoughts will take hold and a new challenge for him will begin.

Lang is a tough nut and I know he'll bounce back.

Training today was intense, productive, concentrating on quality. Everyone looks in excellent shape, peaking nicely for the big game. The pitch looks excellent and the English squad is in disarray due to some late injuries, while our preparations have been almost spot on. It's amazing how much positive publicity we have been getting and, conversely, the enormous amount of negative stuff that's been aimed at the Poms. We must be careful not to take notice of either of these impostors, but rather to keep a check on what we are doing and what processes we need to follow if we want to succeed.

July 3 *Birmingham*

ANOTHER THOROUGH AND PURPOSEFUL TRAINING session, aided by Gary (brother of Matt) Hayden's 150-odd balls and by Queenslander Joe Dawes, who came down from league cricket to bowl to the lads, helped the quality and intensity of batting in the nets. Lang and I found time to have a more meaningful discussion on his demotion. I found his thoughts fair and well expressed, and I'm sure he felt better with it off his chest.

Today is our big day in regard to team preparation. All our meetings take place, so tomorrow is free for each player to mentally and physically prepare for the match. The tactical group of Gilly, Warney, Pigeon, Buck and myself gathered for 30 minutes before the rest of the guys got together, to go through our plans in batting, bowling and overall strategies. Keeping it simple was the theme; doing our jobs and sticking to the three Ps — Patience, Pressure, Partnerships.

Once all the lads were assembled we watched a video showing the English batsmen and their recent dismissals, followed by an analysis of their bowlers. When looking at their line-up, we went though the top order one by one, trying to identify their weak points, until we reached the tail, who are generally summed up with some good short stuff, then back into the 'corridor of uncertainty'. With Graham Thorpe out, their three key batsmen are probably Mike Atherton, Marcus Trescothick and Nasser Hussain, who all are prone to jab tentatively at good-length deliveries and are often caught behind when the bowlers bowl in that corridor, on a length just outside the off-stump. Line and length are obviously the keys.

As to our batting, we summed it up by saying, 'Know your own game, have a plan and be sharp and alert.' My speech centred on us being disciplined in everything we do. If we achieve this no one can beat us. However, if we stay away from this basic ingredient we are fallible, like anyone else. But I believe that the hunger and will to succeed is too great in this squad for this to happen. I finished off by saying the benefits of our efforts and toil in India will come through at some stage when the stakes are high and the game is in the balance. Often you don't know the gains you have made until the next difficult opportunity presents itself. We are a tougher unit for the loss in India and England will find in us an even better side than the one they are expecting to face.

July 4 *Birmingham*

DAYS OFF THESE DAYS ARE not really days off. Even though training was optional, we all had to turn up for the inaugural presentation of the trophy to be handed annually to the No. 1 Test-match team in the world. This was a nice piece of recognition for all the hard work we have put in and the £30,000 prize was proudly accepted by all of us.

After some treatment on my niggly left knee, aimed at preventing it getting any worse more than making it better, it was back to the ground for the match referee's meeting. These are normally tedious affairs but at the same time essential, because they do offer a forum where a significant point could be made.

The main issue today was totally out of the blue — the match referee will now be the tosser of the coin. This is an initiative of the International Cricket Council (ICC), and I think it is a joke, a decision made without consultation with any players and for what reason? Surely, as a captain, you have the right to either toss the coin or call it, but now only one captain will have any input. Obviously, they don't trust the captains, which

Fancy a stroke with these guys?

By SHARON HENDRY

IF you thought cricket was boring, take a look at these hunks and think again.

The Ashes spins into action at Edgbaston, Birmingham, tomorrow when England take on Australia.

But don't fall asleep just yet. At least there will be 22 fine specimens of the male species on display every time the teams do battle on TV. If your fella is a cricket follower, conversation

WE RATE CRICKET'S ASHES HUNKS

will be full of confusing babble about spin bowling, strokeplay, bouncers, bails, and LBWs.

SW's philosophy is: "If you can't grasp the rules – at least appreciate the talent."

So to help you understand that cricketers are a bit of all white, we've rounded up some of the sexiest Brits and Aussies who will be on display – fitness permitting – and rated them, using cricket balls.

And columnist Debbie Barham has prepared a special guide, right, to help you bat your way through the jargon.

BRITS

Nasser Hussain, 33

FAVOURITE POSITION: Batsman.
BACKGROUND: The Madras-born England captain is a good all-rounder with a "wide range of strokes". Made his Test debut against West Indies in 1989 and is known for his "great powers of concentration".
STATUS: Married to Karen, dad to three-week-old Jacob.
YUM FACTOR: His brooding good looks and strong leadership have girls going wobbly behind the wickets. Nass is skinny for a sportsman – but his dazzling dark eyes more than make up for it.

RATING

Craig White, 31

FAVOURITE POSITION: Bowler.
BACKGROUND: Craig was born in Morley, West Yorks, but brought up in Australia. Apparently, he's vital to England because of his unique ability to "reverse swing his balls". That should be worth watching!
STATUS: Married to Liz, dad to Megan and Isabella.
YUM FACTOR: This sexy Tyke could bowl you over with his rugged looks and roguish charm. Catch him in the right light on the pitch and he's a dead ringer for Mel Gibson.

RATING

Ian Ward, 28

FAVOURITE POSITION: Batsman.
BACKGROUND: Plymouth-born "Wardy" is a top toff – he attended posh Millfield public school. He made his debut for Surrey in 1996.
STATUS: Married to Joanne, dad to Robert and Lennox.
YUM FACTOR: He may only be 5ft 8in but Ian is strong and very well-built – and an impressive catch on or off the cricket field. Ian combines classic good looks with trendy attire, which sits well on his superbly masculine physique.

RATING

Darren Gough, 30

FAVOURITE POSITION: Bowler.
BACKGROUND: Barnsley-born Darren is known as "Rhino" (hnnn!). He was offered a place at Rotherham FC and Yorkshire Cricket Club at the same time but decided his equipment was best suited to a good long innings.
STATUS: Married to Anna-Marie, dad to Liam and Brennan.
YUM FACTOR: Goughie is small in stature but big in departments where it counts – like personality. Tanned and toned, it's not just the batsmen who look forward to his approach.

RATING

AUSSIES

Steve Waugh, 36

FAVOURITE POSITION: Batsman.
BACKGROUND: The Sydney-born captain has played in Test cricket for 15 years and is regarded as "tough, competitive and highly skilled".
STATUS: Married to Lynette, dad to Rosalie and Austin.
YUM FACTOR: Although Steve is no spring chicken – and that floppy fielding hat and menacing stare leave a lot to be desired – he redeems himself with a superbly toned body and those strong forearms. You'll go phwoaar at Waugh.

RATING

Brett Lee, 24

FAVOURITE POSITION: Bowler.
BACKGROUND: New South Wales-born Brett is known for his thrilling technique. It's been described as follows: "He approaches the crease at a gallop thrusts his front arm high, then releases at thundering speed from a nicely-balanced side-on position."
STATUS: Hurrah, girls, he's still single
YUM FACTOR: As one of the few singles playing, Brett gets a head start. His blond, pretty-boy looks are not everyone's cup of tea in the pavilion but wait until you see him bowling from behind!

RATING

Adam Gilchrist, 29

FAVOURITE POSITION: Wicketkeeper and batsman.
BACKGROUND: New South Wales-born Adam, the Aussie vice-captain, is described as "reliable, enthusiastic and athletic" – and one of the game's foremost strokemakers!
STATUS: Married to Melinda.
YUM FACTOR: OK, so he's not exactly pin-up material, but Adam is still worthy of inclusion as an Ashes hunk for his cheeky grin and knowing eyes. And let's face it, those well-toned legs and tanned, muscular arms are wasted on a cricket pitch.

RATING

Glenn McGrath, 31

FAVOURITE POSITION: Bowler.
BACKGROUND: Glenn is from New South Wales and is famous for "preferring bounce to pace".
STATUS: Married to Jane, dad to James.
YUM FACTOR: Glenn's long, lean limbs and fresh-faced grin make him a firm favourite. But girls hopping to share more than a cucumber sandwich with this hunk should be warned that he is hopelessly devoted to his equally attractive wife.

RATING

The captain and two of the vice-captains (Ricky Ponting was the third) during our 16-Test winning streak with the trophy we received for being officially recognised as the No. 1 Test side.

makes for a sad day. More importantly, why don't they deal with some real issues rather than one as mindless and ridiculous as this one?

But enough of such negatives. The fight for the Ashes is less than 24 hours away. Personally, I'm really looking forward to the cricket. I'm feeling amazingly relaxed at the crease at the moment, and am sure that if I concentrate well I'll get some runs, while on another level I'm really excited about captaining my country in an Ashes Test for the first time.

England will have noted how India took us on, and they will have learned from that. I expect them to try to get in our face a bit, to have a real go at us. I'm sure, beyond what they saw of our matches in India, they'll have memories of 1997, when they killed us on the first day, setting up a Test victory for them. The first session can have a real bearing on the outcome of the Test, and there is no doubt in my mind that the way the first Test evolves will have a significant bearing on what happens for the rest of summer.

I expect our pace attack to test England's batting line-up, but it's not going to be as simple as just blasting away. We've still got to put the ball in the right spots. This said, if the three of them get it right, they're going to be a real handful.

The England selectors seem to have acknowledged the threat our pace attack holds by their choice of batsmen to replace their injured first-choices, Michael Vaughan and Graham Thorpe. They're obviously looking for players who might be able to blunt our attack, which is why they originally selected Mark Ramprakash and now they've gone back to Mark Butcher. Of course, I'd love to play them at full strength, but the guys coming in are pretty good players with something to prove. They have an incentive to do well, to keep their places for the rest of the series, so perhaps England might even be bolstered by the changes forced upon them.

My main concerns, though, are for my own team. Have we done the right thing leaving Lang out? Will Punter's electric form continue? Who should I open the bowling with — Lee or Gillespie? Or both? I pondered these and other questions as I spent the afternoon devouring chocolate with the kids during a visit to the local Cadbury's factory. Austin has definitely got my sweet tooth and had enough chocolate for 10 kids, while Rosie enjoyed the kids' playground and rides, traversing the ropes, bars and equipment like an Olympic gymnast of the future.

SOMETIMES LIFE TAKES A TURN for the unexpected or fate deals you a hand that stops you dead in your tracks. At 9.35pm tonight we were confronted with a life-threatening emergency. On hearing what sounded like someone in pain, moaning loudly but somewhat incoherently, Lynette and I turned down our TV to try to establish where this ghastly noise was coming from. Our initial instincts told us to check the children, who were asleep in our adjoining room. They were fast asleep, and we realised there was a problem somewhere close by. The noise continued, actually increasing in intensity and frequency. When we opening our hotel-room door, we could hear clearly these blood-curdling sounds, and I feared that a child was in distress. Then, down the hall, we saw what looked like a human limb, jutting out from a doorway about six rooms from ours, and then we heard a plea, for, 'Help! Help!'

As I rushed down the corridor, I wasn't sure what to expect. Even so, being confronted by a naked man, barely conscious and lying on the carpet, was shocking. My first thought was that he might simply have been sleepwalking, then gone back to sleep, but that was only for an instant as I quickly realised that he was in serious trouble. He had no colour, almost ashen grey and pale, and his breathing was almost non-existent. He was halfway out into the hall when I reached him, wedged against the door, and there was a pungent odour emanating from the bathroom. I asked him if he was okay, but he said nothing.

Was he hurt? 'No,' he mumbled.

And with that, realising he'd been found, he lapsed into unconsciousness. I yelled to Lynette to call for an ambulance.

By this time an off-duty cameraman, here for the cricket tomorrow, had arrived on the scene. The two of us entered the man's room to try to put together the pieces, and discovered that the bathroom was like a set from a murder plot. The bath was full of vomit floating on the top. There was an empty aspirin bottle on the mantelpiece, a smashed bottle of spirits on the floor, blood on the walls and most chillingly, a pâté knife placed on the rim of the bathtub. It was quite obvious that this man had attempted suicide by overdosing on the pills and had at least contemplated using the knife. Thankfully, he didn't complete his mission. Meanwhile, hotel staff had arrived and were helping to comfort the man, who was lapsing in and out of consciousness. He was placed in the recovery position, while we gathered some towels to keep him warm. Soon after, paramedics arrived, much to everyone's relief, and immediately revived him with smelling salts. It was established that he'd taken 24 aspirin and soon he was confirming that he had attempted suicide. 'I want to die!' he kept yelling, 'I want to die!' Judging from the jagged scars that weaved their way up his arms, it seems that he had been unsuccessful in the past.

I couldn't help but feel sorry for him, a bloke who would have been in his mid-40s, no more. What makes someone book a hotel room for themselves, have all the tools of destruction lined up and then try to end their life? Such a waste and such a shame. I only hope he gets the help he needs to make his life livable and not such a battle, which it obviously is for him at present.

Getting back to sleep wasn't easy. I kept on thinking. Did this man have a family? Did anyone care about him and what does the future hold for him? I also found it strange that no one else came out to help this guy in distress. Why were Lynette and I the only ones to hear his pleas for help? Whatever the reasons, I just hope that the guy survives and, somehow, gets better.

July 5 *Birmingham*

At Edgbaston
First Test — Day One
England 294 (MA Atherton 57, AJ Stewart 65, AR Caddick 49*; SK Warne 5–71) v Australia 2–133 (MJ Slater 76*)

THE TENSION ON THE BUS is always heightened on day one of a Test. Today, it was further magnified by the fact that it was the opening day of a series, and completing the occasion, this is an Ashes series.

I was fully conscious of the positive energy on our bus, and couldn't help wondering whether the English vibes would be so upbeat. They should be a much tighter unit than in recent Ashes series, bound together by the spirit that comes from enjoying five unbeaten series in a row, but in terms of personnel they are not much changed — a fact that should not to be underestimated, for mind battles can be the most strangling of all problems. If you cannot put the past aside, it will always come back to haunt you and nourishment of the thought process will not occur. This makes it almost impossible to move forward, with retreat or stagnation the only options.

As we'd stressed at our team meetings of the past few days, if we can reopen a few old wounds, it will be very difficult for the likes of Atherton, Butcher, Hussain, Stewart, Gough and Caddick to prosper and deliver the goods that their talents deserve and desire.

I had a double win at the toss. Not only did I call correctly, but I did so wearing the baggy green while Nasser Hussain had donned a sponsor's cap. To me, a sponsor's cap is important but it has a time and place and the toss is not one of those. This issue aside, I wouldn't have minded losing the toss, as the pitch looked a good one to bat on and also appeared to be the sort of wicket that would turn later on. However, the thought of having first crack at a batting line-up that has a hint of inexperience about it, with Ian Ward and Usman Afzaal debuting against us, was too tempting. Our attack is made up of wicket-takers capable of setting the game up for us. To win a Test you need 20 wickets and it makes sense to me to get 10 straight away, therefore potentially eliminating our second innings if we bat well enough in our first. This also takes out the weather factor as the result can be achieved in four or less days if we are good enough.

I'm not sure what it was, but we were very slipshod in the first session, missing chances, fielding poorly, playing without our usual discipline. Perhaps we were trying too hard, but any excuse is one too many and we needed to improve. Gilly appeared very nervous, missing chances along with regulation catches of balls coming through to him. He's had such an outstanding introduction to Test cricket since he made his debut in November 1999 that one forgets his relative inexperience at this level, and that today was his Ashes debut. This was a fact that had escaped my attention but obviously not Gilly's. His uncertainty was a wake-up call for all of us that we can't take anything for granted and to keep others in mind when the natural thing to do is to be concerned totally with oneself.

Fortunately, Warney struck for us in his first over, immediately before lunch, to leave us reasonably placed at the break (England 2–106). This breakthrough, coupled with the fact that the home team had certainly had things go their way to that point, had us believing that we only needed to tighten up our bowling a little and lift somewhat in the field to swing things our way upon the resumption.

Having experience in a team is invaluable, because it enables you to trust what the outcome will be. If you have been through a procedure before you know what the likely results will be if you stick to your guns and be professional. Discipline has been our theme for the whole tour; if we keep it both on and off the field, we've kept reminding ourselves, we will be successful as the talent and skill are already there. We have to be dedicated to the tasks and causes we have set for ourselves, and follow the routine ball after ball. The lunch-to-tea session was a clear demonstration of this. It went our way,

While Andy Caddick and Alec Stewart discuss their batting exploits, I ponder what we need to do to break their stunning last-wicket partnership. They ended up adding 103, the second highest 10th-wicket stand ever by an English pair against Australia.

ALLSPORT

with Warney being the star, and very well backed up from the other end. Partnerships are more associated with batsmen, but it is just as important for bowlers to work in tandem, creating pressure and forcing errors by being consistent and persistent.

A spanner was thrown in the works when, after reducing England to 9–191, Andy Caddick and Alec Stewart proved that cricket is such a great game because it's never predictable. They smashed 103 for the final wicket and didn't appear to be in much trouble either, while in contrast Binga looked a bit rusty and lost his way and confidence. We must rally behind him because this is only temporary — we all know what a match-winner he is. The only good news to come out of this partnership was the fact that it showed that the pitch was playing well. If a No. 11 can score 49 not out, then specialist batsmen should really prosper.

With England on a high from this stirring performance, Matthew Hayden and Michael Slater had the job of reversing the momentum. The reply couldn't have been any swifter, better or more dramatic than the one that stunned the Edgbaston crowd. Slats demolished Darren Gough's first over, slamming 18 runs from it including three beautifully struck boundaries and one streaky one. It was mini Bon Jovi at his best, as he signalled his intentions with power, class and supreme confidence. This is the beauty of Slats — he can turn a match in the blink of an eye. Haydos looked the goods again until Craig White took one of the all-time great catches, hauling in a missile at mid-wicket with one hand.

What a day of Test cricket: 12 wickets for 427 runs. The longer form of the game is well and truly alive. Long may it continue to prosper.

July 6 *Birmingham*

UNLIKE YESTERDAY'S WARM SUNNY DAY, we were confronted with a dull grey sky that hung over the ground, giving no sense of depth with its mist-like appearance. These were just the conditions suited to swing and seam bowling and England knew nature had given them an excellent opportunity. My thoughts of a morning of viewing Slats and Junior at their finest quickly vaporised when Gough shattered the stumps of our opener in his first over of the morning.

I gathered my gloves, bat and helmet as quickly as I could, so I wouldn't be arriving in the middle with the Poms waiting for me on their turf. I was able to take guard before they got set, so they were on my turf. It may have been a small victory, but it left me feeling in charge of proceedings. My first ball, from Gough, was an absolute beauty as it spat off a length catching me high on the bat and jamming my index finger on the right hand. This was actually a well-played shot; I went forward when I could have just as easily gone back, but if I had played back I would have been in trouble, struggling to keep the ball down.

It's amazing what a confidence boost you can get from a well-executed defensive shot. I immediately felt this was going to be my day. Of course, you can't get carried away because you think you are going to score runs — you obviously still have to concentrate and play each ball on its merits, but a positive thought process is the key if you know how to manage it.

As a batsman, I feel that if you get to 15 you should go on and make a big score, as you have had the chance to adjust to the conditions, you know the pace and bounce of the pitch and you've hit enough balls to gain your confidence. My first 30 runs today came at a run a ball, thanks to some opportunities off my legs and wide of the stump, probably my two strongest areas. Feeling relaxed, yet alert, is my ideal state as a batsman and that's exactly how I felt today. In contrast, Mark looked tense, but to his credit he batted through these tough times. His 49 and our 133-run partnership may be overlooked in the final wash-up, but it was a vital stand that gave us the initiative and took away England's hopes of what would have been a crucial first-innings lead.

By the end of the day I had completed my 26th Test century and Marto, on his return to Test cricket, looked made for it, being unbeaten on 34. I think the wickets over here suit my style of play, because I'm a back-foot player and you get a little bit more time. The first 20 or 30 runs were as good as I've hit the ball for a long while. The conditions were difficult and I thought Darren Gough bowled superbly, troubling all the batsmen. I know some people have been critical of the wicket, but it's a good cricket pitch in a way because it gives everyone an opportunity: the batsmen never feel really set, but if you're brave enough to play your shots you're getting good value. The occasional ball has looked ugly, kicking up or keeping low, but all in all it is providing a very good test for all the players. As a batsman it is vital to keep trusting your technique and not to be concerned about the odd ball that will move so far away from the outside edge that you would never be able to touch it. That ball won't get you out so why worry about it.

To score a 100 is always special but to do so when your team needs it, in difficult conditions and by playing technically extremely well, is very rewarding. This is why I said following the day's play that it is among my top half-dozen Test-match hundreds. The press conference where I made those remarks was both enjoyable and predictable. The former because it's always easier talking about good things and the latter because the local scribes are already writing their own team off, after just one ordinary day.

While the journos went back to pen their negative articles, I couldn't help thinking about how wonderful it was to have walked off Edgbaston at stumps and see my wife and two kids clapping and waving alongside my in-laws, as they all are a part of my success. And then there was the chance to share my joy with my comrades. Coming into a cricket change-room after scoring a hundred is one of life's great joys. You can feel the genuine warmth of your teammates as they share your moment in the sun. Everyone will come and shake your hand, offer a few words and then you get a chance to gather your thoughts. My thoughts, however, were somewhat interrupted by tumultuous applause and extremely vocal encouragement from the boys for Pat Rafter as he came back from the dead to put away Andre Agassi in a men's singles semi-final at Wimbledon.

The heartfelt cries of support by our lads every time Agassi served late in the fifth helped our Pat get across the line. Or at least that's what we believed. The lads really were quite passionate about this result, which goes to show what respect and admiration we have for the guy.

July 7 *Birmingham*

**At Edgbaston
First Test —
Day Three**

England 294 and 1–48 v Australia
576 (SR Waugh 105, DR Martyn
105, AC Gilchrist 152; MA Butcher
4–42)

A DECENT NET SESSION THIS morning, followed by a massage, had me in a good frame of mind to face the second new ball today, but once I got out in the middle I couldn't find that state of mind I reached yesterday. Almost inevitably, I was lbw, playing from the crease to an excellent delivery from Darren Gough that kept a little low and nipped back at me.

England must have felt they were back in the match and had they taken their chances they may well have been. However, as we've seen many times already in his short Test-match career, Adam Gilchrist can destroy any attack when he's 'on song'. Today, he looked as if he was playing in a game of social cricket with a few of his mates while he waited for the steaks on the barbie to be cooked. He pulverised all comers, while Marto continued his well-crafted innings to the point where at tea he was 99 not out, on the crest of a dream.

Reaching your first Test hundred is always memorable and at the same time, to some extent, a relief. Marto had to wait eight-and-a-half years from his Test debut — and that 20-minute break in play — to reach this milestone, but having climbed the summit he slipped and fell at the hands of a part-timer, Mark Butcher, for 105, exactly the same total as me. This innings was further confirmation, if anyone needed it, that this guy is going to be a real force for a long time to come. Butcher then enjoyed a run of wickets, which meant Glenn McGrath came into bat with, once again, someone in the 90s at the other end. And, once again, Pigeon came through for the team. He and Gilly put on 63 runs for the last wicket, which was invaluable to the team.

Gilly produced a couple of stunning episodes, taking an Australian Ashes record 22 (three sixes and a four) from one Butcher over, and scoring his last 52 runs (100 to 152, featuring six fours and four sixes) in 25 balls. Glenn McGrath contributed one run (another 50 nipped in the bud as he so often laments!) and one leg bye to the last-wicket stand of 63,

This has to be one of the most amazing shots ever played to reach a Test-match hundred. Gilly scoops a short ball over the keeper's head for four, just one memorable shot from one of the most explosive hundreds ever scored in Ashes cricket.

and that one run didn't come until after the partnership had gone past 50. This was clean hitting at its best by Gilly. He has already scored three great Test hundreds, all made at a run-rate of a run-a-ball or less. In time, I reckon, he will rewrite the history books on keeper/batsmen and redefine the role for future generations.

Before the close, we had claimed the hardest of all English scalps, when McGrath sent back Atherton for a 14th time in Tests in exactly the manner we had plotted — a good length delivery that caused him to fend away from his body and edge a chance to the waiting slip cordon. The form of Warne and Gillespie looks ominous for England, especially Dizzy, who is due a big haul sooner rather than later. Tomorrow promises to be a winning day if we maintain our discipline and if our other bowlers, especially McGrath and Lee, continue to improve.

PICS: ALLSPORT

*Right: **Damien Martyn has just reached his first Test hundred.***

*Below: **Martyn, Gilchrist and Waugh,** Australia's three centurions from the first Test.*

July 8 *Birmingham*

England 294 and 164 (ME
Trescothick 76; JN Gillespie 3–52,
SK Warne 3–29) lost to Australia
576 by an innings and 118 runs

A FEW WORDS BEFORE THE start of play today from Justin Langer, the man we'd so unfortunately had to leave out of the Test, played a significant part in our victory. Lang felt that we mightn't have been switched on enough, with the rain being about and most critics having written off England's chances. His words hit home. We made a pact that we were going to play very good, disciplined cricket, make our opponents work hard for their runs and take our chances. Being sharp and hungry is what it is all about, and it took Lang to remind us of that fact.

The plan for this morning was simple: make it very difficult for England to score by bowling good lines, backed up by energetic fielding and a good team presence. Straightaway, Pigeon and Warney did superb jobs, giving Marcus Trescothick and Mark Butcher little in the way of easy runs. Even though we didn't get an early breakthrough, you could feel the tense atmosphere and the build-up of pressure on the batsman.

One could sense that one wicket would lead to a couple more quick ones and that's exactly what happened. Gillespie was inspirational, combining speed and skill, while Binga regained some confidence when he claimed the initial breakthrough with a beauty that reared off a length, catching the edge of Butcher's bat. Things went from bad to worse when the aptly named 'Poppadom fingers' Nasser Hussain had to retire hurt after Dizzy exploded one off a length, catching the batsman on the little finger of his right (bottom) hand. We could tell from Hussain's immediate reaction that another digit had been broken.

The England captain's frustration and anger at knowing this emerged before he aimed up to the next delivery. When Punter encouraged Dizzy to 'follow it up with another good one', Hussain spun around and gave him a filthy look. If Ricky's remark is sledging, then we do it, but for me the entire incident was an excellent example of what Test cricket is all about: testing your opponent, physically and mentally, when he's vulnerable. People who think that back in the good old days cricketers didn't try to win a psychological edge on the field are wrong. I've spoken to Test players from past eras and they've confirmed that there has always been that element of talk out there. Perhaps now there is more than before, but it has always been there. We're not going to stop talking out in the middle, and we will always play hard but fair.

Unluckily for England, Hussain was unable to continue and with him went their desire for a tussle. Under menacing skies, it was all over shortly after lunch.

For us, the result and the way we achieved it was the perfect start to the series. We were thorough, clinical, professional and entertaining. Everyone contributed and perhaps that is the most pleasing aspect of such a convincing win, as it suggests most of the players are in form.

In the media conference afterwards I described Jason Gillespie as being 'as good a bowler as I've seen'. He was magnificent today — in one inspired spell breaking Hussain's finger, having Stewart caught at slip, hitting White's off stump and trapping Afzaal lbw —

as England lost their final seven wickets for just 22 runs, to give us victory by an innings and 118 runs. However, while that final margin suggests a thrashing, in truth England were in the game quite a few times. We didn't pull away until yesterday afternoon.

During this match we jettisoned convention in relation to the role and duties of the 12th man. This for too long has been an unrewarding, unappreciated role that goes beyond the limits of being a good team man and paying your dues. Too often in the past, a consistent 12th man has suffered the consequences of a complete lack of cricket as well as never getting a break from the mundane tasks associated with the role. For this series, as a squad, we decided that the duties would be shared among the six reserves. Further, on any given day some of these guys had the option of having a session off or even a day just to recharge the batteries and give

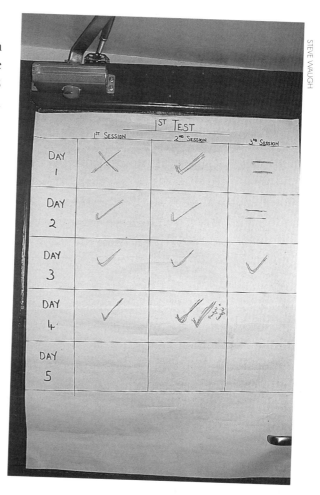

This sheet in our dressing-room served as our guide to how we went in each session of the Test. X indicates we lost the session, = says it was equal, a tick says we won.

the guys time for themselves, to practise or to keep their fitness levels up. Flem was the designated 12th man, because of his attitude and recent form, while Kat was the first choice if we needed a substitute fielder.

Celebrations were, of course, rowdy and energetic, with plenty of beer ending up on the floor and headaches brewing everywhere. We had a good five or six hours, remembering past tours, analysing the current match and talking of the future. The team song, as it always is, was a time to treasure. It may only be short in length, but it is the one sure way of bringing the group together. Once you've been in the circle, arms linked, beer in one hand, gathered around a table with Punter on top, it stays with you forever. It permeates your whole body; the passion, the pride and the love of playing for Australia seems to multiply and you want time to stand still. Let's hope we have the chance to experience this moment many more times on this tour.

Rain and lack of discipline are our two dangers for the Tests ahead. As one of these is in our control I don't see why we can't create history.

Winning is a Habit

Getting this Australian side to play positive cricket is about as hard as getting the kids to follow La La, Po, Tinky Winky and Dipsy as they frolic around the grassy hillsides. To win Test matches you obviously have to take 20 wickets and to me the best way to do that is get the opposition in first so you can make some inroads into that target. Of course, how often we implement such a tactic during this series, as we did in the first Test, will depend on the nature of the wicket and the strengths of the opposition, but with our wicket-taking bowlers we will more often than not end up batting last.

To many brought up on the mantra that you should always bat first when you win the toss, this is bordering on ridiculous. By the fourth innings, these seasoned critics argue, the pitch is generally wearing and bouncing erratically. In my view, to consistently send opponents in requires no more than a different mental approach from that held by the teams of the past. We see it as a challenge to be embraced.

When we scored 6–369 in the fourth innings to beat Pakistan in Hobart in late 1999, led to victory by magnificent rearguard innings from Adam Gilchrist and Justin Langer, we defied everyone's opinion that you couldn't score that many on the final day and achieved one of our best ever Test wins. From that moment on, batting last has been both challenging and enjoyable rather than intimidating, because we truly believe that our positive attitude can carry us through in most situations.

Setting attacking field placements has been another trademark of the side in recent times. Bowlers, of course, have to be talented and disciplined to bowl to such fields, and they also have to be comfortable with the many wide open spaces that are presented to the batsman because so many fieldsmen are in catching positions. But, as captain, I hate to see an opportunity fly through the slip cordon because I've plugged up a gap to nullify a poor delivery. Bowlers, as with all cricketers, like incentives to stimulate their skills and aggressive fields not only make them stick to the team's game plan, they often improve their performance because they have to be spot on in everything they do. To have plenty of men in catching positions, ready for a chance, there needs to be flexibility among the squad in terms of where guys are able to field effectively and great skill from all fieldsmen so that they are able to accept any half chances that come their way. Giving all the lads varied fielding practice sessions gets them out of their 'comfort zones' and also gives us the opportunity to identify specific catching and fielding talents that might otherwise remain dormant if not encouraged. Rotating fielding positions during matches keeps players from becoming complacent and bored, and also shows faith in their abilities wherever they are put.

To score 300 runs on every day you bat is the perfect way to set up a Test victory. Such a rate of run-scoring puts an onus on the opposition bowlers to stem the run flow and also exerts the sort of pressure that often eventually leads to opponents capitulating. Of course, you need the right type of players to follow through on this course of action, and they must show courage to achieve this goal. Having aggressive openers such as Michael Slater and Matthew Hayden allows us to often set the tone and tempo for our entire innings,

Above: **The joy on the faces of Punter, Warney and Gilly are in marked contrast to the gloom of Darren Gough, out lbw to Shane for a duck on the final day at Edgbaston.**

Right: **The victorious Australian team after the first Test.** Back row (left to right): **Gilchrist, Ponting, Langer, Gillespie, Lee, Katich, McGrath;** Front: **Warne, Slater, S Waugh, Martyn, Hayden, M Waugh.**

opening a path for natural strokemakers such as Ricky Ponting, Mark Waugh, Damien Martyn and Adam Gilchrist to keep the momentum going.

Batting in this fashion is enjoyable to watch for spectators and teammates alike. It is both inspiring and stimulating to score quickly and is often contagious to the point that so-called tailenders join in when they get to the crease.

If you want to succeed in any contest, whether it be cricket, marbles or monopoly, you must play to win, be positive and back yourself. This is the way we are brought up in Australia. There's no second prize, so get in there, roll up the sleeves and have a good stack at it. Unless you have a go you'll never know what you can achieve. For a sportsman there can be no greater crime than unfulfilled potential.

We're all determined that will never happen with this Australian team.

July 9   *London*

IT TAKES SOMETHING SPECIAL TO ask for a 7am wake-up call the morning after a Test-match win, but seeing Pat Rafter in a Wimbledon final definitely fitted into this exclusive category. Attrition rates for sight-seeing tours or anything requiring advance bookings is usually around 50 per cent, but this morning only two fell by the wayside. Binga, after a month's abstinence, had taken himself down and was consequently out of the picture for today's adventure, while Funky Miller didn't know what all the fuss was about. When a last-minute call was placed to let him know the bus was about to leave for the tennis, he replied, 'What tennis?'

Enough said, we were on our way, and I for one couldn't wait. It was almost too good to be true, winning a Test in four days and then having the men's final between Rafter and Croatia's Goran Ivanisevic held over until Monday because of inclement weather, which gave us the chance to see it live. My good fortune continued when, 30 minutes prior to the match beginning, I was escorted by former Wimbledon champion and long-time Australian Davis Cup coach, Neale Fraser, to the change-rooms to have a chat with Pat and his entourage. What an opportunity! To tell you the truth I wasn't exactly sure what to say, except, 'Well done, enjoy the day, all the boys are here to support you, and we're wearing our baggy greens.'

Pat was remarkably relaxed, almost as if he was about to have a game with his buddies, as he smothered himself in sun cream while meandering around the room. He did manage, as all Queenslanders do when they win an Origin series, to ask me whether or not I'd seen the footy score!

There was one surreal moment. The cheering of the massive Aussie contingent in the crowd gained all of our attention, and we looked up on the small television mounted on Pat's dressing-room wall to see that they were applauding the cricket team I was captain of as the guys were ushered to their seats. My turn was about to come when I entered the stadium and was immediately spotted by the fans from down under. To have my name being chanted on centre court at Wimbledon will remain one of the weirdest experiences of my life. It was awkward, humbling and something I'll never forget. Most of all, it made me feel proud to be Australian. Earlier, I'd also had the chance to meet John McEnroe, an old hero of mine, courtside, when Warney and I did a quick interview with the BBC's Sue Barker.

What a superb match the final was, played by two guys who the crowd clearly loved. The mood of the whole arena was upbeat, with rowdy support for both players, until the final pulsating set where immortality was on the line. I don't think I've ever been as nervous as I was late in that final set, my heart beating strong and fast, as the likely outcome continually oscillated. One thing that will stay with me was the look on Ivanisevic's face when he got his first match point. He was on the precipice of breaking down, mentally and physically, with tears welling in his eyes at the knowledge that a dream was about to turn into a reality, if only he could win that final point. Unfortunately, Pat couldn't get the fourth match point back in play and the stadium erupted, with both sets of fans giving the two combatants a sustained standing ovation to acknowledge a magnificent sporting contest. One could feel the elation of the Croatian fans but also the despair in the Aussie camp. We were just thankful that we were there.

For me it was back to London for a week with my family. Shane, Glenn and I have the next match off, and we won't be reunited with the boys until next Monday, July 16, when they return to London. As I've explained previously, we are trying to give the guys time off when their families are over here, and now is the moment for the pregnant wives of the players and their kids. It's also beneficial to get away from the grind of a tour, and the prying eyes and minds of the media, to recharge the batteries for the battles ahead. The rest of the boys headed back up the motorway to Birmingham, from where tomorrow they'll journey to Taunton for a game against Somerset. No doubt they'll watch a couple of videos to help kill the time on the road, most probably two out of *Planes, Trains and Automobiles, Dumb and Dumber, South Park* and *Kingpin*.

Right: Anyone for Pimms and lemonade? Slats does the barman thing while Goran Ivanisevic and Pat Rafter warm-up for the 2001 Wimbledon men's singles final. Simone and Brooke Warne are in the front row.

Left: A fantastic tennis match has just been won by a very popular champion.

At Taunton
July 13–16

Australians 3–348 (declared:
RT Ponting 128, JL Langer 104*,
ME Waugh 55*) and 4–335
(declared: DR Martyn 176*,
WA Seccombe 76) defeated
Somerset 267 (Aamer Sohail 50,
DW Fleming 6–59) and 240
(M Burns 59, MJ Wood 51) by
176 runs

THREE OF THE LADS DECIDED to confirm their allegiance to the Australian cause while they were in Taunton. They did so in a very permanent way by having tattoos placed on their anatomies. Slats had the No. 356 put on his ankle, in recognition of the fact that he was the 356th man to be selected to play Test cricket for Australia. Junior had 349 and 105, his Test and one-day numbers, branded onto his ankle, while Punter now has 366 and 123 on his lower back. All three had the stars of the Southern Cross emblazoned alongside their career numbers.

Seeing brother Mark sporting a tattoo was quite startling, but even more astonishing was hearing that the tattooist performed his duties while chatting on the phone at the same time. The quality of his work must surely come under scrutiny.

It was just coincidence that these operations occurred at the same time as a number of England players were admitting that they didn't really want to be captain of their country. Mark Butcher was one who reputedly wasn't keen, being quoted as saying, 'Being England captain does not hold too many good memories for me, and at this stage in my career and life, I just want to enjoy myself. I think I could do without such distractions.'

This issue caused much debate, until the England selectors went with the safe option of Michael Atherton. The positive for the home team of his elevation again to the top job is that he knows what to expect, how to handle it and he is very capable of doing it well. Alternatively, they could have looked to the future and blooded someone such as Marcus Trescothick. Some have argued that this would have put too big a workload on relatively inexperienced shoulders, which is true to some extent. But surely if you are scoring runs and have been earmarked as a future captain then how is one match going to destroy you, particularly as the team lost the previous match and you have nothing to lose?

Only time will judge the wisdom of the English selectors. What I couldn't believe were the players such as Butcher who said, 'I don't want the job.' What greater honour is there than to captain your country? Once again, there are two ways of looking at this and their honesty has to be admired, even though I can't understand it.

I must admit I could not believe that I was looking at my younger brother sporting a tattoo. Still, his loyalty to the team and love of playing for Australia will now always not only be in his heart but on his body. As a fashion statement, the guys' tattoos certainly put Funky's 'candy floss' hair in the shadows for a few hours, although the lime green zinc he wore quickly had him back on centre stage. I can't wait to see what shade he has in store for the old folk at Lord's. Let's hope there are plenty of paramedics on standby.

Above: The toss before the first Test. Channel 4 commentator Mark Nicholas is to Nasser Hussain's right, while match referee Talat Ali of Pakistan is the other gentleman in the photograph.
Below left: Mark Waugh has just caught Mike Atherton during England's first innings.
Below right: Michael Slater continues his assault late on the opening day at Edgbaston.

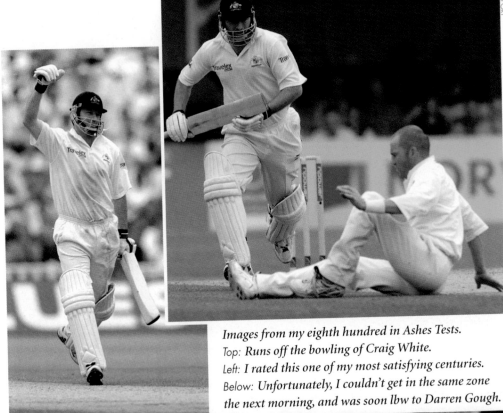

Images from my eighth hundred in Ashes Tests.
Top: *Runs off the bowling of Craig White.*
Left: *I rated this one of my most satisfying centuries.*
Below: *Unfortunately, I couldn't get in the same zone the next morning, and was soon lbw to Darren Gough.*

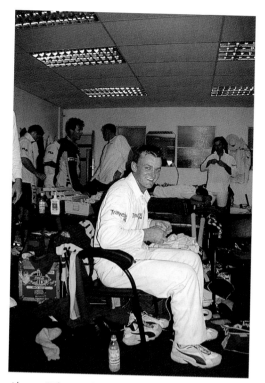

Above: Why wouldn't the boys be smiling! Gilly (left) has just smashed 152 as if he was playing in his own backyard, while Marto (right) has completed the first of what I'm sure will be many Test centuries.

Below: One-nil up in the series and the boys are pretty rapt to be a part of it.

Scenes from our dressing-room at Edgbaston during the first Test.
Left: Glenn McGrath (sitting closest to camera) takes in the celebrations after our victory.
Below: Brett Lee sharpens up the guitar skills that he sometimes puts to good use with the band Six and Out.

Above: Slats finds time for a brief kip during a rain delay.

Right: Dizzy and Warney reflect on the way our bowlers dominated the match.

How lucky were we to be at the 2001 Wimbledon men's singles final?

PICS: STEVE WAUGH

THE LAWN TENNIS CHAMPIONSHIPS WIMBLEDON

CENTRE COURT
UNRESERVED SEATING

North Open Entrance H

Miss C. Cooper, Lady Champion

Price as displayed

This portion does not admit to Ground without a passout

CENTRE COURT

Admit Bearer to Ground

This portion to be given up at the entrance to the Ground

Notice
This counterfoil is not valid if detached from ticket

Left: The boys decided to wear the Baggy Greens as a sign of support for Pat Rafter.

Right: Tennis 'tragic' Steve Waugh meets Pat Rafter just 30 minutes before the final. Pat seemed a lot calmer than I was!

Left: I'm not sure exactly how he did it, but Matt Hayden somehow managed to find a decent wave on a rare day away from the cricket.

Right: Warney and I with legendary commentator Murray Walker at Silverstone on July 15 for the British Grand Prix. This was the last time Murray would call a Formula 1 Grand Prix on his home soil.

Left: Two other celebrities we met at the Grand Prix were the Benetton team's No. 3 driver, Australia's Mark Webber, and the very glamorous Kylie Minogue.

Our four frontline bowlers at Lord's during the second Test. Clockwise from top left: *Glenn McGrath, Brett Lee, Jason Gillespie and Shane Warne.*

Above: **The 2001 Ashes tourists at Lord's. Back row (left to right): Campbell, Katich, Lee, Gillespie, Fleming, Martyn, Langer; Middle: Alcott, Slater, Miller, Hayden, Noffke, Seccombe, Walsh; Front: Ponting, McGrath, Buchanan, S Waugh, Gilchrist, Bernard, Warne, M Waugh.**
Below: **Rosie and Austin join in the celebrations on the Lord's balcony after the second Test.**

July 17 *London*

TODAY WAS SHAPING UP AS one of those days where there are a million things on and you know you are going to have to grit your teeth and just get through it. It all started at 7.30am with a photograph at the apartment my family had been living in for the past four-and-a-half weeks. It was for an in-house magazine to help promote their accommodation facilities. From there it was straight to Lord's on the team bus for a three-hour session at the nets. Again our intensity and quality of work were impressive and everyone looked ready and well prepared for the Test that starts in two days time.

Brett Lee came through a solid workout with no problems, as did two other two injury concerns, Slats and Haydos, which gave us a full squad to pick from. Obviously, Flemo came into consideration for this Test after his seven-wicket haul against Somerset. While it caused headaches in the conference call between Gilly, Trevor Hohns and myself, this is exactly the position we want to be in, where competition for places ensures that everyone stays sharp and hungry. While it's hard to change a winning team, if we can improve a successful combination we will. In this case, we decided to sick with the same XI who played at Edgbaston.

Just before warm-ups, I had to give the Aussie contingent of journalists their pre-match interview so they could make their deadline back in Australia. It's important to work with the media and try to give each other a bit of breathing space, because we are tied to each other and we may as well try to make the relationship work the best we can. With this done, I had to see Errol Alcott for some treatment, mainly maintenance work on my knee and shoulder, followed by a bat signing session involving some 300 bats. Then it was time to change into the tour suit for a luncheon at the Café Royal.

Damien Fleming confidently shouts for lbw during his excellent bowling performance at Taunton.

This turned out to be an enjoyable event, with Slats and Gilly executing a fine double act taking the mickey out of each other. Gilly had the locals in stitches as he described the fine set of listeners he is blessed with, which make his melon look like the FA Cup, while Slats killed them, especially our squad members, when he dropped a 'magic' word before realising he wasn't with the boys in the change-rooms but at a suited function for 800 people. The one thing that did bug me, besides the late finish, was the constant theme from all the local speakers, who bagged the English team unmercifully while praising us to the skies. I found it all a bit sickening and pathetic. I just wish these Poms would stand up, be counted, show a bit of ticker and support for their side. Six weeks ago England were unbeatable but now, after one loss, they can't play. Of course, the gushing comments about us are much nicer than being bagged, but tonight it reached the stage where the audience was clapping but I was no longer listening to what was being said.

With a spare 40 minutes or so before the tactical group of S. Waugh, McGrath, Gilchrist, Warne, Buchanan and new guest M. Waugh were scheduled to meet, I had time to squeeze in an article that was due to be written, and another that had slipped my mind. The think-tank meeting was relatively short, with the main focus on how we are going to play and not so much on what the opposition might do. The full team meeting that followed was very relaxed and fairly short in length, suggesting that we are ready to go. My final comments centred around England's desire to prove, especially to themselves, that things have changed. I'm sure they will want to show that they are a tougher side than their performance suggested in the first Test.

Much has been said and made of England's heavy defeat at Edgbaston, and most of the comments have been scathing and demeaning to the local side. Of course, it was a decisive loss in the final analysis, but in reality England had their chances and if they had taken them the result may have been very different. The press are also getting plenty of mileage out of the fact that England have only won one Ashes Test at Lord's in 105 years, but that means nothing to me. We can't worry too much about history. Instead, we need to focus on making our own. In fact, their woeful record at Lord's might be a spur for them; it should be a special occasion for any English cricketer, and perhaps they'll be inspired by the opportunity.

England's batting has been bolstered by the return of their best batsman, Graham Thorpe, and the re-selection of Mark Ramprakash, who also missed the first Test because of injury. Added to the bowling is the paceman, Chris Silverwood, a quick outswing bowler who has promised much with his talent but has yet to display these natural gifts at the highest level. He does look to be in good form at the moment.

I believe England may adopt a less aggressive approach this time, with ring fields and a third man in place. On paper, I believe their line-up this time is actually stronger than the first Test team. While Hussain has done well at the helm, I can't or couldn't see him scoring runs with his unusual and unorthodox technique, so his absence because of that broken finger may actually strengthen the batting. However his appetite for a battle is a quality that we shouldn't underestimate.

Continuing with our habit of including an honoured guest at our final team meeting before a Test and dinner afterwards, Lang invited South African rugby legend Francois

Pienaar to join us. Pat Rafter actually began this tradition back in 1999–2000, when he joined us before the first Test of the summer, against Pakistan in Brisbane. Francois gave us an insight into his profession and how the South Africans operated, which was not unlike our operation. His talk was very modest in nature, but highly impressive for what it revealed, and certainly showed why he is recognised as an icon of his game. When I talked to him later on at dinner he told me his recipe for success. The four Ds, as he calls them, are essential for success and are as follows:

1 — Desire
2 — Determination
3 — Dedication
4 — Discipline

Embrace them, and it will lead to DELIGHT.

Unfortunately for me, an ugly migraine had developed during the evening and I still had some work to do before hitting the sack. In our quest to travel down the 'Road Less Travelled' and embrace new ideas and concepts in order to stay one step ahead of the opposition and to occasionally break the mould of traditional cricket thinking, Buck and I went way left field tonight. Buck, in his wisdom and desire to leave no stone unturned, decided to try to locate the famed lateral thinking genius, Edward De Bono. When I asked him why, our coach said, 'I'm not sure what's going to happen or come out of it, but he might have one idea that we haven't thought of before that could help us improve or change our way of thinking.' So he tracked him down, somewhat amazingly I reckon, to an address in Mayfair and contacted him. A time slot was arranged, and before we knew it, the black cab had rolled up to the entrance of his apartment. A phone call by the permanently stationed security guard acknowledged the fact that we were at the right place, invited as well as expected.

This was a stimulating experience to say the least, and the nature of the challenging conversation turned my migraine into the 'vice like' category, with dizzy spells coming rather too frequently to take in all the concepts. One observation he did have about one-day cricket, after we explained that the aim is to restrict the opposition scoring by either taking wickets or stemming the flow of runs, was quite simple and common sense. He enquired, 'If someone is not scoring quickly and struggling, why wouldn't you want to keep him in?'

This line has often been trotted out during a match, but our natural instincts are, of course, to attack and try to remove all opposition batsmen. Thus, the suggestion has always been laughed off. But should it be? Already we could see that picking the brains of someone smarter than us could give us an edge we would otherwise never have.

A more in-depth continuation of the possibilities that we haven't explored in cricket will continue in Australia in October, when Mr De Bono is touring. I for one can't wait. Tonight was a real learning experience. Life is exciting when you try to broaden your horizons and delve into areas that haven't been stimulated before.

July 18 *London*

THE CONCEPT OF 'TAPERING OFF' in the same way as athletes do before big meets is still very new to cricket, but has gained instant approval among the boys. Again, as before the first Test, today was a non-compulsory training session for the guys, with most taking up the option of resting in preparation for an Australian player's ultimate Test. Of course, there were still commitments to be met such as the team photo on the hallowed turf and happily accommodating a request from the MCC to photograph Warney, Pigeon and me for the Club. This was taken inside the famed Long Room.

An afternoon spent with the family was enjoyable and somewhat tiring. The fact my family has a home-like base not far from the team hotel has made an enormous difference as it allows the kids to get settled into a routine. A visit to the National History Museum kept Austin and Rosie enthralled, especially when they came upon the dinosaur display that featured a moving T. Rex devouring a fallen victim. I guess this experience will ensure either a lifelong love of the beasts or a million and one nightmares for the 'tin lids'.

As a player I can't wait to get out on the hallowed turf, maybe for the last time, so I'm going to savour the moment. My confidence is peaking right now, with my net form as good as it's ever been, and I'm feeling relaxed and in control of my emotions. Concentration and enjoyment are my two key words, and for the team we keep on going back to discipline as our motto.

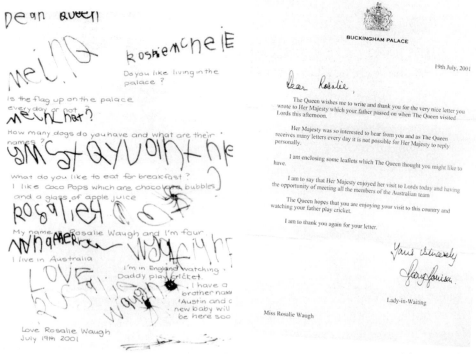

While in England, Rosie wrote to the Queen. A reply from the Queen's Lady-in-Waiting was a tour highlight for my daughter.

Marylebone Cricket Club, Lord's Cricket Ground, St, John's Wood, London NW8 8QN.

AUI

ADMIT TO GROUND
BY NORTH GATE
WHICH WILL OPEN AT 9:00 AM

THE SECOND TEST MATCH

England v Australia

Thursday19th July 2001
Start 11:00am

First Day

No spectator may bring into the Ground more than 2 pints of beer OR 75cl of wine. NO FURTHER ALCOHOL will be permitted on any subsequent re—entry.

Enter stand by

Staircase FF

COMPTON STAND
UPPER TIER

Row
E

Seat
55 **£42**

Complimentary

6 506320 500557

TO BE DETACHED BY GATEMAN
NOT VALID FOR ADMISSION
WHEN DETACHED

AUSTRALIAN RUGBY UNION LTD. ACN 002 898 544,
LEVEL 7, RUGBY HOUSE, 12-14 MOUNT STREET, NORTH SYDNEY, POST OFFICE BOX 188, NORTH SYDNEY, NSW 2059, AU
TELEPHONE (02) 9956 3444, FACSIMILE (02) 9955 3299,
RUGBY WEB SITE: WWW.RUGBY.COM.AU

*Australian***Rugby**

Fax

To:	John Buchanan & Steve Waugh
Company:	Australian Cricket Team
From:	Rod Macqueen
Fax No:	0015 4420 7361 1991
Date:	19/7/01

Pages Inc Cover sheet: 1

PRIVACY AND CONFIDENTIALITY NOTICE - CAUTION - The information contained in this facsimile is intended for the named recipients only. It may contain *private and confidential information* and if you are not an intended recipient, you must not copy, distribute or take any action in reliance on it. If you have received this facsimile in error, please notify us immediately by a collect telephone call to (61-2) 9971 5709, and then destroy the original message. Thank You.

Dear John & Steve,

Thank you very much for your messages of support leading up to the final Lions Test- It was greatly appreciated.

We had John Coutis (the man with no legs) speak to the team before the Test. His message was all about self belief, so our call going into that test was

"BELIEVE IN YOURSELF"

I am sure the team will (once again) put the *Pommies* away and that you will believe in yourselves as much as we do.

All the best

ROD MACQUEEN

Scenes from the Lord's dressing-room as we wait for the weather to clear on the opening day of the second Test.

Left: Lang chills out, listening to a tune or two and reading what might be a motivational book.

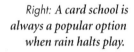

Right: A card school is always a popular option when rain halts play.

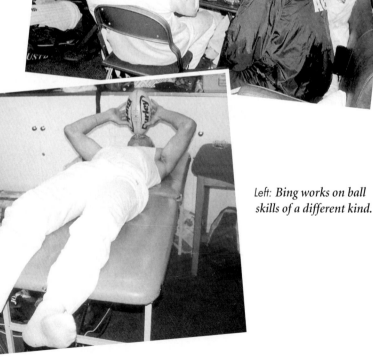

Left: Bing works on ball skills of a different kind.

July 19 *London*

At Lord's —
Second Test —
Day One

England 4–121 (MA Atherton 37;
GD McGrath 2–29)

FOR ME, A TEST MATCH at the Home of Cricket is still the highlight of playing at the highest level. Lord's has a certain aura, combining history, tradition and a unique character to leave you feeling a little jittery in the stomach when you walk up the stairs, pass the elderly members on the way and into the best and most spacious change-rooms in world cricket.

I didn't see this morning's toss with restored English captain Michael Atherton as having any real significance, until overcast conditions, creating a heavy atmosphere ideal for swing and seam bowling, blew in. My mind was now made up and when the specially minted coin featuring Sir Donald Bradman and the Queen came down with The Don looking skywards I had no hesitation in sending England into bat.

Unfortunately, what followed developed into a frustrating day, as we had to come off many times for rain interruptions, which didn't allow either side to get into any sort of rhythm. To be honest, the stop-start day probably helped us more than England, as each delay allowed our bowlers to come back fresh and attack more often than we would otherwise have been able to under normal circumstances. From a batting point of view it is always difficult to start, stop and then restart, as it disrupts your concentration and tempo; you continually feel under pressure to build a worthwhile partnership.

When we did get on, our performance up until tea was fairly ordinary (England 1–55), but the solidarity of Mark Butcher and Atherton was admirable. We needed to lift in the last session or give England the initiative leading into day two and fortunately we did so.

One of the great joys of a Lord's Test is that we have the opportunity to meet the Queen, and today's tea break was down as the scheduled time. Unfortunately, the weather threw a spanner into the works — because of the time lost earlier in the day, the timing of the remaining two sessions was altered, which completely threw out the Queen's schedule. The dilemma we faced at lunchtime was whether to leave the first two session breaks as is and play a three-hour final session or go by the rules and miss the chance to meet the Queen. Normally, we would have no choice but to do what the match referee ruled, but here the man in charge, Talat Ali, gave us these alternatives, citing exceptional circumstances. We chose to meet the Queen.

Our next problem was that someone had decided that only the 12 players in our nominated team for this Test would be involved in the introductions. For me, it was all or none, and upon request common sense prevailed and each member of our squad had the chance of a lifetime become a reality.

As captain, I had the task of introducing the squad to the Queen. Believe me, even guys you have known for years suddenly look like strangers as they stand before you waiting for their introduction. I was particularly nervous with Damien Fleming, because I drew a blank last time he stood before royalty and me, at the World Cup Final in 1999. Flemo eased my nerves this time by mouthing the words, 'Remember me,' as he stood in line.

As it has been every time I've had the privilege to meet and chat with the Queen, this was a great honour. I admire her patience and the way she is able to make people feel at ease. Having said that, it's still not easy to initiate conversation. My best attempt was to ask, 'How are your horses going, have you had any winners lately?'

'No, we haven't won for a while and my best horse is lame at the moment,' she replied.

Other favourites are always small talk about the weather and how the tour is going so far.

When we got back on the field, a notable landmark was reached when Mark Waugh equalled Mark Taylor's world record of 157 Test catches by a non-wicketkeeper when he caught Butcher. Junior seems destined to break Tubby's mark here because this is a pitch that will see many wickets fall to catches in the cordon. Clearly, we had gained inspiration from our meeting with royalty, because we did come back strongly through the final long session, especially in the last 11 overs, when we gained two wickets, to end the day with England at 4–121. In my view, our noses are just in front.

July 20 *London*

At Lord's —
Second Test —
Day Two

England 187 (GD McGrath 5–54) v Australia 5–255 (ME Waugh 108, SR Waugh 45)

A PERFECT DAY GREETED US as we made the 20-minute drive from the hotel to St John's Wood, eager in anticipation of what might happen during the day. Following on from our impressive final 30 minutes last night, we continued to push the momentum in our favour, with Glenn McGrath bowling an outstanding line and length. He used the famous Lord's slope to his advantage: the problem for all batsmen being that his deliveries occasionally came down the slope — either ducking back into the right-handers or sliding across the left-handers — while most other balls kept their line through to Adam Gilchrist.

As I've said before, if Pigeon isn't already considered a great of the sport, then surely he will be after he's hung up his boots. He is in complete control of his game at the moment, keeping it simple, sticking to basics and exerting pressure to the point where a batsman is virtually suffocated until he relents under the examination that is being performed on him. Today, he hardly bowled a ball that even resembled an ordinary delivery and always seemed on the verge of another wicket. He thoroughly deserved his 5–54, as England crashed to 187 all out.

Statistics are important to all cricketers and to Pigeon they act as a source of inspiration. He is always looking ahead to see who's next on the list of Test-match wicket-takers, and takes enormous pride in achieving 'five-fors' and getting his name on honour boards such as the one here at Lord's (where he has already earned an 8–38 performance from 1997). Not bad for a bloke who only seriously began to bowl at around 16 or 17 years of age.

Our quest for a sizeable first innings lead didn't begin as we had planned. Matthew Hayden, playing in his first Test at Lord's, fell to Andy Caddick during what was as good an over (or in actual fact, five sixths of an over) as he's ever likely to receive in any game of cricket. Caddick swung the first three balls back in, followed it up with a straight one and then ... the crowning moment — a delivery that slanted in, pitched and deviated away, catching the outside edge to the delight of the whole English team and the English public. The place was buzzing.

After Matty's phenomenal tour to India the game is now testing him out, seeing whether he can fight off a couple of low scores and come back. This is why cricket is such a great game — we can never take it for granted. To be successful, those involved must keep looking to improve and work hard. I'm sure Matty will figure prominently before the tour is over, but for now he has to get back to basics and keep believing in himself.

Michael Slater's innings here was in complete contrast to the one at Edgbaston, where he began at such breakneck speed. There, he smashed and slashed his way to 16 off Darren Gough's first over; today it took Slats 15 overs to reach the same total. Adapting to different circumstances and conditions is what being a Test batsman is all about, and Slats proved his versatility by working his way through a difficult period. He would have felt short-changed at his exit for 25, just when he looked settled and on top of the situation.

Mum and Dad must be proud their boys put on a century partnership at Lord's, and that we are now both on the Lord's dressing-room honour boards after Mark's century. His was a classy effort from ball one, with his first 20 runs coming mainly on the legside,

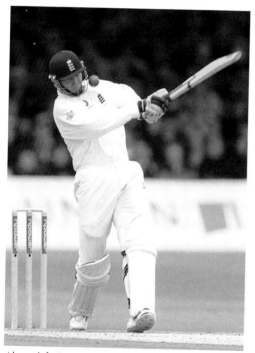 

ALLSPORT

Above left: Dominic Cork gets a good look at the ball during his dramatic battle with Glenn McGrath on the second day of the second Test. Above right: I was very proud to be in the middle when Mark scored his first Test century at Lord's.

due to either some ill-advised theories from the England camp or, more probably, poor bowling. So smoothly did he bat from the jump that it seemed that he got to 20 without anyone knowing. Once Junior had his confidence there was an air of certainty about his three-figure score, with elegant authoritative strokeplay featuring prominently. He did, however, become shaky in the 90s, perhaps reliving memories of his 99 here eight years ago when Phil Tufnell got one to come off both bat and pad before ricocheting into the timber. Today, Mark made it to 100 with an inside edge, which proves that the wheel does go around if you keep persisting.

Unfortunately, Mark's plans for a big one were cut short by a freakish piece of fielding from Darren Gough, while I gloved a delivery from Cork that took off from just short of a good length and was caught by Alec Stewart down the leg-side. For me, this was a real waste, as I felt in good nick and in command of the situation at the time. Cricket can be enormously frustrating at times, but the way I see it, if I keep on doing the right things and preparing well, then my time will eventually come. Today, it wasn't to be, but if I continue to play the same way the odds that success will follow will be in my favour.

After my dismissal, Adam Gilchrist and Damien Martyn negotiated a testing phase in the last 10 overs and set us up for a match-winning first-innings lead, so long as we bat intelligently tomorrow.

Late in proceedings, two moments of play occurred that revealed the different moods of the two sides. One was Darren Gough's poor body language and continual dropping of the ball after it had been tossed to him by his own fielders, which suggested both frustration and dissent at what was going on around him. The other was a Marto back-foot drive off Gough that will be remembered as the shot of the summer, such was its aesthetic and technical brilliance.

July 21 *London*

WHAT A WAY TO START the day and what a way to inspire the boys to great things today . . .

The atmosphere when we commenced our daily trek to Lord's changed dramatically when the ever-alert Justin Langer spotted a commercial being shot on the footpath to the left of the team bus. He quickly became very animated, shouting, 'It's Elle! It's Elle!' Sure enough, it was Elle Macpherson, and you've never seen four hands of cards and various newspapers leave lads' hands so quickly. Doing the teenage boy thing, we began belting the windows to attract her attention, though at first she seemed to be thinking, 'Here's another bunch of yobbos big-noting themselves.' But her disinterested look turned into one of pleasant surprise when she read the wording on the side of the bus and realised who the gawking faces belonged to. There was chaos on board, with lads scrambling over the top of each other to get a close view, and Jock Campbell came close to crushing his bugle on the windowpane in his attempt to put out the right vibe. Onward bound we continued, content that we had spotted an Aussie icon and that she had smiled and waved in our direction. Jock was still starry-eyed as we alighted from the bus; the poor bloke looked in need of a very cold shower.

Our good fortune continued on the park, with Gilly being dropped four times as he compiled yet another match-altering contribution. Before the first over of the day had been completed he was calling for the attention of the 12th man, with an extremely unusual request — he had forgotten to put his lucky yellow wallaby scarf across the Lord's balcony and asked for it to be hung up there. But even before we were able to comply with his request Mark Butcher at second slip put down a regulation offering. If this had been taken, the Test might have headed in a very different direction. It wasn't, Gilly kept batting and Marto continued his outstanding form, amassing another half century before, to everyone's surprise, he was out when another hundred looked a formality.

A 214-run lead was, I believed, more than enough for us not to bat again. This effort extended our average first-innings lead over the past 19 Tests to 164, which isn't a bad effort. England, to their credit, fought hard in their second innings, but a couple of wickets in quick succession — Mike Atherton and then Graham Thorpe — left us in a position to conquer our opponents tomorrow morning.

The big wicket was Thorpe and even more weighty was the manner in which he was dismantled. A menacing spell from Brett Lee, who for the first time on tour really let himself go, produced searing pace and some hostile body language. Binga really worked Thorpe over, and I was able to adopt more aggressive field settings, which added to the intimidation and aura factors we love to cultivate. It was later revealed that Thorpe had not only been completely outmanoeuvred before playing back to a full-length ball (lbw Lee for 2), but that he had also broken a bone in his hand from a steepling riser that crushed his digits to the bat handle before he could release the grip pressure.

At Lord's —
Second Test —
Day Three

England 187 and 4–163 (MA Butcher 73*, MR Ramprakash 40) v Australia 401 (DR Martyn 52, AC Gilchrist 90; AR Caddick 5–101, D Gough 3–115)

We are in an outstanding position, but the lessons of Calcutta and Chennai hang heavy in the air and the foot won't be coming off the pedal in this Test match until we have a 2–0 series lead.

July 22 *London*

At Lord's —
Second Test —
Day Four

England 187 and 227 (MA Butcher 83; GD McGrath 3–60, JN Gillespie 5–53) lost to Australia 401 and 2–14

ANOTHER SURPRISE GREETED US AS we gathered for warm-ups in the nets directly behind the spaceship look-alike media centre. Kato had been creating a masterpiece poem during the first three days of the Test and unleashed it to the boys as he stood alone inside a circle of linked arms belonging to the whole squad. It was a gem of a recital, capturing the vital moments and the essence of what had transpired over the previous sessions. One of the great things about giving people opportunities and responsibility is that they often surprise and invigorate those around them. Kat's work was just the tonic we needed to relax and focus on the job ahead.

My words to the team before play were simple and to the point: 'It's not over yet, we have a lot of work to do before we can think about winning.' It was a precautionary talk, but deep down I believed we could win around lunchtime if we took an early wicket. And that's exactly what happened, after I swapped Dizzy around from the Pavilion End, where he had been bowling last night, to the Nursery End to allow the slope to help his natural away-swing. Pigeon took the other end, which he virtually owns, being triumphant every time he walks on the hallowed turf.

I also pulled somewhat of a surprise by giving Junior the first over instead of Warney, but that decision was based on more than a hunch. Over the years, Alec Stewart has often padded up to right-arm off spinners and been given out lbw, and it's common knowledge that he prefers the quicks to the slow men. The element of surprise that came with Mark bowling so early nearly worked first ball, when he got one to turn and bounce and it narrowly missed Stewart's off stump. His first over was so good, he deserved another just to see whether he could snare us a bonus wicket, and it was here that the hunch got a crunch and three fours flowed from the blade of Stewart, thus ensuring that Junior's spell was over.

From then on, all the bowlers were inspirational, with Gillespie joining his partner-in-crime on the honour board with a thoroughly well-deserved five-wicket haul. I reckon Dizzy has been our best bowler in the last six Tests we've played, but hasn't got the wickets he was entitled to, so it was brilliant that he snared a few today. Many bowlers are considered seam bowlers, but I'm sure no one in the history of the game can keep the stitching on the ball as upright as Jason has so far in this series. By having the skill to perform this art he keeps the batsman guessing as to which way it's going to deviate off the pitch, and keeps our slip cordon on edge, always expecting the ball to fly their way.

From 4–188, England disintegrated to 8–193. McGrath initiated the collapse by dismissing Stewart and Ian Ward with the second and third balls of his third over. Craig White survived the hat-trick ball, but Dizzy immediately had Mark Butcher caught behind and five runs later Dominic Cork was caught at first slip, Pigeon's third wicket of the morning. White and Caddick then did enough to make us bat again, but that was all.

A couple of minor hiccups occurred in our 14-run chase for victory, with Slats trying to swat Caddick over the top as he charged down the wicket, only to deflect it to Butcher at slip. There's one thing for sure when you're watching Slats: life is never boring. Expect the unexpected. Sometimes he'll look like he's thrown his wicket away, but his vulnerability on occasions is far outweighed by his brilliance during many other efforts. Unfortunately for Punter, he had to go out and finish the job just when he had probably switched off and was thinking about singing the team song. He fell to Gough, playing across the line.

At the press conference after the post-match presentations, the media lads wanted my view on the form of Punter and also Brett Lee. I was quick to point out that Ricky has been a little unlucky so far in this series, while Binga is still on the way back from a serious injury, and probably won't be seen at his peak until perhaps as late as the final Test, at The Oval. I emphasised, too, the value of Bing's explosive spell at Graham Thorpe on day three.

Matthew Hayden acknowledges the Australian dressing-room after hitting the winning runs in the second Test.

'Ricky's played three Test innings here,' I said, when one journo wanted to harp on the point. 'In one, the ball kept low, another, the ball took off on him and at Lord's he got out when the Test was over, when the emotion of the win had probably got to him and he didn't expect to bat. I know he's a quality player. He'll come through. He's done that before, backed up a couple of low scores with a couple of big ones. He's certainly hitting the ball as well as anyone.'

I was also asked if I thought we could emulate Warwick Armstrong's great Australian team, who at home in 1920–21 became the only team to win all five Tests in one Ashes series. To be honest, I didn't realise that they were the one side to do that. We're more aware of the history we're trying to create. Hopefully, our results will speak for themselves — if we manage to win 5–0, that's fabulous, but it's a long way off.

As far as this Test was concerned, although we played really well in all aspects of our game, I do think that the fielding was the main difference between the two sides. England missed a few chances while, in comparison, we were pretty sharp. This had a huge impact on the outcome of the match, and caused, or at least exacerbated, the difference between the teams. I know, as batsmen, that we had to work hard out there. England are a very competitive side.

I reckon part of the cause of England's ordinary catching is the pressure we put on them. I know when we played against the great West Indies sides, against the likes of Viv Richards when they were at their best, we knew that we had to take any chances that came our way. Perhaps our opponents are a little bit too tense and wanting it too much. They know they have to take their chances, they tense up, and they drop them. This is especially true when a bloke such as Gilly is at the crease. If you drop him you're really going to pay the price, because he scores so quickly and can change a game if he stays at the wicket for any length of time.

Our victory here continued Australia's remarkable record of only losing one Test at Lord's since 1896 and also made us good things to retain the Ashes. In a break from tradition, we invited our families to celebrate with us in the change-rooms. It was wonderful to be able show Lynette, Rosalie and Austin where I sit and to show them around and let them soak up the experience. So often in the past families have been relied upon to prop us up when we are struggling for form or suffering an injury but are often forgotten when things are running along nice and smoothly. Very rarely do they have a chance to celebrate with us, which, of course, they should do as they play a significant role in how we perform. Here, the mood in the rooms was amazingly relaxed, even with kids tearing about the place, which shows how much the modern game has changed from the days when the Australian team and the Lord's Pavilion were 'boys only' clubs.

A new name had been quickly added to the honour board by the time we started celebrating. The makeshift inscription read: 'Mark Waugh 158 catches World Record'. Fair enough, too, for his new mark is a tremendous achievement, which couldn't have been timed any better — Darren Gough nicking Gillespie to Junior at second slip to end the innings and give Dizzy a five-wicket milestone at the same time. At one point, while Slats was imitating Bon Jovi on the benchtop, someone asked how the name,

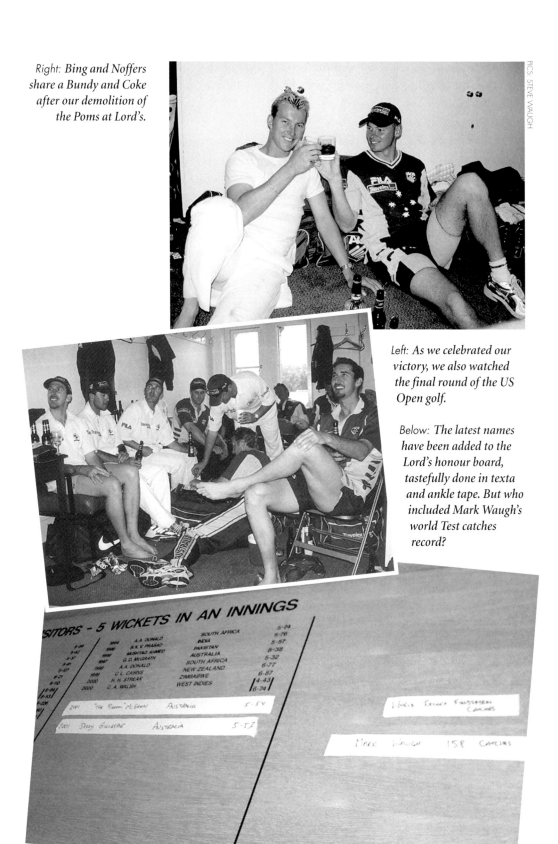

Right: Bing and Noffers share a Bundy and Coke after our demolition of the Poms at Lord's.

Left: As we celebrated our victory, we also watched the final round of the US Open golf.

Below: The latest names have been added to the Lord's honour board, tastefully done in texta and ankle tape. But who included Mark Waugh's world Test catches record?

scrawled on plaster and stuck on the board, had got there. Amid great laughter, it was revealed Mark had in fact put his name up himself. 'Well no one else would have done it,' he said sheepishly.

I love being part of this team!

Kato had added a few verses to his epic poem, and he read them out while surrounded by the lads on the balcony. This was followed by a presentation to Pete, our champion 'roomie', by Lang, who gave him a signed Test shirt in appreciation of his tireless work. Punter finished off a famous day by singing the team song in 'Healy-like' fashion, not breathing, veins bulging, hunched over, eyes glazed, demanding more from each of us. I'm sure no other cricket team celebrates like we do, and when I'm finished many of these times will be the most enduring memories of my career.

July 26 *London*

A DAY OFF BECAUSE THE second Test finished a day early meant bonus hours with the family but it also involved a couple of obligations that had to be met. One was an article for the London *Sunday Telegraph*, with whom I'm contracted during this tour, and it proved to be an uncomfortable experience. It wasn't a written piece, rather a round-table discussion chaired by the journalist Scyld Berry, with Mike Atherton, Nasser Hussain and me, and inevitably featured questions about why we are so good and why England are so bad. It was not the sort of 60 minutes any of us wanted and for me an experiment that will never be repeated.

A dinner put on by FICA (Federation of International Cricketers Associations) at which the team and I received awards filled in that evening and was made memorable by the fact I was seated next to John Major, the former British Prime Minister. One of the things we talked about was the sense of defeatism in the England camp. A classic example of this was a column penned by Marcus Trescothick in last Sunday's press in which he suggested that we were an 'awe-inspiring' team who played the game at 'a different level to anyone else on the planet'. Personally, I'd rather players in my team didn't go to such extraordinary heights to praise the opposition, especially when those views were published right in the middle of a Test match. I guess it was an honest column, so I'll give him credit for that, but there's a psychological battle going on and by writing in such a way I think he's conceding an edge to us.

The following day, we attended a six-a-side corporate day, which kept us busy. Sadly, the standard of our play was poor, and probably best exemplified by Funky. Feeling the effects of a deceptive drop known as 'Pimms and Lemonade', he attempted a quick single after miscuing an attempted huge heave to square leg, but got his legs crossed after pirouetting around, entangled himself and fell flat on his face to the hysterics of all around.

Another promotional event followed on the 25th, when Warney and I were enlisted to help promote the build-up to the Commonwealth Games to be held in Manchester in 2002, starting exactly a year from now. A huge press contingent gathered in Trafalgar

Meeting the great decathlete Daley Thompson (second from right) was the clear highlight of a promotional event for the 2002 Manchester Commonwealth Games that Warney and I attended. At far right is another outstanding British athlete, Darren Campbell, the 200m track silver medallist at the Sydney Olympics.

Square to see me take on Sarah Fitz-Gerald, the world's No. 1 squash player on a specially erected court, while Warney had to shape up to English rugby union's Lawrence Dallaglio in a boxing ring. The highlight of the morning for me was meeting Daley Thompson, a hero of mine and one of the greatest sporting personalities of the 20th century.

WINNING A TEST MATCH IS special, but so is playing with the kids in the park and just watching their zest and love of life is both invigorating and infectious. The days over the past few weeks when we have been a family together — which doesn't happen too often on a cricket tour — have been fantastic.

The 26th was our last day as a family before we went our separate ways and a sadness came over all of us because this may well be the last time we come to England together under these circumstances. We've all had such a great time. Having the family settled at one base has made a tremendous difference, as it has enabled the kids to settle into a routine and given Lynette and her parents a chance to enjoy some home-cooked meals and an environment similar to what they have at home. It was much more relaxing for them and let them get their bearings in London, enjoy their time and have a chance to see the sights.

From an Australian cricketer touring England's perspective, it's important for families to be comfortable when they're over here, as that definitely puts the player in a more relaxed frame of mind and thus makes him better able to perform to the best of his ability.

July 27 *Southampton*

GOODBYES ARE NEVER EASY AND bidding my family farewell never gets any easier; in fact, it's getting much harder. Rosalie is nearly five and wanting more of my attention and time, while Austin is a very active youngster approaching two years old. And then, of course, there's bub number three, who is eight weeks away from making his or her presence felt. Lynette has done an amazing job with them, basically as a sole parent, although her parents Phil and Ethel have been terrific as well.

So the team bus headed off to Southampton, while the family prepared for their British Airways flight tomorrow night. It's hard to come up with an answer when your daughter has tears in her eyes and says, 'I don't want you to go and I'll miss you.' All I could say was, 'Rosie, whenever you get lonely or are missing me, just remember I'll be missing you just as much. You'll always be in my thoughts, because I love you.'

With a couple of spare hours to kill because my room wasn't ready when we arrived in Southampton, I wandered off in search of a much-needed haircut. I expected to find a salon with an opening without a problem, but it was one-and-a-quarter hours later before I finally tracked one down. By then, with the temperatures having crept into the 30s, I was a lather of sweat. The good news is that they're predicting more of the same weather-wise, which should mean flatter pitches, which is where we play our best cricket.

A night at the flicks watching Travolta's new flick *Swordfish* was both relaxing and enjoyable. I had an extra interest in the film because I had met one of the co-stars, Australia's own Hugh Jackman, during the Sydney Olympics, and was very impressed by his presence in real life then and by his on-screen performance this evening.

Before going to bed, I had a quick chat with Buck, during which I outlined my thoughts on how we should proceed for the rest of the tour. There's a month of the tour to go. Let's refocus on winning our remaining games and give the rest of the tour our undivided attention. We have only three Tests and two other first class games to perform in before having a break away from the game. In my strong opinion, we should win each of those matches.

**At Southampton —
July 28–30**

Australians 97 (AA Noffke 28; AD Mullally 5–18, JEK Schofield 3–25) and 9–389 (declared: ML Hayden 142, SM Katich 59, SR Waugh 40; SD Udal 4–149) lost to Hampshire 354 (DA Kenway 70, RA Smith 113, NC Johnson 88; AA Noffke 3–66) and 8–134 (NC Johnson 37; B Lee 3–17, SK Warne 4–31) by two wickets

July 28 *Southampton*

FOR A VARIETY OF REASONS, our team selection for this match is very unorthodox, with six bowlers, a keeper and just four specialist batsmen. Our main goal here, of course, is to win the Test series and our preparation is geared 100 per cent towards achieving that objective. In any case, it makes life interesting when you challenge conventional ways that might have become a little too ingrained over the years.

Outlining my visions for the remainder of the tour certainly had an effect on the boys — we were all out 97 and Hampshire ended the day at 3–238. This was probably one of the worst days ever put in by an Aussie touring side and hopefully just one of those days that can be put down to everything going wrong. A lack of discipline and poor shot selection, coupled with an inability on our part to properly assess the match situation caused our batting embarrassment. As all our specialist batsmen had been dismissed before the completion of the seventh over, our final total was actually more than many people expected.

Our bowling was marginally better but four dropped catches and a wicket off a no-ball compounded an inept display on a pitch that definitely had something in it for the bowlers. For Hampshire, Alan Mullally's quest for a return in English colours gained momentum, but in reality his figures were flattering and his loss of pace due to injuries might count against him. One player who still looks the goods was Robin Smith (79 not out at stumps), a player who got pensioned off by the England selectors far too early considering he averages in the mid-40s in Tests and relishes a tough battle. Today, he played with increasing authority and to me is still a better player than half the current incumbents in the England XI.

The stand-out feature for Australia today was our hair, or more appropriately, the variety of colours on show. Funky's 'peacock' green shone like a beacon, while Warney's 'snowflake' white looked as if someone had tipped a truckload of flour over his dial. Flemo's 'boot polish' black gave him a debonair touch, matching Dizzy's 'vegemite' tint and disguising a 'silver fox' undergrowth. Binga's 'top deck' look of dairy milk chocolate bottom half and white chocolate top just overshadowed Haydos' blond streaks, and there was even a whisper that Marto's locks have been touched up.

So much for the macho Aussie male! Maybe we need a hairdresser, not a coach!

The Southampton scoreboard tells a sad story as last wicket to fall Colin Miller walks off. Australians all out 97.

July 29 *Southampton*

AFTER YESTERDAY'S DEBACLE, I MENTIONED to Buck that there needed to be a chat about what happened and how we are going to rectify the situation today, but that the talk shouldn't come from either of us but rather from the players themselves. When we got together it was quickly obvious the lads are embarrassed about the performance and promised to be more professional and disciplined for the rest of the game. We resolved to show everyone in England that we can come back from adversity, not just win from in front. Today we turned things around to a position where we not only hope to save the game but perhaps even win it. Taking seven wickets for 116 was more like it, with new boy Ashley Noffke bowling impressively to take three wickets from his 22.1 overs. 'Noffers' looks a Paul Reiffel-type bowler, with a hint of McGrath thrown in. He has improved on each outing since he joined us, and appears to be settling in well for a guy who never expected to be here at all.

The real positive of the day was that Matt Hayden spent considerable time in the middle. In doing so, he was able to finally get a feel for the pitches over here and a chance to work on and put into place his powers of concentration that have so far not been as commanding as they were in India. He was unbeaten on 92 at stumps. Justin Langer and Simon Katich also looked impressive, with the former fighting back with all his powers to try to win back the Baggy Green while the latter continues to edge closer to his dream of a Test appearance. At stumps we were 1–176, still 81 runs behind, but much better placed than we had been 24 hours earlier.

The England team for the third Test was announced today. The injured Hussain and Thorpe were missing, but otherwise it was fairly predictable, with the only real selection mistake in my book being Robert Croft preferred to Phil Tufnell. You only have to play against both of them to realise one is in a different league from the other.

The ever diligent Wade Seccombe on 12th-man duties. In fairness, this photograph was taken during Chuck's time off, and he was outstanding all tour long with his attitude and efforts.

July 30 *Nottingham*

THERE WAS ONLY ONE THING on my mind as we gathered together in our huddle before the start of warm-ups this morning, and that was for us to record an unexpected win. I outlined this to the boys, with instructions to bat normally to lunch, by which time the deficit would be wiped out, go on and get a 100-odd run lead after the break and then bowl Hampshire out in the final session on a wicket that was still favouring the bowlers.

This approach almost came off. Even though we narrowly lost the match after setting Hampshire 133 in 26 overs, everyone enjoyed the challenge and stimulation of the situations that presented themselves. Tour games are often dull, one-sided affairs, mainly because counties these days put out second-string teams. To Hampshire's credit, they put out the best side available and covered themselves in glory, competing tenaciously and believing in themselves to the point where it seemed that they almost expected to win.

A defeat was obviously not the result we were after, but the positives from this match far outweigh the negatives. Matt Hayden's 142 was a colossus of an innings on a dangerous pitch. His presence, balance and relaxed demeanour at the crease suggest big Test runs will follow. Brett Lee's spell today was awesome, mixing pace, hostility and skill, with the magic ingredient for all bowlers — rhythm — added in. Bing looked sure of himself today, and for the first time on tour managed to sustain his pace for a prolonged period, which indicates that he is on the improve and will produce at least one decisive spell before the Test series is over.

In one spell, Bing had their opener, Giles White, caught behind after he couldn't avoid an awkward, rising ball, set up his partner, Derek Kenway, with a bouncer barrage that ended with a skied catch to square leg, and yorked Lawrence Prittipaul as the batsman sat back waiting for a bouncer. He would have had a fourth wicket soon after, Will Kendall caught in the slip cordon, had he not been called for a no-ball.

Brett Lee knocks over Hampshire's Lawrence Prittipaul during the exciting final afternoon of our three-day game at Southampton.

Warney also turned back the clock, producing a ball equal to the famous one Mike Gatting could do nothing about back in 1993. This time, Shane ripped out Shaun Udal with a ball that pitched outside leg stump before gripping, turning and fizzing past his blade and knocking his off stump out. It was cricket nirvana and a massive morale boost for Warney (or 'Hulk Hogan' as we've begun to call him whenever he dons his bandana).

A quick shower and then it was on to the motorway for a 'junk food stop' before arriving in Nottingham shortly after 11pm. Before I could go to sleep I called Rosie for her fifth birthday and talked to her as she opened her presents, one of which was a Cinderella music box I bought for her when we were in Disneyland. My daughter is growing up so quickly. I can't believe school is around the corner; it seems like yesterday that she was entering the world.

July 31 *Nottingham*

IT WAS A TOUGH TRAINING session today, mainly because it came so soon after the Hampshire match and the long bus trip that followed that game. Afterwards I had a browse at the Trent Bridge pitch, which looks quite good, in contrast to the undulating outfield that is way below Test-match standard. In my view, it is not far from being dangerous, with damage to ankles and knees a real possibility, and should be rectified, especially considering how much money big cricket generates these days.

The chaotic scene in our dressing-room at Trent Bridge. As usual, every single centimetre of space has been taken.

Tonight's team meeting was fairly brief, with discipline, hunger and pride dominating our thoughts. Credit was paid to the lads who again missed out on selection for their attitude and dedication to the team. Punter, in a Lonely Planet style, gave us a quick summary of his four-day trip to Venice with his girlfriend.

And then it was off to the team dinner, which was organised by Slats. Unfortunately, we got lost trying to find his chosen pub, and to rub salt into the wounds our intrepid opener took possession of the bus microphone and gave us a guide to all the prominent landmarks we were passing, such as an elderly couple pruning the hedges of their garden, plus important information on the breeding backgrounds of the local 'Mutleys' (dogs) walking past. Thankfully, we located our destination after around 20 minutes and alighted with some alacrity and plenty of relief.

August 1 *Nottingham*

EVEN THOUGH TRAINING WAS 'OPTIONAL', quite a few of the lads, including myself, took it up. Warney claimed it was the lesser of two evils, citing fitness work as the least desired of the two choices on offer. It was a brisk workout in which I spent my batting time trying to play in the 'V' between mid-off and mid-on, while I also had a good session working with Lang, concentrating on his footwork. His attitude has been outstanding — as has that of Chuck, Kat, Flem, Funky and Noffers — and has helped keep everyone sharp and on their toes.

My usual pre-Test media conference with the English boys turned out to be rather eventful. I had talked with the Aussie contingent the day before, so they could meet their deadlines, and talked mostly about captaincy. Consequently I'd forgotten about the hullabaloo Buck's misplaced team notes — prominently featuring the fifth century Chinese warrior/philosopher Sun Tzu — had caused. After the obligatory first few half-volleys from the Pommie journos the bouncers started coming thick and fast. Question after question came about these treasured documents and their magical words. I think it is a storm in a teacup, as all Buck's scribbled comments are designed to do is to instigate comment and thoughts among our team. Many people have started calling Buck things ranging from a crackpot to Plato and plenty in between, but I see him as a 'performance manager', rather than merely a 'coach'. In my opinion, he's ahead of his time, a bloke I have always found helpful and stimulating.

Of course, many a spin was put on the notes, and in particular on the paragraph Buck included about the England team's excuses. In part the memo states: 'Overall this English team is hanging on to excuses (eg, injuries, toss, bad luck, dropped catches, etc). By gradually taking each of these away, ultimately there is no place to hide.' This was not meant in any way to be derogatory to the opposition; all Buck was doing was putting down on paper what the English camp has been saying. Despite what some papers are shouting, it's hardly dramatic stuff, and it is for each individual within the team to use it as he wants. If you want to take it on board then you do, if you get something out if it, great, but I know brother Mark, for one, read four words and said it was rubbish so he threw it out.

Near the end of the press conference I suggested that anyone outside the Australian team who had the document was in possession of stolen property and instead of publishing the notes they should have handed them back. I likened it to finding a wallet and deciding whether to keep the cash. Maybe this was stretching the point a little, but it certainly quietened the scribes down for a moment. Then they were off again and my patience was wearing thin. It culminated in one gentleman asking, 'Did you purposely put the notes under a journalist's door?' My response was immediate and to the point. You could have heard a pin drop, but the issue was now dead.

This is how the *Mirror* newspaper saw coach John Buchanan's now infamous memo. Buck related where our Ashes campaign had reached to Sun Tzu's philosophy on the nine types of ground needed to be covered for a battle to be won, as written in *The Art of War*. Buck's thoughts were as follows:

August 2   *Nottingham*

At Trent Bridge —
Third Test — Day One

England 185 (ME Trescothick 69,
AJ Stewart 46; GD McGrath 5–49)
v Australia 7–105 (ML Hayden 33;
AR Caddick 3–39)

DAY ONE OF A TEST match is always special and the mood on the bus during the 20-minute journey to Trent Bridge reflected the apprehension and sense of expectation the players were feeling. Some short motivation videos helped pass the time.

Another capacity crowd confronted us on a day where the weather forecast was mixed and the pitch looked a little uneven, strangely not as solid as it had a couple of days back (or perhaps I just looked more closely this time, or

Dispersive Ground: We enter the last phase of the tour with partners having just left, or not far off (leaving). If these thoughts occupy our minds, we leave ourselves vulnerable.

Facile Ground: We have won two Tests of a five-Test series. Now is no time to ease up, as we have only done part of the job.

Contentious Ground: The contentious ground which neither side has claimed yet and which is critical to success is discipline for the whole game.

Open Ground: Open ground could relate to selections. Let us do what we wish to do about our selections but not interfere or attack English selections — give them no 'fuel' or insights into our thinking.

Ground of Intersecting Highways: We have joined hands with public, sponsors and media about the way the English team plays its cricket and thus its 'ability' to play Australia. Consequently, we have currently gained 'psychological control'.

Serious Ground: We have damaged England, not only by our performances but also by the way we have achieved these results and our manner, behaviour and image. It is essential that these standards are maintained to ensure we do not have to spend unnecessary time and energies on putting out 'bushfires'.

Difficult Ground: This ground may be typified by difficult wickets, conditions, game circumstances. It is our belief that we are capable of adjusting to difficulties/challenges in order to keep going forward rather than treading water and waiting for something to happen.

Hemmed-in Ground: This is ground that is 'foreign' to us. However, we must be better prepared to face such situations, as they will inevitably arise (eg, India). In order to devise and enact appropriate strategies to win unwinnable positions, it will require flexibility in our thinking, creativity and initiative.

Desperate Ground: This ground requires good and skilful leadership when we are really up against it (ie, opposing batsman in full flight/on flat wicket/fast ground/ball soft/new ball long way off; or opposing bowlers taking wickets quickly and regularly). While the captain is charged with ultimate decisions, he requires the clear thinking and alternatives provided by all his leaders to be able to strike swiftly and decisively.

had been influenced by all the pre-match talk that suggested that this wicket was one of the best in the country). Small plates of the pitch moved when I pushed them, which suggested to me that we'd be playing on a two-paced, two-heights type of wicket. It was a good toss to lose and Michael Atherton elected to bat even though his selectors had decided to include another bowler in their quest to get back into the series. For us the only change was bringing Lang into the 12th-man role, a reward for his attitude and enthusiasm of late.

The job of captain is always a challenging one, because you have to be able to make decisions, change your plans and adapt quickly. In the back of my mind all morning was the idea of throwing Binga the new ball after his encouraging form against Hampshire. In giving him this chance, I thought, his confidence would be enhanced further and he'd be eager to turn in an eye-catching performance. But in the end I decided to leave the 'Dumb and Dumber' dynamic duo intact. Then, with Atherton gone within two balls, I changed my mind because I was keen to expose their No. 3, the left-handed Mark Butcher, to an inswing bowler, that being Brett Lee. Butcher, I had noticed, had fallen lbw to the inducking ball many times for Surrey, but until now it wasn't something we had tried to exploit. As it turned out, Bing didn't pick up a wicket, but the plan nearly came off perfectly when the first ball he bowled to Butcher ducked back and caught him not offering a stroke. Unfortunately for us, the delivery was doing too much and would have missed the leg stump.

The English players and fans no doubt felt aggrieved by Atherton's quick-fire dismissal (replays indicated it came off his arm guard), but to us it sounded like two noises, which normally indicates a bat or glove in there somewhere. Going against what

Ricky Ponting at third slip is about to catch Mark Butcher on the opening day of the third Test.

had occurred throughout the series to date, the replay of this contentious dismissal was shown time and time again on the big screen at the ground, which inevitably infuriated the spectators, who, of course, then directed their anger at us. Under normal circumstances, such a replay would not have been shown, and I don't know why it was this time because all it did was stir up trouble.

That problem aside, the first two sessions went according to our script, with McGrath again magnificent in claiming his 20th 'Michelle' (as in Michelle Pfeiffer, rhyming slang for five-for) in Tests. Gillespie and Warne took two wickets each, while only Marcus Trescothick and Alec Stewart managed to get more than 14. Overall, today's effort represented another skilful exhibition by our bowlers, as I thought England's total of 185 was about 120 below par and presented us with the ideal opportunity to secure the Ashes, if we could nail down a big total ourselves.

However, following on the theme of ball dominating bat, we collapsed to be 7–105 at stumps, which thankfully came three overs early due to bad light. The way things were going we may well have been all out if we had had to continue, because England were on a roll and we had no answers to Andy Caddick and Alex Tudor, who had orchestrated the collapse. This early finish may well turn out to be crucial, because it gives us a chance to stem the flow, start again and whittle down the deficit. And, of course, with Adam Gilchrist at the crease anything is possible. It's amazing what a bit of sun on a batsman's back can do to his batting. All of a sudden the pitch becomes benign, the ball doesn't swing and he feels much more comfortable in his surroundings. This is what we're hoping will happen tomorrow.

My innings was cut short by a Caddick special, seaming and bouncing away, catching my edge as I dithered between being aggressive or defensive. Indecisiveness is a batsman's worst failing and will nearly always lead to one's downfall. For me, it was a huge disappointment, because I again felt in great touch, with every ball hitting the middle, bar one, which, of course, was my undoing. That's why it's 'Test' cricket: you can't afford any lapses, as you get punished for them on most occasions. It's no consolation to know this; all I can do is make sure I learn from the experience and prosper next time.

August 3   *Nottingham*

At Trent Bridge —
Third Test — Day Two
England 185 and 6–144 (MA
Atherton 51, ME Trescothick 32;
SK Warne 5–25) v Australia 190
(AC Gilchrist 54, JN Gillespie 27*;
AR Caddick 3–70, AJ Tudor 5–44)

THIS MORNING'S FIRST SESSION WAS quite obviously a crucial one, with England having their first real opportunity to move into a dominating position in the series if they could take our last three wickets quickly. The weather again was very mixed — one minute blue skies, the next a thick, dull, grey atmosphere. This should have suited the bowlers, but Gilly took over once again while England captain Mike Atherton seemed caught between wanting to try to take his wicket and also wanting to try to stop the flow of boundaries.

Adam has a fantastic ability to sense a weakness or poor body language, and he upped the ante and hammered a brilliant 50 before the Poms knew what had hit them. Not for the first time in this series, he tore into Darren Gough, who he fancies as a bowler more than the others. Perhaps this is because Goughie has a flatter trajectory than, say, Andy Caddick, which allows Gilly to hit through the line regardless of the length. Gilly has probably influenced the outcome of around half the Test matches he has played in with the bat, which represents a phenomenal start to a career that will surely lead to greatness. In support, Jason Gillespie, as always, was the man for the job, giving Gilly the vital back-up in a partnership that went a long way towards giving us our five-run lead instead of a nasty deficit. While this was only a marginal advantage for us on the scoreboard, it meant much more because it took away that feeling of us being behind the eight ball. A first-innings deficit of any kind, added to the fact that we have to bat last on a pitch that was already hard work to bat on, would have been a testing handicap to overcome.

England began in fine style in the quest to leave us a substantial victory target. We needed an ounce of luck or something special to turn things around and both came just in the nick of time. A perfectly executed sweep by Trescothick cannoned into Matthew Hayden's calf at short leg before lobbing up in the air for what seemed an eternity. A lunging Gilchrist reacted quickest, gathering the freak chance centimetres above the ground.

The strange but constant booing of the crowd that followed this dismissal suggested something was amiss. As is customary these days, the umpires had called for the third umpire to confirm or deny the appeal, but it was quite obviously out — extremely unfortunate for England but a huge break for us. Then we realised that the boos were coming as the big on-ground TV screen kept repeating the image of Warney's foot landing fractionally over the popping crease as he delivered the ball responsible for Trescothick's dismissal.

The debate over uncalled no-balls really began during the England–Pakistan series, when the TV replays were able to show that at least a couple of English wickets had fallen off balls that could have been called because the bowler had overstepped the mark. But I truly believe the issue of no-balls has been overstated. A no-ball from a spinner is, technically, an indiscretion, but in reality it affects nothing and should be seen as that, rather than being made into a major issue. The umpires are only human and I am sure the odd no-ball has been missed since the game began, or at least since the front-foot law came into being.

Surely the last thing we want is for the game to become too clinical or Americanised. The variables and vagaries of cricket are part of its attractions and are why people watch it and talk about it. Some critics are suggesting that there should be a video umpire employed only to spot no-balls, but the introduction of too much technology could leave the game like American football, with stoppages galore. That would benefit no one. One of the strengths of this series has been the pace at which the games have rolled along. There has been continuity, a minimum of stoppages and the tempo has been high, giving the fans full value for money.

In any match there are turning points and, whatever the crowd's reaction, we Australians felt confident that those replays on the screen were repeatedly showing an important one. We also knew it was time to drive home the advantage. Mark Butcher went next, just as we had planned, playing across the line to an inswinger and being trapped dead in front. The big scalp wasn't far away, and again it was controversial, with Atherton falling victim to a caught behind decision off Warney. This was a curious one, as both keeper and bowler were certain of a thin edge while Junior at first slip didn't bother to appeal. Judging by Atherton's laboured exit he obviously wasn't impressed by the verdict, which must have been particularly frustrating for him as he looked settled and ready to make a big score. From there, England's middle order was exposed, with Mark Ramprakash cracking under the weight of expectation and the presence of pressure.

An example of the psychological edge we try to gain over our opponents happened when Ramprakash made his way to 14 not out. He had been dismissed for 14 in the first innings here, amazingly the fifth time out of the last six innings against us that he'd made precisely that score. A fact such as this is one that can be used by his opponents to create doubts and to shift the batsman's concentration away from where it should be. I began with, 'Let's make it six 14s for Ramps,' and immediately gained the impression he knew what I was on about. A change in his body language was accompanied by a succession of play-and-misses and we knew he was ours. By now the lads had made the number 14 a favourite of ours. Warney piped in with, 'let's chip up on number 14', a casino reference to the roulette wheel. On this occasion, Ramprakash did get past his bogey number, but it made no difference — now he was being reminded that he was

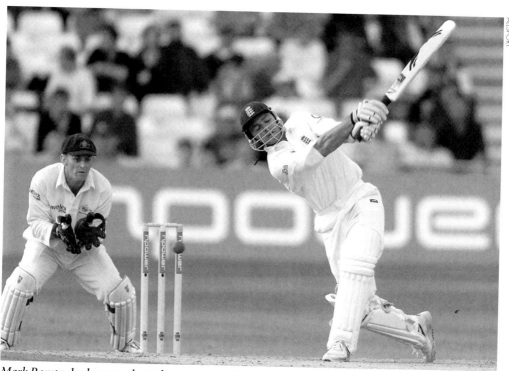

Mark Ramprakash succumbs to the pressure and is stumped during England's second innings at Trent Bridge.

entering unknown territory. And soon enough he succumbed, stumped Gilchrist bowled Warne. To me this is gamesmanship, or mental disintegration, but it's not sledging, which is what some people like to tag everything that's said in the middle. This is Test cricket — any weakness will be exposed.

A fantastic day was capped off when we took a sixth wicket from the second-last ball of the day. This time the captain lunged forward at silly point to take a one-handed diving catch to rid us of Craig White. At the time, White was being swarmed upon by a pool of sharks looking for a kill as our champion leg-spinner put him under the microscope.

Even with great players such as Shane confidence can play a part, and that ball he bowled Shaun Udal at Southampton has given him an enormous injection of self-belief. Of course, we eventually lost the Hampshire match, but the boost to Shane's confidence as a result of his spell on the least day there is proving far more significant than the defeat. Here, there have been no full tosses and barely a loose ball as he picked up his 18th five-wicket haul in Test matches. Warney looks relaxed and back to his best and that is an ominous sign for those teams facing him over the coming weeks and months.

Jason Gillespie has to take some of the credit for Warney's five wickets, as he bowled equally well at the other end without the same reward. Batting has always been about building partnerships and bowling is much the same. Ask anyone in the dressing-room, and they will acknowledge how well Jason bowled, ensuring there was no escape for the batsmen if they got away from Warney. This was another illustration of the value of teamwork — while individuals take the headlines, in reality the sum of the whole is almost always greater than the individual parts.

I'm sure a lead of only 139 runs with four wickets remaining wasn't how England would have foreseen the stumps scoreline when play began this morning, but the game is still there for the taking. There's no doubt, though, that we have firmed into clear favouritism.

An invitation to see Notts County play West Ham in a pre-season football friendly was taken up by the lads tonight, but due to our late finish we missed all three of the goals. Still, we had a chance to take our seats to a chorus of boos and chants of 'England! England!' We felt like responding with '2–0! 2–0!', but being horrendously outnumbered we bit our tongues and enjoyed the view.

August 4 *Nottingham*

At Trent Bridge — Third Test — Day Three

England 185 and 162 (JN Gillespie 3–61, SK Warne 6–33) lost to Australia 190 and 3–158 (ML Hayden 42, ME Waugh 42*, DR Martyn 33*) by seven wickets

JASON GILLESPIE RECEIVED HIS REWARDS for yesterday's heroic performance by claiming three of the remaining four English wickets, while Shane got the other to finish with a very impressive and well-deserved 6–33. It was a pleasing morning's work for both the team and myself. As a captain, many successful moves can go unnoticed but the mistakes certainly don't. Subtle field changes for Robert Croft, Andy Caddick and Alex Tudor may have contributed to their downfall, and for that reason I felt very satisfied because in each case I had followed my gut instincts. The only thing I didn't enjoy was copping a Caddick cut shot on the forearm just above the wrist after it leapt off the hills and valleys outfield (or, rather more appropriately, what we're calling the 'minefield'), which gave me an instant lump combined with a numbing of the fingers due to a nerve being crushed.

Chasing a small target such as we had in front of us can often be hard work, because you often keep looking at the end result and as a consequence change your normal game plan. My only words to the batsman were, 'Let's be positive; play our way, back yourself and have fun.' And straightaway, the Slater–Hayden partnership was energetic and full of positive body language. This final point is vital, because it sent out a message that we had a job to do and we were serious about doing it.

My turn at the crease came with 70 runs to get. I wasn't 100 per cent sure about batting, as my wrist had stiffened up and become very sore whenever I exerted any pressure on it. But I wanted to be out there, so to help me make it through I opted for a little bit of extra help in order to get the job done. It came in the form of a gift loaned to me by Bob Radford (the former CEO of New South Wales Cricket) after our victory at Lord's Test — a gold medallion presented to Victor Trumper for being a part of NSW's victorious Sheffield Shield team of 1903–04. Only two of these medals are known to be in existence, and to have the honour of wearing the one given to Australia's first great batsman of the 20th century was a special experience.

But how quickly and unexpectedly life can change. Feeling strong mentally and physically secure with the inflamed wrist taped up and helped by taking two painkilling tablets before batting, I believed it was my destiny to be there at the end when we claimed the Ashes. However, things suddenly turned very sour after I clipped the first ball I received, from Alex Tudor, behind square leg to get off the mark . . .

Jason Gillespie starts the new day in the best possible way. Ian Ward is lbw without a run having been added to England's overnight total.

At the precise moment I was injured, I was surprised — no, shocked — and at the same time, of course, was suddenly feeling all the pain associated with what had happened. Moments later, reality set in and the thought that I was now facing weeks of rehabilitation was actually more distressing than the physical grief I was experiencing. What had happened was that, on setting off for the first run I had suddenly become overwhelmed by a searing pain in my lower left leg. I stumbled up to the bowler's end, fell over and stayed down until a motorised stretcher came out to get me off the ground. From there, it was just about straight to hospital, where I remained while Junior and Marto knocked off the runs we needed to retain the Ashes.

It's difficult to describe the emotion I felt when the team's physiotherapist of 17 years, Errol Alcott, rang to tell us at the hospital that we'd just won the Ashes for an Australian record seventh consecutive time. Part of me was elated at a magnificent job done by the team but there was another part concerned at the extent of the injury that I'd just sustained. The sterility of the hospital further confused my thoughts, somewhat suppressing an overwhelming urge to feel totally ecstatic.

The fact that I was sitting in a wheelchair, in a fair degree of pain and not being totally sure of my future had made me very apprehensive as I waited my turn in the claustrophobic chamber known as an MRI machine. A further hour passed before my diagnosis was confirmed as being a 5cm long tear in the lower calf and a 2cm tear high up in the calf. This, of course, wasn't great news but in a funny sort of way it was reassuring to know that I was now in the process of making my way back. The bottom of the barrel had been reached and now it was time to look for some positives. The first of these was the fact we had won a difficult Test under pressure and showed everyone that not only are we good frontrunners but we're also capable of fighting back and showing some steel when it is required. To win an Ashes series remains a special feeling, as it is still cricket's most sought-after if elusive trophy, played between two countries with proud and combative histories.

The fact that I'm captain adds to my pride at retaining the Ashes. I have felt an extra responsibility to make sure Australia's golden winning run didn't end during my reign. We have played outstanding cricket, scoring runs quickly, attacking England with the ball and catching well enough to make sure we never entered a fourth day in terms of total hours played. Obviously, we've had individual stars but our collective effort has been the secret to our success. This has been our hallmark over the past few years, a trait that I hope continues, because it ensures an even share of responsibility, pressure and workload on all team members. With such a settled line-up, there are inevitably going to be players regularly missing out. These guys are known as the 'dirt trackers' but more realistically they are 'gold nuggets'. In the Australian set-up they invariably retain a positive outlook and put the team ahead of their personal needs, encouraging the lads on the field while putting up with the many chores that come with being on the bench. We also have a support staff who rarely get any kudos but who allow the players to enjoy the tour while at the same time looking after their well-being and future. The squad ethos that we are trying to encourage and develop binds us tightly in times of difficulty or need and certainly pulls us through when we most need it.

The catches that took Mark Waugh past Mark Taylor as the leading non-wicketkeeping catcher in Test history. Above: Junior snares Mark Butcher on the first day of the second Test, at Lord's, to draw level with Tubby. Below: The last dismissal of the game — Gough caught M Waugh, bowled Gillespie — is Junior's 158th catch of his Test career.

Above: Mark Butcher drops Adam Gilchrist early on the third day, one of four let-offs our champion all-rounder took full advantage of.
Below: Gilly smashes another boundary on his way to 90 from 121 balls.

The way Brett Lee softened up arguably England's No. 1 batsman, Graham Thorpe, was one of the highlights of the Lord's Test. Above: Thorpe struggles to come to terms with a riser.
Below: *He walks sadly off after being trapped lbw.*

Above: Each morning before the start of play during the Tests, Jock Campbell would give the 'dirt trackers' some extra physical work. Here at Trent Bridge, while John Buchanan looks on, Jock delights in putting Wade Seccombe and Simon Katich through a testing tyre-pulling routine. Below: While the England team heads back to their dressing-room on the day before the third Test, Buck tries to explain The Art of War to the media. Good luck!!

Two crucial catches from the third Test. Above: Gilly reacts quickest after a Marcus Trescothick sweep rebounded off the heel of short-leg Matthew Hayden. Below: The captain dives forward to snare a useful grab from the bat and pad of Craig White, to end the second day's play.

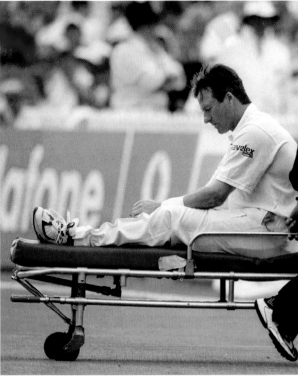

The end of my tour?
Above and above right: **The pain of the double muscle tear in my calf was nothing compared to the ignominy of being carted off on a stretcher.**

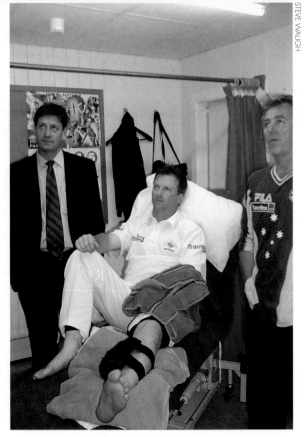

Right: **In the physio's room with Steve Bernard and Errol Alcott, watching endless replays of my demise. I've got ice packs on my torn calf muscles and also on my first injury of the day, a bruised wrist.**

PICS: STEVE WAUGH

Right: Schkimpy our mascot shares Brett Lee's joy after we retained the Ashes. He is a gift that was given to Buck by a fan during the 2000–01 Australian season and is now our constant companion. He's even got his own Baggy Green!

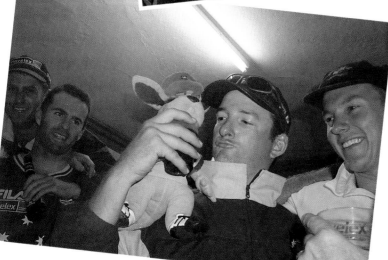

Left: Junior, overcome by the excitement of winning the series, lines Schkimpy up for a celebratory kiss.

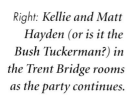

Right: Kellie and Matt Hayden (or is it the Bush Tuckerman?) in the Trent Bridge rooms as the party continues.

Left: *Punter (back to camera) is atop a Trent Bridge table, firing the boys up — in particular Buck — as he belts out* Under the Southern Cross.

Right: *Buck looks pretty pleased with himself — and so he should! — after a week in which the press lampooned him because of the leaked 'Sun Tzu' document.*

Below: *Seven Ashes series wins in a row (a feat Dizzy thought was pretty special) … and my second ever set of crutches.*

PICS: STEVE WAUGH

At 7–102 late on the first day most observers believed we were in trouble — and realistically we were on the brink of conceding a sizeable first-innings deficit, on a pitch that was only going to get worse. In this situation I guess most critics would have expected an air of tension in our camp, but in fact we talked our position through and after that believed that we could get a first-innings lead. And even if we didn't, we knew we'd get close enough so that the Test would virtually come down to a one-innings battle, which we believed we would win. Many would say this is arrogance, but in my view that word is one that too often gets confused with confidence. Confidence is arrogance with belief and hard work thrown in; arrogance is confidence without belief and hard work.

By the time I made it back to the change-rooms, the lads had been celebrating with family and friends for a good hour and a half. I quietly slipped into my corner on my crutches, sat down and thought to myself, 'It doesn't get any better than this.'

To sit back and observe in this situation was a worthwhile exercise. It gave me a chance to get a perspective on what our achievement means to everyone in the squad. Lang, as usual, was ecstatic, pouring drinks and slapping backs in his infectious way. Haydos had flogged a supporter's hat that looked like the Bush Tuckerman's and was busy grabbing anyone within reach and then proceeding to give them a headlock. The old heads of Warne, Mark Waugh, and McGrath were more subdued, but clearly equally satisfied, while the new boys, Katich, Noffke and Seccombe, were lapping it up, no doubt imagining similar times to come for them in the Baggy Green. Buck, meanwhile, looked

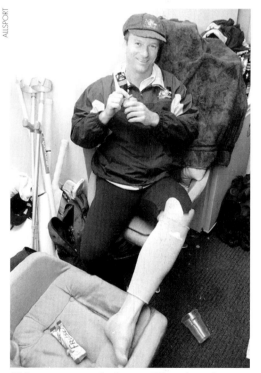

This was not exactly the way I'd envisaged our moment of triumph, with a set of crutches, ice bags and a leg guard on or around me, but the important thing was that the precious urn was with me too.

a contented man. He's been called anything from a crackpot to a man who should be wearing a straitjacket rather than a tracksuit, but he didn't need to respond to those wild, headline-grabbing lines. His record and the success of his methods speak for themselves.

I wished time would stand still, but it was also a time I knew we could never take for granted. I needed no reminding of this fact: I'm still the only current player who has experienced the pain and self-doubt that comes with losing an Ashes series. One day we'll again know and taste defeat against the non-bread stealers, but I hope that day is still a long way off. By 10pm the ice had numbed my calf and chilled my southern and coke, and I was in the best place in the world — among friends with whom I'd played a part in creating our own history.

Alighting from the team bus after six hours of victory celebrations in the change-rooms occasionally presents a few problems due to the 'wobbly boot syndrome'. This time I had to negotiate the steps with two crutches and a leg that felt as if a tiger had just had a chew on it. As I hobbled back to the room I knew my celebrations had come to an end, which was a real letdown considering winning the Ashes is a highlight for any Aussie cricketer. Instead, for me it was a night of ice packs for 20 minutes on the hour, followed by 40 minutes off, as many times as I could before falling asleep. Eventually 3am came around ... by morning, the bed was soaked from the remnants of a pillowslip full of ice cubes.

The scene at Trent Bridge the day after we retained the Ashes. If England had only dug in a bit more, the game might have been saved.
Opposite: Unused tickets to the scheduled, but not needed, fourth and fifth days of the third Test.

A Team Without Stars

Something we have been working towards during my time in charge of the Australian side is to create a team without stars. That might seem an odd thing to write given that we have players of the calibre of Glenn McGrath, Shane Warne and Adam Gilchrist, especially as all three took the plaudits during our Ashes-retaining victory.

But our belief is that any sustained success has to be based on the combined efforts of the team rather than relying time and again on the same individuals. The three I have mentioned have regularly made match-winning contributions, but we want all our players to be capable of doing it and everyone in our current line-up has done just that. If someone fails in one match or, like myself yesterday, gets injured, it is up to the others to step up and fill the void. That is the foundation on which our record-breaking run of wins was built and it is a philosophy we try to carry into every match.

An example came in the first Test at Edgbaston. We topped 500 but that total was not down to just one or two players. Everyone contributed and that is the kind of dominance that creeps up on the opposition and overpowers them.

Every player will have his own game plan, but at the same time we also want the players to be flexible enough to recognise different situations and adapt to them, to back themselves and take control of key moments. There is a belief that everyone in the side is capable of that. Coach John Buchanan and I are keen to get players outside their comfort zones, to push themselves that extra yard to produce something special.

August 12 *Birmingham*

At Hove
August 8–10

Sussex 4–355 (declared:
MW Goodwin 105, RR Montgomerie
157, CJ Adams 66*) and 5–67
(declared: DW Fleming 3–20, B Lee
2–27) lost to Australians 2–86
(declared: MJ Slater 46*,
ME Waugh 32*) and 2–339
(AC Gilchrist 114, RT Ponting 147*,
SM Katich 40*) by eight wickets

At Belfast
August 12

Australians 1–86 (ML Hayden 52*)
v Ireland: game abandoned due
to rain

HAVING COME BACK FROM VARIOUS ailments over the years, ranging from hamstring and groin strains to stress fractures in the legs, knee and back, plus broken bones to the fingers and nose, I can honestly say, don't tear your calf. It makes the others look and feel like a stroll in the park.

My last eight days have been totally consumed with the need to make sure I'm doing everything I possibly can to get back as quickly as is humanly possible. Wherever Errol Alcott has gone, I have gone, meaning that while the rest of the team is in Ireland, I am here with the team physio in Birmingham, while he visits some long-time friends.

In the 24 hours after I suffered the injury I went through a whole range of emotions. My first thought as I hobbled away from Trent Bridge on crutches was that I should go home. If I did so, I could see my family again and concentrate on getting my leg right for the new season at home. At that point, however, my wife Lynette took a hand. I'm sure she would have been happy at the prospect of me returning early,

The fun pier at Brighton will never be the same again. Knocking cans down with an accurate throwing arm, shooting baskets and grabbing toys with a mechanical claw are easy pickings for serial amusement park stalkers such as Lee, Gillespie and McGrath. Such was the pillaging on the night before this photograph was taken that one basketball stall closed down for fear the boys might lob again. That they did, and this time team masseur Bec Lauder went along to gather and look after the winnings. She's pictured here with Pigeon, who proudly displays his prized catch — a stuffed tiger that will do well to make it back to Oz.

especially as she is expecting our third child next month. But when I told her about my situation she said that because this was likely to be my last Ashes tour I should stay and savour it, and give myself every chance of being right for The Oval.

With support like that, as well as encouragement from my teammates, the answer to the question about what I should do suddenly became clearer. Errol and I began to plan my schedule of recovery and rehabilitation and with each day I could see some improvement. By the night after I'd been stretchered off I had tossed away the crutches and by the time we left Brighton, on the morning of August 11, after our three-day game with Sussex, I could walk without a limp.

I haven't set any timeframe for my return and haven't even discussed it with Errol Alcott. I'd rather focus on what I have to do for each given day, and try to achieve what's set out in front of me. I see it as being like a game of Test cricket in that, if I stick to the required process, the end result will take care of itself. However, if I lose sight of that and keep thinking about what I want to happen, I'll take my eye off what's required and lose my way.

Being injured, of course, does affect your mental state and it's very easy to get down about things. My way of coping with my situation was to firstly say, 'It's happened and I can't change that fact.' The other option would have been to say, 'Why me? I can't believe my bad luck.' But if I'd taken that attitude I would have quickly become disenchanted about the whole situation and what I was going to miss out on. I guess in some ways, however, this is natural response, but I dealt with it by saying to myself, 'Yes, it's disappointing, but I'm going to come back stronger and more determined than before.'

Many factors can help motivate you in times of adversity. For me, the main one was waiting to get back into that Baggy Green as quick as possible. Another spur was an article written back in Australia by the veteran cricket writer, Peter McFarline, who suggested I am going to struggle to come back as strong as I was, and that now that I'm older it's going to take extra time. For me, saying something can't be done is the best possible stimulation I can get. For it ignites a desire and passion within that I can't allow to lie dormant.

In a situation such as I am facing, I reckon that once you've taken the step to be positive and proactive, you are on your way. All I then needed was discipline, quality treatment and mini goals to aspire to. My first one was to get rid of the crutches and start to walk unaided within 48 hours. It's amazing how one little act like this can get you fired up; after I made it I realised that there was light at the end of the tunnel and that the only way to go was up.

Today's rehabilitation work was typical of what I have put myself through over the past few days. The program reads as follows:

7.30pm — Pool session: stretching followed by swimming 12 laps (six of breaststroke, six freestyle), then four laps kicking on back. Then exercises: calf raises in pool, running on the spot, running up and down steps in waist-deep water, all up one-and-a-half hours.

10am — Massage: deep friction. Then stretching and walking for one-and-a-quarter hours.

4pm — Pool: same routine as morning for one hour.

5pm — Gym session: stationary bike for 20 minutes, then treadmill (10 minutes), walking, then calf raises (6 x 5) plus balancing work.

6pm — Massage: deep friction for one hour, featuring intense pain, verging on agony (I'd give it nine and a half out of 10 for pain).

8pm — Hot water bottle, then 'stockings' on to stop the swelling as well as a 'thermoskin' to keep it firm.

After each session I rate how I'm feeling and also give myself a percentage chance of playing in the fifth Test at The Oval, which starts on August 23. Today's rating read: 'Mentally, leg feels almost like a leg again. Can almost walk without a limp but the muscle has wasted away and I need to get that stimulated and back to what it used to look like. Pain is intense with the hands-on treatment but I know it's doing me good so must put up with it. Percentage chance of playing: 10 per cent.'

I find that by putting my thoughts down I remain positive and on top of things. But I'm also conscious not to push things too quickly, as the body can sometimes trick you into believing all is well when you are still vulnerable.

Ideally, I want to play again on this tour, but if it isn't possible then so be it. I am quite content with what's been achieved in the first three Tests. We have won the series, I have no worries about the players available to take my place and I can look back on my four Test tours of this country with some fantastic memories. Even if I don't make it back in time to play I still have a role on this tour as a selector, which is important and carries enormous responsibility. And it will be interesting to observe the team from a different viewpoint and may, in the long run, be beneficial for me to observe from this perspective how the squad functions as a unit. I'm happy to put my knowledge to use if it can be of benefit to anyone.

I'm sure the boys will survive without me in the same way they did against the West Indies during the last Australian season, when, under Gilly's leadership, they decisively won the third Test.

August 13 *Leeds*

THE OBVIOUS DOWNSIDE TO MY calf injury is, of course, that I'll have to sit out the upcoming Headingley Test. This is especially frustrating because I have many fond memories of runs and victories here. Batsmen lucky enough to make it at the international level never forget their first Test-match hundred — my 177 not out in the first Test of the 1989 Ashes battle came in my 27th Test. It was a period in my career where I was unsure of my ability and, to be blunt, wondering whether I belonged among giants such as Allan Border, Ian Botham and company.

We won that Test in '89, and again in 1993 and 1997 pleasant memories were the outcome for all the Aussies involved. It was here in '93 that Allan Border and I put on 332 for the fourth wicket, in the process scoring 200 not out and 157 not out respectively. However, it wasn't the score that I recall from this match, but the fact that it was here that my 'lucky red rag' first emerged. For much of my innings I was signalling to the 12th man for a cloth so I could wipe the sweat from my brow. Struggling to fulfil my requests, the lads ended up carving up a few of the towels that were actually designed for use after the showers at the conclusion of play. That red rag has been with me ever since and acts as a type of security blanket, giving me reassurance and a sense of confidence whenever I see it dangling from my hip pocket.

Cricketers are a very superstitious lot, often preferring not to tempt fate by changing anything that has previously had even the vaguest connection with their success. Damien Martyn is a prime example of this. The shirt he wore at Edgbaston during his first Test century instantaneously became his most treasured possession and the most guarded item in his kit bag. Unfortunately for Marto, though, the sponsor's logo was on the wrong sleeve and he had to change shirts for the third Test match. Thankfully the outcome was positive for everyone, with Damien breaking the 'hoodoo' and the sponsor getting value for money from the new shirt.

August 14 *Leeds*

AN 8AM CONFERENCE CALL BETWEEN Adam Gilchrist, Trevor Hohns and myself to select the side for the fourth Test. A number of players were discussed in relation to the starting XI, with the major decision obviously involving my replacement. The choice between Simon Katich and Justin Langer in the end came down to two considerations — whoever played would be batting at No. 6 and the player needed some current form to get the nod.

On both counts, Kato had the answers. I felt it would be unfair for Justin to bat in an unaccustomed position, especially as his recent form hasn't been that good. I have no doubt he could have handled the assignment, but Simon was our final decision, which means he'll be the first batsman to debut since Gilly a bit less than two years ago. The last specialist batsman to make his debut before Kat was Darren Lehmann against India in March 1998.

It will be a rare experience for me, watching a Test match from the sidelines, but I'm excited about watching another 'Baggy Greener' make his debut. Kat possesses an admirable temperament, excellent technique and gets on with the job in an uncomplicated and simple way.

A 10am session was our last full get-together before the Test and the intensity of the workout was satisfactory at the end after a tardy start. Buck, Gilly and I could sense an air of casualness and I just hope the boys can switch on in time for the match after their two days of generous hospitality in Ireland. Kato was quite obviously ecstatic at his

The Aussie lads at the Kinsley dogs. What at first I thought would be a dud sponsor's event actually turned into an enjoyable night out.

selection as Australian Test cricketer No. 384, while Lang accepted his exclusion with the professionalism that we've come to expect from him.

For me, another day of torture awaited, with pool and gym sessions interspersed with painful massage and current therapy to stimulate the muscles. And there were the endless stretching routines.

Tonight's team meeting was all positive stuff, with a video catalogue of dismissals of English batsman in the three Tests to date setting the mood nicely. The development of our game plan was a real team effort, with many players contributing to a strategy that, when cut back to basics, involves executing the three Ps — Patience, Pressure, Partnerships. The fact that we can make our own history was also discussed, with the potential 5–0 series scoreline obviously on our minds, although again we reminded ourselves to stay in the present. I also suggested that the Poms might come at us more aggressively in this Test. What we agreed upon was that with only two weeks to go we will give our all and focus on the cricket, and not get distracted by thoughts of going home that inevitably are starting to play on our minds.

A Travelex (our tour sponsor) function at the Kinsley greyhounds was on the night's agenda. God knows how or why we ended up at a country dog track that seems to have a maximum capacity of around 500 spectators, but it ended up being a fun night, with the races being named in honour of the lads. My night was somewhat mixed, with relaxation being prominent until I managed to swallow a stray mosquito halfway through a TV interview — I'm very sure will end up on a 'bloopers' tape. On our return to the hotel, I squeezed in a quick workout on the bench with Hooter, before heading back to a room that was as hot as an oven thanks to a malfunctioning air conditioner.

Dear Tugga . . .

While on tour we get a mountain of correspondence, some supportive, some clever, some bizarre and some downright angry. One fax I was very happy to receive came just before the Trent Bridge Test, and came from our former fitness co-ordinator Dave Misson. 'Misso', who among his many duties used to provide us with inspirational poems or quotes before important matches, is now working for the Sydney Swans. His note read:

Tugga, 'Beware the enemy with nothing to lose.' I don't know whether Sun Tzu said that, but maybe it's applicable. From here it looks as if we are really building towards a supreme performance. The blokes who have missed out in the last two Tests, I'm sure are about to produce.

'There are many ways of going forward, but only one way of standing still,' — FD Roosevelt.

Good luck, Misso.

Of course, not all the correspondence is quite this positive. After the third Test, I received this crudely typed message . . .

You are a lot of whingeing kangaroos. I sincerely hope that when you get back to Australia you and your families will contract some fatal illness.

In the 3 tests so far you have intimidated the umpires into giving decisions in your favour. In the last test played at Trent Bridge Mike Atherton was NOT OUT and you damn well know it, the same applies to Marcus Trescothick.

If you can not play the game fairly then why do you not withdraw as a Test playing nation. You are all a disgrace to the players who have gone before you and are not fit to wear the Baggy Green Cap. The late Sir Donald Bradman must be turning in his grave to see the way you lot behave.

If you had played each test match fairly and in the spirit of the game it would be England who were leading 3–0 and certainly not you. The England players play the game fairly and squarely and unlike you DO NOT CHEAT.

On a different theme, I received this letter from a bloke living in County Durham . . .

Dear Steve,

Ever since I became interested in cricket as a child the Baggy Green cap worn by the Australian cricket team has impressed me. When your team take to the field, all wearing the Baggy Green cap, there is no finer sight in cricket, as far as I am concerned. Subsequently, ever since childhood I have longed to have a Baggy Green cap of my own. On 24th August 2001 I will be 40 years old and your team will have started the final Test of the series, probably on the way to a 5–0 whitewash. I wondered if it would be possible for you to arrange for me to be sent a Baggy Green cap of my own.

This would clearly be a wonderful piece of memorabilia for me, and an ideal way to celebrate my birthday, as well as a reminder of a series of watching one of the finest teams in recent history.

August 15 *Leeds*

FIRST UP, IT WAS BACK into the pool, followed by a gym session that involved some new exercises that continue to aid and test my rehabilitation. I'm totally in the hands of Errol Alcott and his knowledge of what to do, when and how. Again the session ended up with some manual work from his magic fingers, and even though the pain was at times excruciating, I knew it was beneficial. Some of these new exercise routines have left me discovering new muscles, which has left me with some aching body parts and meant I required a 90-minute loosening up from Bec.

With this Test being Kato's debut, I then went off in search of a person of respected credentials to present him with his Baggy Green before the start of play tomorrow. To my delight, Richie Benaud agreed to perform the task and seemed genuinely excited to be asked to do so. The moment will become a great memory for the young West Australian, and I hope it signals the start of a special career.

At Headingley
Fourth Test —
Day One

Australia 4–288 (RT Ponting 144, ME Waugh 72; AR Caddick 3–97)

At Headingley
Fourth Test —
Day Two

Australia 447 (DR Martyn 118; D Gough 5–103, AR Caddick 3–149) v England 2–155 (ME Trescothick 37, MA Butcher 47*, N Hussain 45*)

August 16 *Leeds*

TODAY IS NOT ONLY SPECIAL for the fact that it features the opening day of an Ashes Test, it is also Lynette's and my 10th wedding anniversary. Again, we are apart, as is the case for most celebratory events, but I guess it won't always be the case and, as I've said many times, sacrifices have to be made if you want to achieve your dreams and ambitions.

The Headingley pitch is not what you'd usually expect here. Normally, it would have a thick covering of white thatchy-looking grass, but this one is dry, cracked on the surface and with an intermittent green grass cover. Consequently, it was very difficult to assess how it would play. We came to the conclusion that it will deteriorate, making it a 'bat first' wicket for whoever won the toss.

As I had in the first three Tests, Gilly backed Sir Donald to come up trumps at the toss, and had no hesitation in electing to bat when the special coin fell his way. Interestingly, the English left out their specialist spinner, Robert Croft, going instead for Alan Mullally, which we considered to be a somewhat negative move considering Mullally has lost the zip he once had and is now a consistent bowler more than an attacking one. Obviously his job will be to bowl long spells into the breeze and give the strike bowlers time to recuperate.

Michael Slater and Matthew Hayden began well, but both perished after they felt that the hard yards had been done. Nothing is anywhere near as frustrating as that for an opener. Ricky Ponting's third ball again brought the technology debate to the forefront. He tried to drive Caddick on the up, but edged it to Ramprakash, who took it low down at third slip and there was a confident all-round appeal. It was a close thing, so Punter rightly stayed his ground while the umpires asked the third umpire to use his replay screen to deliver a verdict. Unfortunately for bowlers and fielders, nine times out of 10 the replay in such a situation is inconclusive because the definition on the close-up video is not sharp enough to distinguish a gap between the ground and the ball in the hand. This was the case this time, and it proved a defining moment. In our dressing-room, we instinctively felt it was going to be Ricky's day and, boy, it sure was. He was utterly brilliant. Not content merely to survive, he took the challenge head on, dominating with audacious strokeplay, driving with authority on both sides of the wicket, and offering a lesson for all young cricketers in hooking and pulling. Strange, isn't it, that if the law makers have their way these exciting back-foot strokes will disappear from the game? It was an innings that was waiting to happen, such has been Ricky's overall tour form, but even so he would not only have been delighted to play it, but also quite relieved.

Once again the Tasmanian showed his character and sheer will to overcome a difficult phase in his career. Six Test matches in a row without a half century would weaken many players resolve, but with Ricky it only enhanced his desire to score runs. At the other end, Mark Waugh again displayed his determination and a slight change in batting philosophy to accumulate and wear down the bowlers for a well-earned 72. Unfortunately, he was out to the fifth ball of the final over of the day. But considering there was a bit of uneven bounce in the pitch, it has still been a great day for us.

The two captains head to the centre for what I believed would be a very important coin toss.

**At Headingley
Fourth Test —
Day Three**

Australia 447 and 1–69 (RT Ponting
30*) v England 309 (MA Butcher 47,
N Hussain 46, MR Ramprakash 40,
AE Stewart 76*; GD McGrath 7–76)

**At Headingley
Fourth Test —
Day Four**

Australia 447 and 4–176 (declared:
ML Hayden 35, RT Ponting 72) v
England 309 and 0–4

August 18 *Leeds*

THE AMOUNT OF RUNS SO far scored in this match almost defies belief, firstly because Headingley has become in recent seasons something of a bowlers' paradise and secondly because this particular wicket is uneven in bounce and pace. The standard of batsmanship to date has been outstanding and has presented spectators with excellent value for their money. It seems to me, from my vantage point off the ground, that Test cricket is alive and well, contrary to reports of its demise and of standards dropping. From the first day of this series, where 12 wickets fell and 427 runs were scored, the cricket has been great value in terms of action and aggressive play.

Like Ricky Ponting on the first day, Damien Martyn's century belonged in the 'master class' of batting. Marto's batting has been simply awesome during this trip, culminating today in an effortless looking 125-ball century. He is a player who has almost reinvented his game, from a dashing debonair 20-year-old to today's master of concentration and playing-to-one's-strengths. He is proof to any youngster watching the game that change is possible and it's okay to be your own man and do things your way.

England's run chase then produced some of the most extraordinary cricket you're ever likely to witness at this level. After digging in and toiling hard against the initial

onslaught from McGrath, Gillespie and Lee, England changed tack and played as if they were in the last 10 overs of a one-day game, taking on a rampaging Lee and a menacing McGrath. It was gutsy, courageous cricket led by Alec Stewart, who at one point played a back-foot slash off McGrath that sailed over the ropes and into folklore. His array of 'duck' hooks also had the pulses racing.

With Mark Waugh having been dismissed off what proved to be the final ball of the first day, Simon Katich was due to begin his maiden Test innings at the beginning of day two. This photograph was taken minutes before he went out to the middle. Kato is a cool customer destined for a long and illustrious Test career.

The response from Brett Lee was intoxicating stuff and Bing's duel with Andy Caddick today was real Test-match cricket. It was not only a skill test, but also one of courage and a battle of wills. Watching from afar, I thought it was a sensational duel, fast man verses fast man, neither wanting to back down or be intimidated. It was a shame to see it all end so tamely (a short ball from Bing hit Caddick either on the glove or the arm-guard and lobbed gently through to the keeper), but until then their confrontation was a classic example of the essence and uniqueness of our game.

The Test has developed into a titanic struggle, but we appear to hold all the aces right now. This said, the desire to be involved in this ruthless battle displayed by our opponents suggests to me that England have something that many scribes haven't given them credit for. You don't win two Test series on the Indian subcontinent without internal fibre and strength of mind ... but then again you don't win 19 out of your last 21 Tests without something special going on either. The last two days of this Test should be beauties. We intend to make our win column click over to No. 20 and to keep enjoying the challenges offered by this great game.

August 20   *Leeds*

At Headingley
Fourth Test —
Day Five
Australia 447 and 4–176 (declared) lost to England 309 and 4–315 (MA Butcher 173*, N Hussain 55) by six wickets

THEY SAY PLAYING THE BEST opposition under the most intense of pressure situations will either break a cricketer or make him. During my time as Australian captain, when we've won a high percentage of our matches, we have been beaten on three occasions virtually by the blade of one opponent. In each case, these have been career bests by the guys involved, whose innings must rank among the all-time great knocks. Brian Lara's 153 not out in Barbados, that won the third Test of our series in the Caribbean in 1999, VVS Laxman's epic 281 in Calcutta earlier this year and now Mark Butcher's magnificent 173 not out here in Leeds were all scored against a team who expected to dominate and win comprehensively.

All three batsmen had confidence coming into their masterpieces, with recent form that indicated that a big score wasn't far away. This is obviously an important factor in producing such fighting knocks, as it must allow the batsman to relax and give him confidence that he can rely on his technical ability to take on the impending battle. All three had made a substantial and classy hundred against us before their epic innings — Lara plundered a superb 277 in Sydney in early 1993, Laxman thrilled the SCG crowd for 167 in early 2000, and Butcher played beautifully in Brisbane in 1998–99 for 116. Significantly these innings were made away from home, which indicates the three batsmen have the right type of temperament and mental toughness to succeed; it is always tougher to make important runs on pitches you aren't used to and to prosper and then flourish in front of a partisan away crowd. Also, none of these three 'prelude' digs led to victories, which must have left their makers somewhat unsatisfied. I know

Mark Butcher gets Glenn McGrath through the leg-field during his heroic hundred that won the fourth Test.

that a critical part of the jigsaw is missing from a major innings if the team's objective has not been reached.

Perhaps the most binding element to the match-winning feats of Lara, Laxman and Butcher was the nature and tempo of their strokeplay. When each of these guys made it to the wicket their team was in dire straits, with the game slipping away and the momentum well and truly in our favour. To be bold enough and courageous enough to not only establish themselves with an air of authority but to then proceed to take on quality bowlers who had the game under control is extremely hard to do. All three no doubt had their plans to counter the major bowlers in the back of their minds, but to execute such strategies over a long period of time is not easy. Placement, timing and shot selection were major features of the three innings — skills that don't just appear overnight. It is hours of work in the nets, planning before an innings and a belief in your ability that allows these traits to come to the fore in the team's hour of greatest need.

To play an innings that turns the fortunes of your side around is the ultimate for a batsman. It is what all those hours of sacrifice in the nets, away from your family on tours, years learning the game are all about. Succeeding on the big stage, against the best bowlers, under intense pressure gives the batsman responsible enormous satisfaction and a confidence they don't realise they've acquired until later, when runs begin to flow regularly for no apparent reason.

In this vein, Mark Butcher's innings was an Ashes epic, but I know that, deep down, he will one day wish that it was scored in a do-or-die Test match. That, for him, must now be a long-term goal.

The result of the fourth Test will no doubt lift cricket in England and rightly so. It sets up the Oval encounter starting in three days time as a special event. We will want to turn around our poor recent record at that historic venue (just two wins to England's six in the last 15 Ashes Tests over 63 years), while England will be desperate to pull back the scoreline to a more respectable 3–2.

August 21   *London*

BECAUSE THE JOURNEY FROM LEEDS to London takes four-and-a-half hours by coach and I needed to fit in a crucial fitness assessment I left early and travelled by car to arrive in London by lunchtime. Errol, Jock and I also squeezed in a running session at Kensington Park, which went reasonably well. I am at about 60 per cent of full pace, but my hamstring tendons are very tender and stiff from all the extra workload they've borne and the strength work I've put in, almost to the point that it disguises the pain in my calf. It's still almost impossible to tell if I'm going to be right or not for the fifth Test, but I've resolved to give myself until the morning of the match to make a decision.

After this morning's phone link-up with fellow selectors Adam Gilchrist and Trevor Hohns, we decided to play Lang in front of Slats at The Oval. This is another tough call

Michael Slater (centre), Adam Gilchrist (right) and I discuss the selectors' decision to leave Slats out of our side for the fifth Test.

that came after lengthy debate, during which we argued for and against any changes. Now came the tough part — informing the players. I invited Slats to my room where, accompanied by the team manager, who needed a few words as well, I gave him the shattering news. It certainly wasn't pleasant and Slats seemed in shock, before he headed back to his room, clearly devastated by his demotion. If it is any consolation to Slats, I felt sick in the stomach and drained both physically and mentally at having to deliver the news. Without doubt, this is the worst part of the job.

Later, we had a somewhat tense team gathering, sitting on the Oval outfield, where we talked through our defeat at Headingley. Buck wanted us to have this meeting at the ground, because he believed that we should start 'owning' the ground as soon as we could. I had my say at the end, before announcing the team change, which went down initially without any problems. However, the discussion that followed started to head off in different directions, until thankfully Lang interjected and put a clear perspective on what the Baggy Green meant to him and to all of us. 'Never take it for granted,' he said. 'You don't know when the last time you are going to wear it is going to be.'

My net session went tremendously well and I feel like I'll be throwing away a 100 if I don't play. However, the fact remains that I need to be able to run for the whole game and at this moment in time, I couldn't quite do that. Hopefully, I'll be ready to go, come 10.30am Thursday, even though that is less than 48 hours away.

Warney, through his legion of contacts, managed to organise tickets for the players and families to see U2 in concert at Earls Court tonight. It was a real rush to get there on time after training finished at 6pm, but we made it and were able to be part of an outstanding concert, stunningly performed by Bono, who appeared despite learning that his father had passed away earlier in the day. Making the event even more enjoyable for me was the fact that younger brother Danny, who I rarely get to see at home, was able to come along.

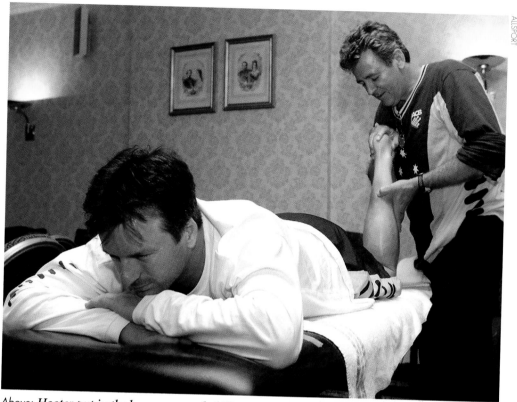

Above: *Hooter put in the hours as my rehabilitation program continues.*
Below: *Kato faces the media at Headingley two days out from his Test debut, while our media manager Brian Murgatroyd stands back to ensure everything is under control. In the background, the English team is warming up for a practice session.*

PICS, STEVE WAUGH

Above: *I'm not quite sure how Bing and Dizzy can get some shut-eye in the Headingley dressing-room while there is music blaring through their headphones.*
Below: *Who is this cricketer? It's actually Marto, showing off the benefits of all those 'tough yards' he's done in the gym.*

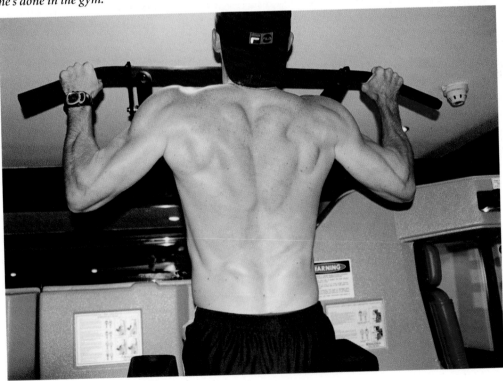

Darren Gough (above left) charges in at Headingley … and Ricky Ponting (above left) hooks him away for four.

Left: *Man of the match Mark Butcher completes a superb performance by hitting the boundary that completed England's outstanding victory in the fourth Test.*

Above: A slog sweep for six during my hundred at The Oval.

Left: After being pinned down in the 90s, I reached three figures with a desperate dive for a single.

Right: Relieved and exhausted in my very messy corner of the Oval dressing-room, after continuing on to 157 not out.

Above: Mark Waugh goes over the top during his century at The Oval. This was the first time Mark and I had scored hundreds in the same innings of an Ashes Test.
Below: Funky Miller in canary yellow. This was how his hair looked on day one of the final Test, before he changed to peacock green on day three and then burgundy red on the final day of the series.

Above left: Shane Warne has just taken his 400th Test wicket. Above right: *Warney and Glenn McGrath, who took 31 and 32 wickets respectively during the series, at The Oval.*
Below: A very satisfied smile from the first Australian and sixth man (after Courtney Walsh, Kapil Dev, Sir Richard Hadlee, Wasim Akram and Curtly Ambrose) to take 400 wickets in Test cricket.

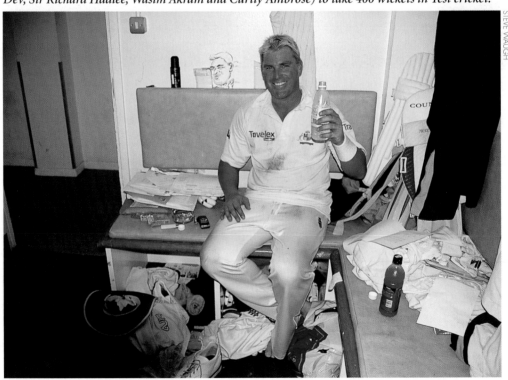

Above: Lang initiates our burning of the match bails at the conclusion of the fifth Test. If they wouldn't give us the real Ashes, then we'd create our own ...

Below: They're finally alight, but sadly they didn't turn into ashes. Note Chuck in the centre of the photograph, with a bottle opener attached to a cord around his neck, ready as ever to assist his comrades if they need any help.

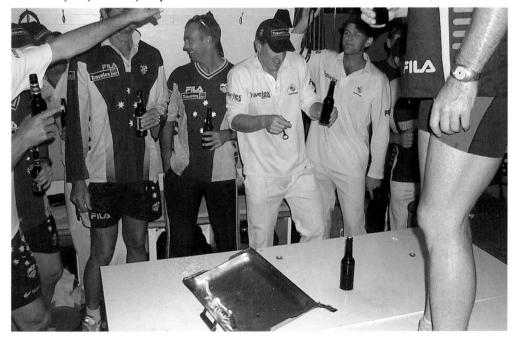

Above: *Our final team song of the tour, and what a beauty it was. Here Haydos has the honour of joining Punter on 'stage'.*

Left: *It's amazing how much luggage you accumulate on an Ashes tour, but it's still a great feeling to be home.*

August 22 *London*

MOST OF THE PLAYERS WANTED an extra practice before the game, so they were with me on the 8am bus to The Oval this morning. The exceptions were the bowlers, who as usual preferred to rest up for the match. At the ground my net form was again excellent and my running between stumps on an imaginary pitch was much better. I ran a series of threes, twos and singles, and then successfully participated in a team fielding drill, which lifted my hopes of playing to 50/50.

This morning's press conference was always going to be a tricky one, with my availability still not confirmed and the choice between Brett Lee and Colin Miller still unresolved. On that one, we want to take one more look at the wicket tomorrow morning. The topic of Slats' omission came up, with the inevitable question being, 'Was he dropped on form alone or was it a disciplinary matter?' In general terms he was dropped because of his form. He has not been completely out of touch, but he certainly hasn't been doing himself justice. A man of his ability and quality should have scored more than one century in his past 30 digs and he has had plenty of starts.

In my view, what Slats needs is to become more task-oriented, to know his game better then ever and to prepare and plan at a new level. He is a brilliant player who is not reaching his potential at the moment, and I emphasise 'at the moment'. This is by no means the end of his career. In fact, I see it as a career-enhancing moment that will eventually bring out the best in him. Obviously, he doesn't see it that way at the moment, but in time I'm sure the bigger picture will become clear.

At the end of the press conference I had another duty to perform, which was to bring attention to a condition known as vitiligo. This is a skin disorder that results in a loss of pigment from the skin that leaves whitish patches and affects one in 100 people worldwide. Vitiligo is not life-threatening and therefore no one had done any research into it, but it is dangerous in that the affected areas are at risk of being damaged by the sun very quickly and the stigma that comes from such damage for dark-skinned people and kids can be very traumatic. Once this was explained to me I was happy to help out. Our hope is that more attention can be brought to the plight of sufferers and that specialists can be convinced that research into the problem is justifiable.

Straight after, Slats did the brave thing and held a press conference of his own. He did a fine job considering the strain and stress he is under, since his cricket world has been turned upside down.

The afternoon was again spent under the care of Hooter, who is doing everything possible to make my leg right for tomorrow. His hands seem to perform miracles each time he gets to work, and at the end of the session I was left feeling even more confident about being involved in the Test. After a relaxing trip to the flicks with Murgers and Lang, I enjoyed a quick feed of noodles with Bing and Lang, two guys who are keen and excited about tomorrow's game. Their enthusiasm had me going to bed looking forward to this match as if it was my first ever Test match.

Diary of an Injury

I can't remember when I hurt my leg whether the muscle tearing made a noise or not, but in my mind I could hear something and I knew straight away that I'd done some serious damage. My initial thought was 'that's the end of my tour', closely followed by 'bloody hell that hurts'. To be carried off on a stretcher is certainly somewhat embarrassing, not to mention uncomfortable, and also rather annoying when you hear the cheers of the crowd as you gradually leave the ground so helpless. I really felt like jumping off and saying, 'Bugger you guys, I'm going back out there.' However, reality set in and on went the ice-packs as Errol Alcott and the doctors at the ground gave the injured area the once-over. Once an MRI scan had been organised and the game looked safely won, I was off to the private hospital.

The following morning I began keeping a separate diary, in note form, of what I was doing to try to fix the injury. Once I set my mind on playing in the fifth Test, at The Oval, as part of this process, I assessed my chances of being right in time.

Here are some of those notes . . .

August 4 (Day of injury)
- It was as if someone had thrown a shot put into the back of my calf. I felt the tear and the spasm that followed
- Zero per cent chance of playing again on tour; I've resigned myself to going home
- Ice every hour for 20 minutes
- Can wiggle my toes only

August 5
- Using crutches to get around; begin to take small steps in the pool
- One per cent chance of playing again this tour (my rating)
- Mentally: more positive after talking to my wife Lynette and waking up feeling better

August 6
- Crutches thrown away — too embarrassing and negative
- Massage extremely painful
- My chances of playing at The Oval: Five per cent

- Mentally: feel stronger, more positive. Will do anything possible to get back for fifth Test
- Walked (hobbled) to restaurant, one kilometre each way

August 7
- Calf raises in the water, walking on toes
- Felt grabbing pain two to three times during rehabilitation
- My chances of playing at The Oval: 10 per cent
- Mentally: on the up, can see some progress

August 8
- Bike ride, 10 minutes, stationary
- Starting to run in the pool
- My chances of playing at The Oval: 11 per cent
- Mentally: saw MRI report . . . not good, moderately severe tear and a substantial one. After feeling depressed decided to be extra determined and to make it back for The Oval Test

The morning after. A sombre media conference with Errol Alcott. At this point I honestly thought my tour was over.

August 9
- Walking up and down stairs.
- Pool/gym sessions increased in length and intensity
- My chances of playing at The Oval: 12 per cent
- Mentally: feeling positive, anything possible. The leg feels like a leg for the first time since injuring it

August 10
- Hopping on one leg in the pool
- Twenty minutes on the bike
- Deep friction massage (excruciating pain)
- My chances of playing at The Oval: 14 per cent
- Mentally: walking almost without a limp; pain has eased off, now it's more tightness

August 11
- Extensive gym and pool session
- Balancing work on calf and ankle
- Deep friction — 10 out of 10 for pain
- My chances of playing at The Oval: 16 per cent
- Mentally: feeling quietly confident.

August 12
- Cross-country machine workout and bike
- 45-minute walk into town and back
- My chances of playing at The Oval: 18 per cent
- Mentally: leg needs more walking, easily fatigued

August 13
- Balance work on boards
- Hamstring curls
- Running up pool steps

- My chances of playing at The Oval: 20 per cent
- Mentally: frustrated at lack of calf muscle and not being able to 'switch' it on. Still optimistic and Errol says it's going very well

August 14
- Leg press machine
- Electric current through calf for 40 minutes
- My chances of playing at The Oval: 22 per cent
- Mentally: Good to actually feel muscle again

August 15
- Treadmill for 10 minutes
- Bike for 10 minutes
- Boxing: three x three minutes
- Stomach exercises for 10 minutes
- My chances of playing at The Oval: 25 per cent

- Mentally: on the way, will be running shortly

August 16 (start of fourth Test)
- Catching and batting practice
- Heat vibration pad to loosen the muscle up
- My chances of playing at The Oval: 27 per cent
- Mentally: Still not confident when jogging but each day brings new hope

August 17
- Balance work, catching balls at the same time
- Pool/gym: increased intensity
- My chances of playing at The Oval: 30 per cent
- Mentally: running with some confidence — big day tomorrow

ALLSPORT

Former teammate Ian Healy joins Errol, Jock Campbell and me for a walk around Headingley the day before the fourth Test. During our stroll Heals had the audacity to suggest I was suffering 'an old man's injury'.

August 18
- Interval work — running/stop/jogging — for 25 minutes
- Net session, then ran two laps of ground
- My chances of playing at The Oval: 32 per cent
- Mentally: running at 50–60 per cent, but hamstring tendon on left leg is sore, though calf feels good

August 19
- Day off from work
- Hot and cold therapy
- My chances of playing at The Oval: 35 per cent
- Mentally: Needs to improve a lot, but it's starting to be a realistic chance

August 20 (end of fourth Test)
- Walk in park
- Deep massage
- My chances of playing at The Oval: 40 per cent
- Mentally: feeling better, but still unsure about my chances

August 21
- Running at 60 per cent of capacity.
- More interval work
- Training at ground: catching, batting, running
- My chances of playing at The Oval: 45 per cent
- Mentally: hitting the ball very well, but need to be start pushing it in running between wickets, turning, etc.

Warney and I run with Errol Alcott on the morning of the fifth Test. This was actually a last-minute check for both of us — Shane had felt a twinge in his right thigh — before the final line-up for the Test was announced at the toss.

August 22
- Training: running ones, twos, threes, up and down pitch at 70 per cent speed.
- Massage, stretching
- My chances of playing at The Oval: 50 per cent
- Mentally: Scared to really push it. I'll give myself until tomorrow to make the team. Tendon on hamstring now major worry. Must get through it and block out the pain

August 23 (start of fifth Test)
Good enough. I'm taking a risk but as captain I must lead the way. Am confident without being unrealistic. Fingers crossed that I'll make it through. Errol says the muscle has healed and shouldn't tear again. Fatigue will be the major worry . . .

August 23 *London*

As we travelled to The Oval in the team bus, a journey that takes 20 minutes, I had plenty of time to think through my final decision as to whether I'd be playing. I knew, to be fair to everyone, that I'd have to make the call pretty soon after the warm-ups. In the end, the decision about whether I should play was mine. Errol told me that the muscle had healed but, of course, there was no iron-clad guarantee that something wasn't going to happen again. I was keen not to put my own desire to play ahead of the team's needs, but as a captain and a player I felt good enough to take my place in the side. In the back of my mind was the realisation that very few players at this level ever take the field without some niggle or other. The key is how you cope with that. My main concern was that I wouldn't be a passenger and it took me until this morning to be clear in my own mind that I wouldn't be. As soon as I had decided that, I declared myself fit.

Once I decided to play, I then started to concentrate on the job at hand and that was to produce a result that was indicative of the standard of our play throughout the series. In my view, 5–0 would have been a just result, but 4–1 will certainly suffice.

Just as I was relaxing, Shane Warne put a scare into the camp when he felt something give in the top of his right thigh. Glenn McGrath was already going into the match with a groin aggravation, so Warney's news wasn't exactly what we needed to hear from our premier spinner on a pitch custom-made for him. Thankfully, he got through warm-ups and took his place in the starting XI.

Colin Miller was left out by the closest of margins, a decision I hope we won't rue at the conclusion of the game. Funky has never let us down in a Test, but we feel Bing is about to hit his straps and the pace and bounce here will aid his cause.

Winning the toss this time was crucial, because it was obvious that the first three days were going to be good for batting while days four and five would be hard work against the spinners. Nasser Hussain must have felt gutted losing his 14th toss out of 15 as captain — odds that are too ridiculous to even work out.

What a day we have had, with Matthew Hayden and Justin Langer doing sterling work up front setting the platform for the rest of us. They are like the bricklayers, with the middle order the interior decorators. Lang's century was a gem, full of grit, character, skill and passion. His attitude today was to enjoy every moment; he smiled at the umpires, opposition, anyone he could lay eyes on. I remember asking him how he felt after his net session this morning. 'It feels like it's Christmas day today,' he replied. This totally relaxed attitude was in stark contrast to his recent 12 months at the crease, where he has been fighting with himself and the elements around him. Today was a superb lesson for not only Lang but for all of us: enjoy the moment.

The instant he brought up his century the team went berserk — genuine happiness for a guy who gives the team so much and whose passion and pride inspires those around him. The opening partnership of Lang and Haydos was the best of the series, and I'm sure their close friendship helped them build their partnership together. When Matt was dismissed, Ricky Ponting came in and continued where he left off at Leeds, confronting the bowlers with great body language and a stunning array of shots.

Lang's innings came to a premature halt when he wore a Caddick bouncer on the helmet, but by the close Mark Waugh had raced into the 40s and I remained unbeaten on 12. We accepted the bad light with eight overs remaining, satisfied our work for the day had been achieved and nothing more could have been gained in the dark.

My nerves today reminded me of my debut Test match, back on Boxing Day 1985. I was very tense, edgy and worried about the outcome. Coming back from a muscle tear is difficult as a fear the injury isn't right constantly plays on your mind, feeding negative thoughts that are almost unavoidable until you actually get out there and do it. My half an hour at the crease was a relief and a confidence boost at the same time, as it gave me the encouragement that everything was going to work out okay.

It has been a great day for us. Late in the day, we could sense that England knew they were in huge trouble for the remainder of the match, especially as the turn had already begun to occur even though the pitch is yet to be worn down by the footmarks.

A game of 'Foccer' (a cross between soccer and Australian football), invented by Damien Fleming and Wade Seccombe, kept the troops amused and involved at the close of play. The inventors say it's not a game for the faint-hearted and truly tests one's ball skills and vision. Dinner was had with a few of the lads and their girls, plus Aussie legend Tim Horan of rugby union fame. I'm always impressed by the rugby boys, by their sense of team and character, and Tim Horan is certainly a guy to admire and look up to.

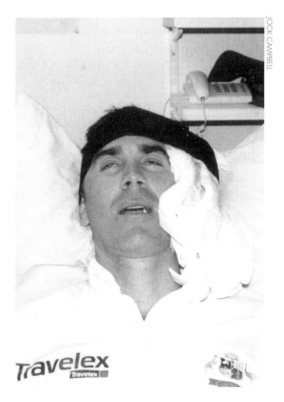

Not too long before this photograph was taken, Justin Langer was punching the air after reaching three figures during his gallant return to the Test stage. However, he then wore an Andy Caddick bouncer on the helmet and had to retire hurt.
I'm not convinced Lang was quite as dazed as his facial expression here suggests. The fact that Jock Campbell took another photo straight after, in which our pocket-sized left-hander gave him a slight grin, indicates that he did know which dressing-room he was in. But there is no doubt Lang took a fearful whack on the side of the head, and definitely needed the icepacks Errol Alcott found for him.

August 24 *London*

A 45-MINUTE WALK THIS MORNING through Kensington Park, in which sits Kensington Palace, the former residence of the Princess of Wales, was exactly what I needed to get some of the residual stiffness from the calf tear and new soreness that had come with the unaccustomed use of other muscles. Even today, there are many messages and flowers placed alongside the wrought iron gates of the palace, most placed to recognise the upcoming fourth anniversary of her shocking death.

Down at the ground, I had a fairly extensive net session in anticipation of the battle ahead. Sometimes, I'll just have someone throw 20 or so balls at me without my pads on to get a feel for the ball on the middle of the pad, at other times I won't touch a bat at all, but today I needed a solid workout to build my confidence in my legs and my strokemaking. When I strode out of the nets I had an inkling a big one was on the cards. Every ball I tried to hit had found the middle and because I'd worked so hard to get here I knew my concentration wouldn't be a problem. A 30-minute session of stretching, massage and exercise left me ready for the day.

The first over from Caddick was eventful in that I straight drove a three and then Mark was put down by Butcher at second slip, a straightforward chance. This wasn't that unexpected — the missed chance, that is — because The Oval is one of the toughest viewing grounds in the world for both batsmen and fielders. On top of this, this morning the bright sun gave off a glare from the pitch that pierced your eyes, and it took a couple of overs to make the necessary adjustments.

For me, all was going well until I reached the mid 20s when, stupidly, I chanced a quick single and immediately felt a twinge in my right buttock. I was confident it was only a nerve thing, because I felt a tightening sensation emanating from my hip and tingling down to my right knee. I've had these before and they are like warning signs that something worse could follow if I don't ease up. I now had two bad legs, although overall my batting was still relatively unaffected. That was soon to change, however, when I felt another jabbing pain as if someone had thrown a penknife into the middle of my calf. The only good thing I could think of was that the pain was not where I'd torn the muscle before, but I felt as if I couldn't run any more than about 30 per cent of my normal full speed between the wickets. I don't like costing the team runs.

It was time for a change of attack and that's exactly what I did, playing the big shots in an attempt to score boundaries and taking the easy ones in between. At lunch I'd made 77 and Mark was on 92, as England began to flounder, losing heart and all planning, setting fields that suggested they were using guesswork. During the break, Buck gave me the confidence to forge on. I felt I was a handicap, not being able to run between wickets, but he said to me, 'You've worked so hard, go on and make a hundred.' These were the words I needed to hear and following on from Mark's ton I eventually got there myself after a frustrating time in the late 90s.

Errol was the man I pointed my bat at when I reached three figures, to acknowledge his work over the past three weeks to get me to this point. I was a bit of a dusty mess when I did so, because the run that got me from 99 to 100 was quite comical. Running out of patience, I decided to make a desperate dash for the other end after a misfield. I envisaged a close finish, so I dived into safety not knowing where the ball was or how close a call it was going to be. In the end there was no need for the dramatics, but this still ranked as one of the most pleasing 100s of my career. I had a gut instinct before the match that I would score a century. To me, this hundred represents further proof that a positive outlook, when combined with mental toughness (the ability to not give in to oneself), can enable any dream to be fulfilled.

I never thought about retiring hurt because I felt I was hitting the ball well enough to make up for my lack of mobility between the wickets and it

An ambition realised — to not only play, but to make a hundred. I felt it was my destiny.

would have meant another player would have to come in and get established. And even though the niggles I suffered weren't the same as the one I came into the match with, I never thought about calling for a runner. I don't think I would have allowed one if I had been in the umpires' position, but in any case I think it is a law of cricket that needs to be reviewed. Bowlers aren't allowed replacements when they get injured so why should batsmen get special treatment? The removal of runners would stop certain players calling for runners on account of cramp when they don't really have a problem.

Mark's 100 was another beauty. He fell trying to smash Goughie over the covers in one-day mode for 120. Adam Gilchrist came in next as we tried to tighten the screws on England's ailing attack. Lang was ready to go but the residual concussion he was still suffering after yesterday's knock, plus our need to attack at all costs, made the change in the batting order common sense. After Gilly's quick 25 ended when he gifted Usman Afzaal a third-ball debut wicket, Damien Martyn strolled to the crease to play a gem of a cameo, scoring 64 from 54 balls. By the time the declaration came I had moved on to 157 and was feeling fresh mentally and comfortable, despite the inconvenience of two 'barking' legs.

It was great to score a century and see Mark do the same, but the most satisfying aspect of today's play was how we followed our goals for the day. We set ourselves to total around 650 with 17 overs left to bowl at the time of our declaration. In reality, we declared at 4–641 with 18 overs remaining in a near perfect piece of execution. In those 18 overs, England scored more freely than I would have hoped, but Michael Atherton perished to a Warne gem, which augurs well for tomorrow's play.

Back at the hotel it was another night of ice packs and room service, broken only by the delight of speaking to my family. Rosie has only five balloons left from the 15 I sent her. Each day she bursts one, until there will be none left, at which time she'll know that I'm on the plane coming home. It's going to be fabulous to see them all again.

August 25 *London*

At The Oval
Fifth Test —
Day Three
Australia 4–641 (declared) v England 8–409 (ME Trescothick 55, N Hussain 52, MR Ramprakash 124*, U Afzaal 54; SK Warne 6–155)

Another 7.30am pool session with Jock and Errol got things moving and the calf and buttock areas reasonably mobile. The 10-minute walk to the gym down the road had already given me the opportunity to assess how bad my injuries from yesterday actually were. In such situations, I find it's always beneficial to wait and give myself until the next morning before getting too down about what I'm thinking has happened.

Yesterday I thought I had torn my calf in a different place, as well as suffering a 'niggle' in my right buttock muscle. While they were both extremely stiff and sore this morning, they loosened up with the walk and improved further after a swim and stretch in the pool. It's hard to know exactly what I've done and I don't particularly want to know either, just as long as I'll be okay for the next three days.

Today's bowling plan was quite obvious. We needed to tighten things up much more than we had bowled last night. On this pitch, Warney is our ace in the pack, but he had to be supported by the quicks, who needed to be very disciplined in everything they did. I wanted them to bowl maidens and apply pressure so Shane could tighten the noose on our opponents from the other end.

Normally, I don't take long to get dressed before walking out for a day's play, but this morning I could barely move with the amount of kit I had to apply in order to keep the legs warm and feeling secure. A pair of exercise bike pants of full length were beneath a thermoskin pair of shorts, giving me a nice shapely look; the downside was that I could hardly move or breathe.

The cricket didn't pan out as we had expected, with England showing a renewed fighting presence after yesterday's mediocre effort. Initially, after claiming the big wicket of Marcus Trescothick in the first over of the day, it felt as if it was going to go according to the script. But Mark Ramprakash obviously read another version, as he busily compiled an accomplished unbeaten hundred that amazingly was only his second in Test cricket. He is a quality player with a solid technique and needs only to sort out his temperament and concentration to be the nucleus of England's future middle order. He has threatened many times this series to convert one of his starts into a big one but has self-destructed on every occasion before today's gallant century.

Watching from the sidelines of Headingley, I saw Ramprakash take one on the wrist from McGrath and he became visibly stronger in his desire and self-belief from that moment. This hundred may be a defining moment in his career, as he now appears more settled in himself and at ease at the crease.

For us, Warney was magnificent claiming his third five-for of the series, from a marathon 39-over tenure at the crease. He also became the first Australian bowler to take 400 Test wickets when he induced Alec Stewart into a loose drive outside off stump, for Gilly to take a smart catch. It has been a colossal effort by Shane, after coming back from two serious operations to quell the doubters and critics who thought his career was over. He appears to be near his best again, letting them rip and owning the pitch when he comes on.

Our three quicks seemed to tire late in the day, probably due to the heat (it was the hottest day of the summer). I'm hoping they can lift in the second innings and give us one more focused, determined performance before we go home to have three weeks off.

August 26 *London*

At The Oval
Fifth Test —
Day Four

Australia 4–641 (declared) v England 432 (MR Ramprakash 133; SK Warne 7–165) and 1–40

AN EARLY MORNING POOL SESSION for Warney and myself helped get us both moving a bit easier for the day ahead. A 39-over day is a huge workload, especially for someone who has no flexibility in his body, so it was vital for Shane to loosen up because today, quite obviously, he holds the key to our success on this wicket.

When play began I was still not sure about whether I should make them bat again, after not sleeping too well again last night. A sleeping tablet around 2am kicked in shortly afterwards and gave me four hours shut-eye. I'm not sure in this case whether it was adrenalin or pain-related sleep deprivation, but I rarely get a full night's sleep during a Test match.

The great duo of McGrath and Warne wrapped the tail up, but not before I dropped a dolly at second slip off Warney. The follow-on was enforced, largely because of our four strike bowlers' willingness to back up again and the cloud cover that had come over and should have suited the quicks. Mike Atherton, playing his final Test innings, succumbed to McGrath for the 19th and final time in Tests, edging to Warne before saluting the crowd as a parting gesture. As a mark of respect we all applauded him off the field. He has long been an admired and respected opponent who was at his best in difficult conditions when the team needed him most. This is

Mike Atherton leaves the Test arena for the last time, after being dismissed at the start of England's second innings on day four at The Oval.

the hallmark of a very fine player and for England's sake his immense knowledge and experience must not be completely lost to the system. As rivals we have not always seen eye to eye, but I have always admired his determination and desire to make the most of his talent.

The stumps scoreline of 1–40 was very promising, but equally frustrating, as the weather only allowed for 22 of the 90 allocated overs to be sent down. The negative, of course, was the loss of time to force a win, but the positive was the rest and recovery time the bowlers unexpectedly got and realistically needed to freshen them up for one final assault tomorrow.

From my perspective, a night at the cinema viewing the supposed English comedy *Lucky Break* certainly didn't live up to expectations, but the walk to the cinema left me feeling more confident about my calf and buttock niggles, which both appear to be on the mend.

August 27 *London*

**At The Oval
Fifth Test —
Day Five**

Australia 4–641 (declared)
defeated England 432 and 184
(D Gough 39*; GD McGrath 5–43,
SK Warne 4–64) by an innings and
25 runs

THE FINAL FITNESS AND REHABILITATION session of the tour was performed with a bit of added zest, knowing tomorrow that we wouldn't have to go through this familiar routine of touring life. Even better than that was today's weather, crystal-clear blue skies, thus ensuring a full day's play. Many outcomes were possible, but I truly believed that we could wrap this one up around teatime.

The morning's get-together out on the Oval outfield began with Buck calling us into a huddle. He placed a baggy green cap and a slouch hat on the turf and then proceeded to touch on the importance and similarities of both and what they mean to those who wear them. Our tour had started in Gallipoli and that experience continues to provide us with a sense of strength. In fact, it formed part of my motivation to work my way back to match fitness. The sacrifice, pain and suffering that is part of the Anzac spirit helped forge our nation and lives in us all, even if what we go through is miniscule compared to what our great fighting men of 1915 endured.

My words to the team were quite simple and to the point: 'All I want from everyone is to never believe that we can't win, no matter the situation. Let's give 100 per cent attention to every ball and never give in.' Then I added, 'Today, I'm going to enjoy every ball and keep up my intensity and desire all day long. Good luck boys, let's put on a good show.'

A 'good show' was a huge understatement during the first hour. McGrath and Warne were simply outstanding, giving away absolutely nothing and creating chances at regular intervals, slowly strangling the life and hope our of England's batsmen. Four wickets fell in that opening 14 overs, with Butcher, Trescothick, Hussain and Afzaal succumbing to the stifling pressure-cooker atmosphere that the bowlers and fieldsmen created. On this morning, being an English batsman was akin to being a fish swimming in a pool full of hungry sharks.

The game was as good as over by lunch, but work still had to be done after the chicken and BBQ sauce followed by ice cream and strawberries were devoured. Jason Gillespie couldn't take a trick, in much the same manner as at Headingley, where he continually went past the outside edge without ever getting a satisfactory result. Dizzy is quick through the air and savage off the wicket, which means the ball is literally doing too much off the seam to catch the outside edge. McGrath, on the other hand, doesn't deviate as much, and with less pace the batsmen always try to counteract the seam and bounce by going with it, which, of course, leads to numerous edges to the awaiting cordon. Binga, meanwhile, cranked it up for a couple of overs, splattering Andy Caddick's stumps in the process before tweaking an intercostal or 'grunt' muscle (under the rib cage), the bane of all quick bowlers.

With my left leg still a little restricted in its movement and my right extremely touchy after Gough creamed a cut shot into my Achilles tendon, fielding at bat-pad was my best option. It's been a while since I've ventured in there, because Punter and Haydos enjoy

Always on the Improve

I reckon our batting for much of this Test series has been phenomenal, considering the English attack has been highly rated and the pitches up until The Oval were bowler friendly. Each of our batsmen can claim at some stage to have tilted at least one match in our favour. And our scoring rate of over 300 runs per day gave us the time to take rain delays out of the equation in our quest for victories, a feat that very few teams have been able to achieve.

For me the standout has been Damien Martyn, who from our opening tour match at Worcester excelled, combining a simple technique highlighted by supreme balance and economy of movement with a hunger for runs, a cool temperament and a steely concentration. Marto improved with every innings and by the time he played his gem of a cameo here at The Oval he looked in complete control of his own destiny.

Our bowling quartet didn't change during the series, a rather unusual statistic but one that speaks volumes for the select four. Glenn McGrath and Shane Warne have both been exceptional, leading by example, always wanting the ball in their hands and always looking for ways to improve. However, for me, Jason Gillespie was the main man in the 'live' Tests (the first three) bowling many exceptional spells that went unrewarded simply because the opposition couldn't lay bat on him. He now looks the finished product, having gained the confidence that his body won't desert him in times of need, and owning a wrist of both flexibility and strength that sees the seam come down onto the pitch gunbarrel straight every time. Dizzy's time in the sun is just around the corner.

We have thoroughly enjoyed a triumphant three months that saw us lift our game to a new level, but we can always improve. For one, our catching was spasmodic and needs to be worked on before the South Africans arrive for the ultimate show during the upcoming Australian season.

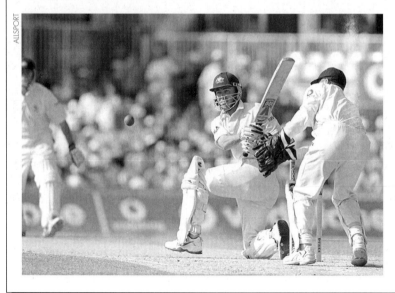

ALLSPORT

Damien Martyn plays a sweep shot during his highly entertaining half-century in the fifth Test.

the 'rush' in close, but I must say I enjoyed the experience, even though it requires courage and patience. The rewards are that you get to have a real feel as to what the tempo and state of the match are and you can sense the body language of the batsmen.

By the time Phil Tufnell ambled in to soak up a few minutes while the presentation party sorted themselves out, McGrath and Warne found themselves in a remarkable statistical equivalent. Both men had taken 31 wickets in the series, claimed three five-fors and had four scalps in this innings. Pigeon had one ball remaining in the over before Warney was to deliver the next. Incredibly, Tuffers did the expected — nicked a drive that flew straight to ... guess who ... Warney at first slip. He gobbled the chance up with those massive havana cigar-like digits. It was all over, a convincing win that was actually a real hiding. Winning by an innings and 25 runs was outstanding in itself, but don't forget that we only lost four wickets in the match, of which two were gifted. That gives a true indication of our dominance.

The satisfaction felt by the whole squad was evident, and the celebrations were about to begin. However, as captain, my media obligations tied me down for around 45 minutes and only then it was time to have a drink with the poms. Mike Atherton was in a relaxed mood — he was now a retired man — while Nasser Hussain told us of his frustration at not having Darren Gough available for England's upcoming winter tours. It was a cordial 90 minutes of cricket talk, by two sides that got on extremely well and didn't have one single problem with each other, on the field or off, during the series.

The series is over, and while the umpires and the defeated batsmen make their way back to the pavilion, 11 very happy and proud Australians gather near the centre. I'm in the centre of the group, shaking hands with vice-captain Adam Gilchrist, while at the right of the group Dizzy Gillespie has his hand on the shoulder of his great partner in crime, Glenn McGrath. To Dizzy's immediate right is Shane Warne, who bowled so superbly in both innings, and took the final catch, appropriately off Pigeon's bowling.

They were quite naturally deeply disappointed by the way a season that had promised so much — and one that they said would give them a good indication of how far they had come during the past 18 months — had turned out.

The atmosphere in our room was not one of wild celebrations, but rather one of relief, contemplation, satisfaction and excitement. Knowing we had done the job we set out to do was very pleasing. Changing the perception of the team and our 'sledging' image was another significant achievement, with match referees, spectators and media people all commenting on our excellent on-field behaviour and the spirit in which we played the game. And after 96 days away there was a joy in knowing that we are heading home to family and friends.

Personally, this match was a triumph and for that I will forever be indebted to Errol Alcott, who inspired and instilled confidence that I could make that fitness deadline. He and Lynette helped me see the bigger picture when I was originally injured, and once I was able to convince myself that I could make it I gave it everything. To be carried off Trent Bridge on a stretcher wasn't the way I wanted to make an exit from Ashes cricket in England; holding the Ashes crystal replica trophy after scoring 157 not out was a far better option.

The team's celebrations were highlighted by a sort of tribal ceremony dance act performed by Haydos and Dizzy. It was an act known as the 'Pig Hunt' when it debuted back in the Port Elizabeth change-rooms on the 1997 South African tour. Today, it evolved into an 'Ashes Urn' quest and Haydos excelled to the point where he could

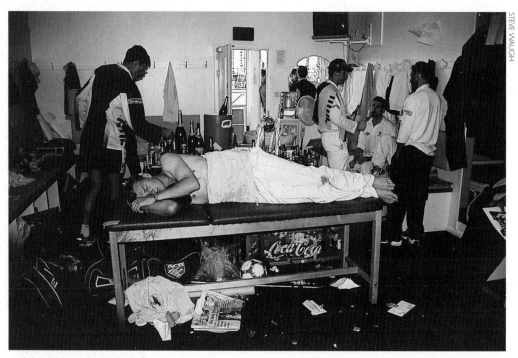

Celebrating is not always what it is cracked up to be. Here, Bing lies in pain with an icepack on his torn intercostal muscle. In years gone by, with the series over, such an injury would have been anaesthetised with a few beers. Today, it's the same.

A Southern and Coke with Hooter, the man who got me on the park for the fifth Test. The Baggy Green is worn proudly under the Slouch Hat. That hat has been on the bus with me all tour, but now it has to be taken off, and packed away with all my other treasures and possessions in readiness for the long trip home …

barely talk or walk at the end of his work. It was a time to enjoy and store in the memory banks for years to come and a performance that will give us many a laugh around the campfire in the future. Punter did his routine with aplomb once again, and then — in an attempt to re-enact the original bail-burning ceremony that led to the creation of the original Ashes urn — three of today's bails were burnt in a tray of kerosene. It wasn't completely successful, but Funky Miller has the remains and one day they may turn up somewhere. It was amusing to see the boys lighting a few cigars off the embers as they sat on top of a table directly beneath the taped-up smoke detectors, all the while savouring the historic moment. It was ironic that later on in the night our team celebration and awards night was severely interrupted by a bomb scare (complete with wailing fire alarms) that left us freezing on the streets outside our hotel for over an hour. By the time we were allowed back in we were all too knackered, so it was time to wrap up the evening.

This was a tame ending to a tremendously satisfying, stimulating and enjoyable tour. I thank my lucky stars that I've had the great fortune to be on four sensational tours here. The Ashes adventure in England is still the highlight for an Aussie cricketer — may that lump-in-the-throat, butterflies-in-the-stomach feeling always be there for future generations whenever they touch the tarmac at Heathrow to begin another campaign.

Test Scorecards and Tour Averages

THE AUSTRALIANS IN INDIA 2001

FIRST TEST, AT MUMBAI, 27, 28 FEBRUARY, 1 MARCH 2001 (TOSS: AUSTRALIA)

India first innings

SS Das	c Hayden b Gillespie	14
S Ramesh	c Gilchrist b McGrath	2
R Dravid	c Gilchrist b Fleming	9
SR Tendulkar	c Gilchrist b McGrath	76
*SC Ganguly	c Hayden b Warne	8
VVS Laxman	c Ponting b McGrath	20
+NR Mongia	not out	26
AB Agarkar	c&b Warne	0
J Srinath	c ME Waugh b Warne	12
Harbhajan Singh	c SR Waugh b Warne	0
RL Sanghvi	c Gilchrist b Gillespie	2
Extras	(b 2, lb 3, w 1, nb 1)	7
Total	(all out, 71.3 overs)	176

Fall: 1–7 (Ramesh, 4.2 ov), 2–25 (Dravid, 12.1 ov), 3–31 (Das, 13.5 ov), 4–55 (Ganguly, 22.3 ov), 5–130 (Laxman, 41.1 ov), 6–139 (Tendulkar, 43.5 ov), 7–140 (Agarkar, 48.2 ov), 8–165 (Srinath, 64.2 ov), 9–166 (Harbhajan Singh, 66.6 ov), 10–176 (Sanghvi, 71.3 ov)

Bowling: McGrath 19–13–19–3, Fleming 15–3–55–1, Gillespie 15.3–4–50–2, Warne 22–7–47–4

Australia first innings

MJ Slater	b Agarkar	10
ML Hayden	c Mongia b Srinath	119
JL Langer	c Dravid b Harbhajan Singh	19
ME Waugh	c Ganguly b Harbhajan Singh	0
*SR Waugh	c Dravid b Sanghvi	15
RT Ponting	c Das b Harbhajan Singh	0
+AC Gilchrist	st Mongia b Harbhajan Singh	122
SK Warne	c Tendulkar b Sanghvi	39
JN Gillespie	c Mongia b Srinath	0
DW Fleming	c Srinath b Agarkar	6
GD McGrath	not out	0
Extras	(b 9, lb 7, nb 3)	19
Total	(all out, 73.2 overs)	349

Fall: 1–21 (Slater, 7.5 ov), 2–71 (Langer, 24.1 ov), 3–71 (ME Waugh, 24.2 ov), 4–98 (SR Waugh, 29.2 ov), 5–99 (Ponting, 30.2 ov), 6–296 (Hayden, 62.3 ov), 7–326 (Gilchrist, 65.6 ov), 8–327 (Gillespie, 66.4 ov), 9–349 (Fleming, 72.6 ov), 10–349 (Warne, 73.2 ov)

Bowling: Srinath 16–3–60–2, Agarkar 12–1–50–2, Harbhajan Singh 28–3–121–4, Sanghvi 10.2–2–67–2, Tendulkar 7–1–35–0

India second innings

SS Das	c SR Waugh b Gillespie	7
S Ramesh	c Ponting b McGrath	44
R Dravid	b Warne	39
+NR Mongia	c Gilchrist b Gillespie	28
SR Tendulkar	c Ponting b ME Waugh	65
*SC Ganguly	run out (Slater/Warne)	1
VVS Laxman	c Gilchrist b ME Waugh	12
AB Agarkar	b ME Waugh	0
Harbhajan Singh	not out	17
RL Sanghvi	b Gillespie	0
J Srinath	b McGrath	0
Extras	(b 4, lb 1, nb 1)	6
Total	(all out, 94.1 overs)	219

Fall: 1–33 (Das, 17.5 ov), 2–57 (Ramesh, 26.2 ov), 3–154 (Tendulkar, 66.5 ov), 4–156 (Ganguly, 72.1 ov), 5–174 (Laxman, 79.6 ov), 6–174 (Dravid, 80.2 ov), 7–193 (Agarkar, 85.3 ov), 8–210 (Mongia, 89.3 ov), 9–216 (Sanghvi, 91.3 ov), 10–219 (Srinath, 94.1 ov)

Bowling: McGrath 17.1–9–25–2, Fleming 15–1–44–0, Warne 28–11–60–1, Gillespie 19–8–45–3, ME Waugh 15–5–40–3

Australia second innings

ML Hayden	not out	28
MJ Slater	not out	19
Extras		0
Total	(0 wickets, 7 overs)	47

Bowling: Srinath 2–0–17–0, Agarkar 1–0–8–0, Harbhajan Singh 2–0–11–0, Sanghvi 2–1–11–0.

AUSTRALIA WON BY 10 WICKETS
Man of the Match: AC Gilchrist

SECOND TEST, AT CALCUTTA, 11, 12, 13, 14, 15 MARCH 2001 (TOSS: AUSTRALIA)

Australia first innings

MJ Slater	c Mongia b Khan	42
ML Hayden	c sub (HK Badani) b Harbhajan Singh	97
JL Langer	c Mongia b Khan	58
ME Waugh	c Mongia b Harbhajan Singh	22
*SR Waugh	lbw Harbhajan Singh	110
RT Ponting	lbw Harbhajan Singh	6
+AC Gilchrist	lbw Harbhajan Singh	0
SK Warne	c Ramesh b Harbhajan Singh	0
MS Kasprowicz	lbw Ganguly	7
JN Gillespie	c Ramesh b Harbhajan Singh	46
GD McGrath	not out	21
Extras	(b 19, lb 10, nb 7)	36
Total	(all out, 131.5 overs)	445

Fall: 1–103 (Slater, 28.5 ov), 2–193 (Hayden, 53.4 ov), 3–214 (Langer, 58.3 ov), 4–236 (ME Waugh, 65.5 ov), 5–252 (Ponting, 71.2 ov), 6–252 (Gilchrist, 71.3 ov), 7–252 (Warne, 71.4 ov), 8–269 (Kasprowicz, 78.6 ov), 9–402 (Gillespie, 123.4 ov), 10–445 (SR Waugh, 131.5 ov)

Bowling: Khan 28.4–6–89–2, Prasad 30–5–95–0, Ganguly 13.2–3–44–1, Raju 20–2–58–0, Harbhajan Singh 37.5–7–123–7, Tendulkar 2–0–7–0

India first innings

SS Das	c Gilchrist b McGrath	20
S Ramesh	c Ponting b Gillespie	0
R Dravid	b Warne	25
SR Tendulkar	lbw McGrath	10
*SC Ganguly	c SR Waugh b Kasprowicz	23
VVS Laxman	c Hayden b Warne	59
+NR Mongia	c Gilchrist b Kasprowicz	2
Harbhajan Singh	c Ponting b Gillespie	4
Z Khan	b McGrath	3
SLV Raju	lbw McGrath	4
BKV Prasad	not out	7
Extras	(lb 2, nb 12)	14
Total	(all out, 58.1 overs)	171

Fall: 1–0 (Ramesh, 1.3 ov), 2–34 (Das, 12.3 ov), 3–48 (Tendulkar, 18.4 ov), 4–88 (Dravid, 31.5 ov), 5–88 (Ganguly, 32.3 ov), 6–92 (Mongia, 34.1 ov), 7–97 (Harbhajan Singh, 38.4 ov), 8–113 (Khan, 43.5 ov), 9–129 (Raju, 47.4 ov), 10–171 (Laxman, 58.1 ov)

Bowling: McGrath 14–8–18–4, Gillespie 11–0–47–2, Kasprowicz 13–2–39–2, Warne 20.1–3–65–2

India second innings (following on)

SS Das	hit wicket b Gillespie	39
S Ramesh	c ME Waugh b Warne	30
VVS Laxman	c Ponting b McGrath	281
SR Tendulkar	c Gilchrist b Gillespie	10
*SC Ganguly	c Gilchrist b McGrath	48
R Dravid	run out (SR Waugh/Kasprowicz)	180
+NR Mongia	b McGrath	4
Z Khan	not out	23
Harbhajan Singh	not out	8
Extras	(b 4, lb 14, w 2, nb 14)	34
Total	(7 wickets dec, 178 overs)	657

Fall: 1–52 (Ramesh, 16.4 ov), 2–97 (Das, 29.4 ov), 3–115 (Tendulkar, 35.6 ov), 4–232 (Ganguly, 66.4 ov), 5–608 (Laxman, 170.5 ov), 6–624 (Mongia, 174.3 ov), 7–629 (Dravid, 175.4 ov)

Bowling: McGrath 39–12–103–3, Gillespie 31–6–115–2, Warne 34–3–152–1, ME Waugh 18–1–58–0, Kasprowicz 35–6–139–0, Ponting 12–1–41–0, Hayden 6–0–24–0, Slater 2–1–4–0, Langer 1–0–3–0

Australia second innings

ML Hayden	lbw Tendulkar	67
MJ Slater	c Ganguly b Harbhajan Singh	43
JL Langer	c Ramesh b Harbhajan Singh	28
ME Waugh	lbw Raju	0
*SR Waugh	c sub (HK Badani) b Harbhajan Singh	24
RT Ponting	c Das b Harbhajan Singh	0
+AC Gilchrist	lbw Tendulkar	0
JN Gillespie	c Das b Harbhajan Singh	6
SK Warne	lbw Tendulkar	0
MS Kasprowicz	not out	13
GD McGrath	lbw Harbhajan Singh	12
Extras	(b 6, nb 8, pen 5)	19
Total	(all out, 68.3 overs)	212

Fall: 1–74 (Slater, 23.2 ov), 2–106 (Langer, 27.3 ov), 3–116 (ME Waugh, 30.2 ov), 4–166 (SR Waugh, 45.2 ov), 5–166 (Ponting, 45.6 ov), 6–167 (Gilchrist, 46.3 ov), 7–173 (Hayden, 48.3 ov), 8–174 (Warne, 50.3 ov), 9–191 (Gillespie, 59.4 ov), 10–212 (McGrath, 68.3 ov)

Bowling: Khan 8–4–30–0, Prasad 3–1–7–0, Harbhajan Singh 30.3–8–73–6, Raju 15–3–58–1, Tendulkar 11–3–31–3, Ganguly 1–0–2–0

INDIA WON BY 171 RUNS
Man of the Match: VVS Laxman

Australia first innings

MJ Slater	c Laxman b Khan	4
ML Hayden	c Ganguly b Harbhajan Singh	203
JL Langer	c Dravid b Harbhajan Singh	35
ME Waugh	c sub (HK Badani) b Bahutule	70
*SR Waugh	handled the ball	47
RT Ponting	st Dighe b Harbhajan Singh	0
+AC Gilchrist	lbw Harbhajan Singh	1
SK Warne	c Das b Harbhajan Singh	0
JN Gillespie	c Ganguly b Harbhajan Singh	0
CR Miller	c Bahutule b Harbhajan Singh	0
GD McGrath	not out	3
Extras	(b 8, lb 10, nb 10)	28
Total	(all out, 115.2 overs)	391

Fall: 1–4 (Slater, 0.3 ov), 2–67 (Langer, 11.4 ov), 3–217 (ME Waugh, 51.2 ov), 4–340 (SR Waugh, 95.4 ov), 5–340 (Ponting, 95.5 ov), 6–344 (Gilchrist, 97.3 ov), 7–374 (Warne, 105.6 ov), 8–376 (Gillespie, 109.4 ov), 9–385 (Miller, 111.2 ov), 10–391 (Hayden, 115.2 ov)

Bowling: Khan 15–5–57–1, Ganguly 2–1–11–0, Harbhajan Singh 38.2–6–133–7, Kulkarni 23–5–67–0, Bahutule 21–3–70–1, Tendulkar 16–1–35–0

Australia second innings

ML Hayden	c Khan b Kulkarni	35
MJ Slater	c Laxman b Harbhajan Singh	48
+AC Gilchrist	lbw Harbhajan Singh	1
JL Langer	c Laxman b Bahutule	21
ME Waugh	c Dravid b Harbhajan Singh	57
*SR Waugh	c Das b Harbhajan Singh	47
RT Ponting	c Dravid b Harbhajan Singh	11
SK Warne	lbw Harbhajan Singh	11
JN Gillespie	c Dravid b Harbhajan Singh	2
CR Miller	lbw Harbhajan Singh	2
GD McGrath	not out	11
Extras	(b 8, lb 6, nb 4)	18
Total	(all out, 97.5 overs)	264

Fall: 1–82 (Hayden, 18.2 ov), 2–84 (Gilchrist, 21.2 ov), 3–93 (Slater, 23.4 ov), 4–141 (Langer, 40.6 ov), 5–193 (ME Waugh, 63.5 ov), 6–211 (Ponting, 71.4 ov), 7–241 (Warne, 79.6 ov), 8–246 (SR Waugh, 87.1 ov), 9–251 (Gillespie, 93.6 ov), 10–264 (Miller, 97.5 ov)

Bowling: Khan 4–0–13–0, Ganguly 1–0–8–0, Harbhajan Singh 41.5–20–84–8, Kulkarni 30–11–70–1, Tendulkar 12–0–43–0, Bahutule 9–0–32–1

India first innings

SS Das	lbw McGrath	84
S Ramesh	c Ponting b Warne	61
VVS Laxman	c ME Waugh b McGrath	65
SR Tendulkar	c Gilchrist b Gillespie	126
*SC Ganguly	c Gilchrist b McGrath	22
R Dravid	c Gilchrist b Gillespie	81
+SS Dighe	lbw Warne	4
SV Bahutule	not out	21
Z Khan	c&b Miller	4
Harbhajan Singh	c ME Waugh b Miller	2
NM Kulkarni	lbw Miller	4
Extras	(b 19, lb 2, w 1, nb 5)	27
Total	(all out, 165 overs)	501

Fall: 1–123 (Ramesh, 41.4 ov), 2–211 (Das, 64.1 ov), 3–237 (Laxman, 70.2 ov), 4–284 (Ganguly, 96.3 ov), 5–453 (Dravid, 138.5 ov), 6–468 (Tendulkar, 144.1 ov), 7–470 (Dighe, 145.6 ov), 8–475 (Khan, 152.2 ov), 9–477 (Harbhajan Singh, 152.5 ov), 10–501 (Kulkarni, 164.6 ov)

Bowling: McGrath 36–15–75–3, Gillespie 35–11–88–2, Miller 46–6–160–3, Warne 42–7–140–2, Ponting 2–1–2–0, ME Waugh 3–0–8–0, Hayden 1–0–7–0

India second innings

SS Das	c&b McGrath	9
S Ramesh	run out (Ponting/Gilchrist)	25
VVS Laxman	c ME Waugh b Miller	66
SR Tendulkar	c ME Waugh b Gillespie	17
*SC Ganguly	c ME Waugh b Gillespie	4
R Dravid	c SR Waugh b Miller	4
+SS Dighe	not out	22
SV Bahutule	c Warne b Miller	0
Z Khan	c ME Waugh b McGrath	0
Harbhajan Singh	not out	3
Extras	(lb 3, nb 2)	5
Total	(8 wickets, 41.1 overs)	155

Fall: 1–18 (Das, 4.6 ov), 2–76 (Ramesh, 19.3 ov), 3–101 (Tendulkar, 24.3 ov), 4–117 (Ganguly, 26.2 ov), 5–122 (Dravid, 27.6 ov), 6–135 (Laxman, 33.2 ov), 7–135 (Bahutule, 33.5 ov), 8–151 (Khan, 39.3 ov)

Bowling: McGrath 11.1–3–21–2, Gillespie 15–2–49–2, Miller 9–1–41–3, Warne 6–0–41–0

INDIA WON BY TWO WICKETS
Men of the Match: Harbhajan Singh and ML Hayden

INDIA WON THE SERIES 2–1
Man of the Series: Harbhajan Singh

Australia Batting and Fielding

Name	Mat	Inn	NO	Runs	HS	Avge	S/R	100	50	Ct	St
ML Hayden	3	6	1	549	203	109.80	66.30	2	2	3	–
SR Waugh	3	5	0	243	110	48.60	43.94	1	–	4	–
GD McGrath	3	5	4	47	21*	47.00	58.02	–	–	1	–
MJ Slater	3	6	1	166	48	33.20	53.89	–	–	–	–
JL Langer	3	5	0	161	58	32.20	63.38	–	1	–	–
ME Waugh	3	5	0	149	70	29.80	47.00	–	2	8	–
AC Gilchrist	3	5	0	124	122	24.80	94.65	1	–	13	–
MS Kasprowicz	1	2	1	20	13*	20.00	23.80	–	–	–	–
JN Gillespie	3	5	0	54	46	10.80	22.13	–	–	–	–
SK Warne	3	5	0	50	39	10.00	52.08	–	–	2	–
DW Fleming	1	1	0	6	6	6.00	28.57	–	–	–	–
RT Ponting	3	5	0	17	11	3.40	36.17	–	–	7	–
CR Miller	1	2	0	2	2	1.00	6.45	–	–	1	–

Australia Bowling

Name	Mat	O	M	R	W	Avge	Best	5WI	10WM
GD McGrath	3	136.2	60	261	17	15.35	4–18	–	–
JN Gillespie	3	126.3	31	394	13	30.30	3–45	–	–
CR Miller	1	55	7	201	6	33.50	3–41	–	–
ME Waugh	3	36	6	106	3	35.33	3–40	–	–
SK Warne	3	152.1	31	505	10	50.50	4–47	–	–
MS Kasprowicz	1	48	8	178	2	89.00	2–39	–	–
DW Fleming	1	30	4	99	1	99.00	1–55	–	–
JL Langer	3	1	0	3	0	–	–	–	–
MJ Slater	3	2	1	4	0	–	–	–	–
ML Hayden	3	7	0	31	0	–	–	–	–
RT Ponting	3	14	2	43	0	–	–	–	–

India Batting and Fielding

Name	Mat	Inn	NO	Runs	HS	Avge	S/R	100	50	Ct	St
VVS Laxman	3	6	0	503	281	83.83	64.90	1	3	3	–
R Dravid	3	6	0	338	180	56.33	42.51	1	1	6	–
SR Tendulkar	3	6	0	304	126	50.66	59.72	1	2	1	–
SS Das	3	6	0	173	84	28.83	38.70	–	1	5	–
S Ramesh	3	6	0	162	61	27.00	49.39	–	1	3	–
SS Dighe	1	2	1	26	22*	26.00	36.11	–	–	–	1
SV Bahutule	1	2	1	21	21*	21.00	34.42	–	–	1	–
NR Mongia	2	4	1	60	28	20.00	50.42	–	–	5	1
SC Ganguly	3	6	0	106	48	17.66	42.74	–	–	4	–
Harbhajan Singh	3	6	3	34	17*	11.33	47.88	–	–	–	–
Z Khan	2	4	1	30	23*	10.00	44.11	–	–	1	–
J Srinath	1	2	0	12	12	6.00	18.46	–	–	1	–
NM Kulkarni	1	1	0	4	4	4.00	10.52	–	–	–	–
SLV Raju	1	1	0	4	4	4.00	26.66	–	–	–	–
RL Sanghvi	1	2	0	2	2	1.00	9.09	–	–	–	–
AB Agarkar	1	2	0	0	0	0.00	0.00	–	–	–	–
BKV Prasad	1	1	1	7	7*	–	30.43	–	–	–	–

India Bowling

Name	Mat	O	M	R	W	Avge	Best	5WI	10WM
Harbhajan Singh	3	178.3	44	545	32	17.03	8–84	4	2
AB Agarkar	1	13	1	58	2	29.00	2–50	–	–
J Srinath	1	18	3	77	2	38.50	2–60	–	–
RL Sanghvi	1	12.2	3	78	2	39.00	2–67	–	–
SR Tendulkar	3	48	5	151	3	50.33	3–31	–	–
SV Bahutule	1	30	3	102	2	51.00	1–32	–	–
Z Khan	2	55.4	15	189	3	63.00	2–89	–	–
SC Ganguly	3	17.2	4	65	1	65.00	1–44	–	–
SLV Raju	1	35	5	116	1	116.00	1–58	–	–
NM Kulkarni	1	53	16	137	1	137.00	1–70	–	–
BKV Prasad	1	33	6	102	0	–	–	–	–

AUSTRALIA IN INDIA, ONE-DAY SERIES AVERAGES

Australia Batting and Fielding

Name	Mat	Inn	NO	Runs	HS	Avge	S/R	100	50	Ct	St
ME Waugh	2	2	1	138	133*	138.00	95.17	1	–	3	–
MG Bevan	5	5	3	218	87*	109.00	79.85	–	1	1	–
ML Hayden	4	4	0	303	111	75.75	92.94	1	2	1	–
AC Gilchrist	5	4	0	172	76	43.00	105.52	–	2	4	1
RT Ponting	4	4	0	137	101	34.25	86.16	1	–	2	–
SR Waugh	5	4	0	93	35	23.25	84.54	–	–	3	–
IJ Harvey	3	3	1	43	25*	21.50	78.18	–	–	1	–
SK Warne	4	2	0	31	18	15.50	62.00	–	–	3	–
DR Martyn	4	2	0	20	19	10.00	86.95	–	–	2	–
DW Fleming	4	2	1	9	9	9.00	112.50	–	–	1	–
A Symonds	3	2	0	12	7	6.00	80.00	–	–	–	–
DS Lehmann	3	3	0	3	1	1.00	25.00	–	–	2	–
GD McGrath	5	2	1	0	0*	0.00	0.00	–	–	2	–
S Lee	1	1	1	25	25*	–	227.27	–	–	1	–
NW Bracken	3	0	–	–	–	–	–	–	–	1	–

Australia Bowling

Name	Mat	O	M	R	W	Avge	Best
SR Waugh	5	6	0	29	3	9.66	3–29
NW Bracken	3	27	3	112	5	22.40	2–21
GD McGrath	5	45.5	1	260	10	26.00	3–52
DW Fleming	4	38	3	188	6	31.33	2–34
IJ Harvey	3	30	1	165	5	33.00	2–49
SK Warne	4	38	0	222	4	55.50	3–38
DR Martyn	4	15	0	100	1	100.00	1–25
A Symonds	3	22	0	118	1	118.00	1–40
ME Waugh	2	9	0	64	0	–	–
DS Lehmann	3	6	0	37	0	–	–
MG Bevan	5	5	0	52	0	–	–
S Lee	1	3	0	11	0	–	–

AUSTRALIAN FIRST-CLASS TOUR AVERAGES

Batting and Fielding

Name	Mat	Inn	NO	Runs	HS	Avge	S/R	100	50	Ct	St
MS Kasprowicz	3	6	3	194	92	64.66	59.50	–	1	–	–
ML Hayden	6	12	1	709	203	64.45	64.45	2	2	4	–
SR Waugh	6	10	2	509	110	63.62	49.03	3	–	6	–
ME Waugh	5	7	0	375	164	53.57	64.99	1	3	9	–
RT Ponting	6	11	1	348	102*	34.80	73.88	2	2	13	–
GD McGrath	4	6	4	66	21*	33.00	54.09	–	–	1	–
JL Langer	6	11	0	346	115	31.45	57.76	1	1	–	–
DR Martyn	2	4	0	115	54	28.75	62.50	–	2	1	–
MJ Slater	6	12	1	270	48	24.54	56.96	–	–	2	–
AC Gilchrist	5	9	0	176	122	19.55	74.26	1	–	18	2
JN Gillespie	4	7	0	116	57	16.57	29.36	–	1	–	–
DW Fleming	4	6	2	64	29*	16.00	39.50	–	–	4	–
BJ Haddin	1	2	0	32	24	16.00	78.04	–	–	1	–
SK Warne	4	7	0	59	39	8.42	44.69	–	–	2	–
CR Miller	4	6	1	8	5	1.60	14.03	–	–	1	–

Bowling

Name	Mat	O	M	R	W	Avge	Best	5WI	10WM
GD McGrath	4	168.2	70	338	21	16.09	4–18	–	–
ME Waugh	5	46	8	133	5	26.60	3–40	–	–
JN Gillespie	4	145.3	39	449	15	29.93	3–45	–	–
CR Miller	4	156.4	34	504	15	33.60	6–90	1	–
SK Warne	4	192.4	40	642	18	35.66	7–56	1	–
RT Ponting	6	23	2	76	2	38.00	2–10	–	–
MS Kasprowicz	3	88.4	13	349	6	58.16	3–68	–	–
ML Hayden	6	15	0	70	1	70.00	1–37	–	–
DW Fleming	4	91	18	299	3	99.66	1–27	–	–
JL Langer	6	1	0	3	0	–	–	–	–
MJ Slater	6	2	1	4	0	–	–	–	–
DR Martyn	2	4	1	11	0	–	–	–	–

THE ASHES 2001

FIRST TEST, AT EDGBASTON, BIRMINGHAM, 5, 6, 7, 8 JULY 2001 (TOSS: AUSTRALIA)

England first innings

MA Atherton	c ME Waugh b Gillespie	57
ME Trescothick	c Warne b Gillespie	0
MA Butcher	c Ponting b Warne	38
*N Hussain	lbw b McGrath	13
IJ Ward	b McGrath	23
+AJ Stewart	lbw b McGrath	65
U Afzaal	b Warne	4
C White	lbw b Warne	4
AF Giles	c Gilchrist b Warne	7
D Gough	c Gillespie b Warne	0
AR Caddick	not out	49
Extras	(b 10, lb 8, nb 16)	34
Total	(all out, 65.3 overs)	294

Fall: 1–2 (Trescothick, 1.1 ov), 2–106 (Butcher, 24.2 ov), 3–123 (Atherton, 31.3 ov), 4–136 (Hussain, 37.4 ov), 5–159 (Ward, 43.2 ov), 6–170 (Afzaal, 46.1 ov), 7–174 (White, 48.3 ov), 8–191 (Giles, 52.2 ov), 9–191 (Gough, 52.5 ov), 10–294 (Stewart, 65.3 ov)

Bowling: McGrath 17.3–2–67–3, Gillespie 17–3–67–2, Lee 12–2–71–0, Warne 19–4–71–5

Australia first innings

MJ Slater	b Gough	77
ML Hayden	c White b Giles	35
RT Ponting	lbw b Gough	11
ME Waugh	c Stewart b Caddick	49
*SR Waugh	lbw b Gough	105
DR Martyn	c Trescothick b Butcher	105
+AC Gilchrist	c Caddick b White	152
SK Warne	c Atherton b Butcher	8
B Lee	c Atherton b Butcher	0
JN Gillespie	lbw b Butcher	0
GD McGrath	not out	1
Extras	(b 3, lb 7, nb 23)	33
Total	(all out, 129.4 overs)	576

Fall: 1–98 (Hayden, 14.6 ov), 2–130 (Ponting, 19.4 ov), 3–134 (Slater, 23.1 ov), 4–267 (ME Waugh, 63.6 ov), 5–336 (SR Waugh, 83.2 ov), 6–496 (Martyn, 117.3 ov), 7–511 (Warne, 119.6 ov), 8–513 (Lee, 121.1 ov), 9–513 (Gillespie, 121.4 ov), 10–576 (Gilchrist, 129.4 ov)

Bowling: Gough 33–6–152–3, Caddick 36–0–163–1, White 26.4–5–101–1, Giles 25–0–108–1, Butcher 9–3–42–4

England second innings

MA Atherton	c ME Waugh b McGrath	4
ME Trescothick	c ME Waugh b Warne	76
MA Butcher	c Gilchrist b Lee	41
*N Hussain	retired hurt	9
IJ Ward	b Lee	3
+AJ Stewart	c Warne b Gillespie	5
U Afzaal	lbw b Gillespie	2
C White	b Gillespie	0
AF Giles	c ME Waugh b Warne	0
D Gough	lbw b Warne	0
AR Caddick	not out	6
Extras	(b 1, lb 5, nb 12)	18
Total	(all out, 42.1 overs)	164

Fall: 1–4 (Atherton, 2.3 ov), 2–99 (Butcher, 24.2 ov), 3–142 (Ward, 32.1 ov), 4–148 (Stewart, 33.1 ov), 5–150 (Afzaal, 35.3 ov), 6–154 (White, 37.3 ov), 7–155 (Trescothick, 38.1 ov), 8–155 (Gough, 38.2 ov), 9–164 (Giles, 42.1 ov)

Bowling: McGrath 13–5–34–1, Gillespie 11–2–52–3, Warne 10.1–4–29–3, ME Waugh 1–0–6–0, Lee 7–0–37–2

AUSTRALIA WON BY AN INNINGS AND 118 RUNS
Man of the Match: AC Gilchrist

SECOND TEST, AT LORD'S, LONDON, 19, 20, 21, 22 JULY 2001 (TOSS: AUSTRALIA)

England first innings

*MA Atherton	lbw b McGrath	37
ME Trescothick	c Gilchrist b Gillespie	15
MA Butcher	c ME Waugh b McGrath	21
GP Thorpe	c Gilchrist b McGrath	20
MR Ramprakash	b Lee	14
+AJ Stewart	c Gilchrist b McGrath	0
IJ Ward	not out	23
C White	c Hayden b McGrath	0
DG Cork	c Ponting b Gillespie	24
AR Caddick	b Warne	0
D Gough	b Warne	5
Extras	(b 7, lb 8, w 2, nb 11)	28
Total	(all out, 63.3 overs)	187

Fall: 1–33 (Trescothick, 11.3 ov), 2–75 (Butcher, 24.4 ov), 3–96 (Atherton, 30.6 ov), 4–121 (Ramprakash, 39.2 ov), 5–126 (Stewart, 42.4 ov), 6–129 (Thorpe, 44.3 ov), 7–131 (White, 48.5 ov), 8–178 (Cork, 58.2 ov), 9–181 (Caddick, 61.3 ov), 10–187 (Gough, 63.3 ov)

Bowling: McGrath 24–9–54–5, Gillespie 18–6–56–2, Lee 16–3–46–1, Warne 5.3–0–16–2

England second innings

*MA Atherton	b Warne	20
ME Trescothick	c Gilchrist b Gillespie	3
MA Butcher	c Gilchrist b Gillespie	83
GP Thorpe	lbw b Lee	2
MR Ramprakash	lbw b Gillespie	40
+AJ Stewart	lbw b McGrath	28
IJ Ward	c Ponting b McGrath	0
C White	not out	27
DG Cork	c Warne b McGrath	2
AR Caddick	c Gilchrist b Gillespie	7
D Gough	c ME Waugh b Gillespie	1
Extras	(lb 3, w 2, nb 9)	14
Total	(all out, 66 overs)	227

Fall: 1–8 (Trescothick, 5.2 ov), 2–47 (Atherton, 16.4 ov), 3–50 (Thorpe, 17.6 ov), 4–146 (Ramprakash, 46.3 ov), 5–188 (Stewart, 58.2 ov), 6–188 (Ward, 58.3 ov), 7–188 (Butcher, 59.5 ov), 8–193 (Cork, 60.6 ov), 9–225 (Caddick, 65.1 ov), 10–227 (Gough, 65.6 ov)

Bowling: McGrath 19–4–60–3, Gillespie 16–4–53–5, Lee 9–1–41–1, Warne 20–4–58–1, ME Waugh 2–1–12–0

Australia first innings

MJ Slater	c Stewart b Caddick	25
ML Hayden	c Butcher b Caddick	0
RT Ponting	c Thorpe b Gough	14
ME Waugh	run out (Gough)	108
*SR Waugh	c Stewart b Cork	45
DR Martyn	c Stewart b Caddick	52
+AC Gilchrist	c Stewart b Gough	90
SK Warne	c Stewart b Caddick	5
B Lee	b Caddick	20
JN Gillespie	b Gough	9
GD McGrath	not out	0
Extras	(lb 9, w 1, nb 23)	33
Total	(all out, 101.1 overs)	401

Fall: 1–5 (Hayden, 1.5 ov), 2–27 (Ponting, 4.5 ov), 3–105 (Slater, 24.1 ov), 4–212 (ME Waugh, 51.3 ov), 5–230 (SR Waugh, 57.1 ov), 6–308 (Martyn, 81.5 ov), 7–322 (Warne, 83.2 ov), 8–387 (Gilchrist, 96.6 ov), 9–401 (Gillespie, 100.5 ov), 10–401 (Lee, 101.1 ov)

Bowling: Gough 25–3–115–3, Caddick 32.1–4–101–5, White 18–1–80–0, Cork 23–3–84–1, Butcher 3–1–12–0

Australia second innings

ML Hayden	not out	6
MJ Slater	c Butcher b Caddick	4
RT Ponting	lbw b Gough	4
ME Waugh	not out	0
Extras		0
Total	(2 wickets, 3.1 overs)	14

Fall: 1–6 (Slater, 1.5 ov), 2–13 (Ponting, 2.3 ov)

Bowling: Gough 2–0–5–1, Caddick 1.1–0–9–1

AUSTRALIA WON BY EIGHT WICKETS
Man of the Match: GD McGrath

THIRD TEST, AT TRENT BRIDGE, NOTTINGHAM, 2, 3, 4 AUGUST 2001 (TOSS: ENGLAND)

England first innings

*MA Atherton	c ME Waugh b McGrath	0
ME Trescothick	c Gilchrist b Gillespie	69
MA Butcher	c Ponting b McGrath	13
MR Ramprakash	c Gilchrist b Gillespie	14
+AJ Stewart	c ME Waugh b McGrath	46
IJ Ward	c Gilchrist b McGrath	6
C White	c Hayden b McGrath	0
AJ Tudor	lbw b Warne	3
RDB Croft	c Ponting b Warne	3
AR Caddick	b Lee	13
D Gough	not out	0
Extras	(b 1, lb 9, w 1, nb 7)	18
Total	(all out, 52.5 overs)	185

Fall: 1–0 (Atherton, 0.2 ov), 2–30 (Butcher, 10.5 ov), 3–63 (Ramprakash, 17.3 ov), 4–117 (Trescothick, 28.2 ov), 5–142 (Ward, 36.1 ov), 6–147 (White, 38.4 ov), 7–158 (Tudor, 43.3 ov), 8–168 (Croft, 45.6 ov), 9–180 (Stewart, 48.4 ov), 10–185 (Caddick, 52.5 ov)

Bowling: McGrath 18–4–49–5, Lee 6.5–0–30–1, Gillespie 12–1–59–2, Warne 16–4–37–2

Australia first innings

MJ Slater	b Gough	15
ML Hayden	lbw b Tudor	33
RT Ponting	c Stewart b Gough	14
ME Waugh	c Atherton b Tudor	15
*SR Waugh	c Atherton b Caddick	13
DR Martyn	c Stewart b Caddick	4
+AC Gilchrist	c Atherton b Tudor	54
SK Warne	lbw b Caddick	0
B Lee	c Butcher b Tudor	4
JN Gillespie	not out	27
GD McGrath	c Butcher b Tudor	2
Extras	(lb 3, w 1, nb 5)	9
Total	(all out, 54.5 overs)	190

Fall: 1–48 (Hayden, 12.6 ov), 2–56 (Slater, 17.1 ov), 3–69 (Ponting, 19.6 ov), 4–82 (SR Waugh, 28.6 ov), 5–94 (ME Waugh, 31.5 ov), 6–102 (Martyn, 32.2 ov), 7–102 (Warne, 32.4 ov), 8–122 (Lee, 39.1 ov), 9–188 (Gilchrist, 54.1 ov), 10–190 (McGrath, 54.5 ov)

Bowling: Gough 15–3–63–2, Caddick 20–4–70–3, Tudor 15.5–5–44–5, White 2–1–8–0, Croft 2–0–2–0

England second innings

*MA Atherton	c Gilchrist b Warne	51
ME Trescothick	c Gilchrist b Warne	32
MA Butcher	lbw b Lee	1
MR Ramprakash	st Gilchrist b Warne	26
+AJ Stewart	b Warne	0
IJ Ward	lbw b Gillespie	13
C White	c SR Waugh b Warne	7
AJ Tudor	c Ponting b Warne	9
RDB Croft	b Gillespie	0
AR Caddick	c Gilchrist b Gillespie	4
D Gough	not out	5
Extras	(b 4, lb 3, nb 7)	14
Total	(all out, 57 overs)	162

Fall: 1–57 (Trescothick, 16.3 ov), 2–59 (Butcher, 17.6 ov), 3–115 (Atherton, 36.6 ov), 4–115 (Stewart, 38.2 ov), 5–126 (Ramprakash, 40.2 ov), 6–144 (White, 48.5 ov), 7–144 (Ward, 49.4 ov), 8–146 (Croft, 51.3 ov), 9–156 (Caddick, 53.5 ov), 10–162 (Tudor, 56.6 ov)

Bowling: McGrath 11–3–31–0, Gillespie 20–8–61–3, Lee 8–1–30–1, Warne 18–5–33–6

Australia second innings

ML Hayden	lbw b Tudor	42
MJ Slater	c Trescothick b Caddick	12
RT Ponting	c Stewart b Croft	17
ME Waugh	not out	42
*SR Waugh	retired hurt	1
DR Martyn	not out	33
Extras	(lb 4, nb 7)	11
Total	(3 wickets, 29.2 overs)	158

Fall: 1–36 (Slater, 5.4 ov), 2–72 (Ponting, 13.2 ov), 3–88 (Hayden, 18.3 ov)

Bowling: Gough 9–1–38–0, Caddick 12.2–1–71–1, Tudor 7–0–37–1, Croft 1–0–8–1

AUSTRALIA WON BY SEVEN WICKETS
Man of the Match: SK Warne

Australia first innings

MJ Slater	lbw b Caddick	21
ML Hayden	lbw b Caddick	15
RT Ponting	c Stewart b Tudor	144
ME Waugh	c Ramprakash b Caddick	72
DR Martyn	c Stewart b Gough	118
SM Katich	b Gough	15
*+AC Gilchrist	c Trescothick b Gough	19
SK Warne	c Stewart b Gough	0
B Lee	c Ramprakash b Mullally	0
JN Gillespie	c Atherton b Gough	5
GD McGrath	not out	8
Extras	(b 5, lb 15, w 1, nb 9)	30
Total	(all out, 100.1 overs)	447

Fall: 1–39 (Slater, 11.1 ov), 2–42 (Hayden, 13.6 ov), 3–263 (Ponting, 59.3 ov), 4–288 (Waugh, 66.3 ov), 5–355 (Katich, 84.3 ov), 6–396 (Gilchrist, 90.5 ov), 7–412 (Warne, 94.1 ov), 8–422 (Lee, 95.4 ov), 9–438 (Gillespie, 98.5 ov), 10–447 (Martyn, 100.1 ov)

Bowling: Gough 25.1–4–103–5, Caddick 29–4–143–3. Mullally 23–8–65–1, Tudor 18–1–97–1, Butcher 1–0–7–0, Ramprakash 4–0–12–0

Australia second innings

ML Hayden	c Stewart b Mullally	35
MJ Slater	b Gough	16
RT Ponting	lbw b Gough	72
ME Waugh	not out	24
DR Martyn	lbw b Caddick	6
SM Katich	not out	0
Extras	(b 5, lb 7, nb 11)	23
Total	(4 wickets dec, 39.3 overs)	176

Fall: 1–25 (Slater, 8.2 ov), 2–129 (Ponting, 28.2 ov), 3–141 (Hayden, 31.4 ov), 4–171 (Martyn, 38.1 ov)

Bowling: Gough 17–3–68–2, Caddick 11–2–45–1, Tudor 4–1–17–0, Mullally 7.3–2–34–1

England first innings

MA Atherton	c Gilchrist b McGrath	22
ME Trescothick	c Gilchrist b McGrath	37
MA Butcher	run out	47
*N Hussain	lbw b McGrath	46
MR Ramprakash	c Gilchrist b Lee	40
U Afzaal	c Warne b McGrath	14
+AJ Stewart	not out	76
AJ Tudor	c Gilchrist b McGrath	2
AR Caddick	c Gilchrist b Lee	5
D Gough	c Slater b McGrath	8
AD Mullally	c Katich b McGrath	0
Extras	(b 2, lb 3, nb 7)	12
Total	(all out, 94.2 overs)	309

Fall: 1–50 (Atherton, 18.4 ov), 2–67 (Trescothick, 22.4 ov), 3–158 (Hussain, 54.2 ov), 4–158 (Butcher, 55.5 ov), 5–174 (Afzaal, 60.5 ov), 6–252 (Ramprakash, 83.5 ov), 7–267 (Tudor, 86.2 ov), 8–289 (Caddick, 89.4 ov), 9–299 (Gough, 90.5 ov), 10–309 (Mullally, 94.2 ov)

Bowling: McGrath 30.2–9–76–7, Gillespie 26–6–76–0, Lee 22–3–103–2, Warne 16–2–49–0

England second innings

MA Atherton	c Gilchrist b McGrath	8
ME Trescothick	c Hayden b Gillespie	10
MA Butcher	not out	173
*N Hussain	c Gilchrist b Gillespie	55
MR Ramprakash	c Waugh b Warne	32
U Afzaal	not out	4
Extras	(b 14, lb 16, nb 3)	33
Total	(4 wickets, 73.2 overs)	315

Fall: 1–8 (Atherton, 2.6 ov), 2–33 (Trescothick, 9.6 ov), 3–214 (Hussain, 54.3 ov), 4–289 (Ramprakash, 71.2 ov)

Bowling: McGrath 16–3–61–1, Gillespie 22–4–94–2, Warne 18.2–3–58–1, Lee 16–4–65–0, Waugh 1–0–7–0

ENGLAND WON BY SIX WICKETS
Man of the Match: MA Butcher

FIFTH TEST, AT THE OVAL, LONDON, 23, 24, 25, 26, 27 AUGUST 2001 (TOSS: AUSTRALIA)

Australia first innings

ML Hayden	c Trescothick b Tufnell	68
JL Langer	retired hurt	102
RT Ponting	c Atherton b Ormond	62
ME Waugh	b Gough	120
*SR Waugh	not out	157
+AC Gilchrist	c Ramprakash b Afzaal	25
DR Martyn	not out	64
Extras	(b 10, lb 13, w 1, nb 19)	43
Total	**(4 wickets dec, 152 overs)**	**641**

Did Not Bat: SK Warne, B Lee, JN Gillespie, GD McGrath

Fall: 1–158 (Hayden, 42.2 ov), 2–292 (Ponting, 72.5 ov), 3–489 (ME Waugh, 123.1 ov), 4–534 (Gilchrist, 134.3 ov)

Bowling: Gough 29–4–113–1, Caddick 36–9–146–0, Ormond 34–4–115–1, Tufnell 39–2–174–1, Butcher 1–0–2–0, Ramprakash 4–0–19–0, Afzaal 9–0–49–1

England first innings

MA Atherton	b Warne	13
ME Trescothick	b Warne	55
MA Butcher	c Langer b Warne	25
*N Hussain	b ME Waugh	52
MR Ramprakash	c Gilchrist b McGrath	133
U Afzaal	c Gillespie b McGrath	54
+AJ Stewart	c Gilchrist b Warne	29
AR Caddick	lbw b Warne	0
J Ormond	b Warne	18
D Gough	st Gilchrist b Warne	24
PCR Tufnell	not out	7
Extras	(b 3, lb 13, w 1, nb 5)	22
Total	**(all out, 118.2 overs)**	**432**

Fall: 1–58 (Atherton, 12.4 ov), 2–85 (Trescothick, 18.5 ov), 3–104 (Butcher, 30.1 ov), 4–166 (Hussain, 50.1 ov), 5–255 (Afzaal, 71.6 ov), 6–313 (Stewart, 86.2 ov), 7–313 (Caddick, 86.3 ov), 8–350 (Ormond, 94.5 ov), 9–424 (Ramprakash, 113.3 ov), 10–432 (Gough, 118.2 ov)

Bowling: McGrath 30–11–67–2, Gillespie 20–3–96–0, Warne 44.2–7–165–7, Lee 14–1–43–0, Ponting 2–0–5–0, ME Waugh 8–0–40–1

England second innings (following on)

MA Atherton	c Warne b McGrath	9
ME Trescothick	c & b McGrath	24
MA Butcher	c SR Waugh b Warne	14
*N Hussain	lbw b Warne	2
MR Ramprakash	c Hayden b Warne	19
U Afzaal	c Ponting b McGrath	5
+AJ Stewart	b Warne	34
AR Caddick	b Lee	17
J Ormond	c Gilchrist b McGrath	17
D Gough	not out	39
PCR Tufnell	c Warne b McGrath	0
Extras	(lb 2, nb 2)	4
Total	**(all out, 68.3 overs)**	**184**

Fall: 1–17 (Atherton, 5.3 ov), 2–46 (Butcher, 14.2 ov), 3–48 (Trescothick, 15.5 ov), 4–50 (Hussain, 16.6 ov), 5–55 (Afzaal, 23.5 ov), 6–95 (Ramprakash, 36.2 ov), 7–126 (Stewart, 48.6 ov), 8–126 (Caddick, 49.1 ov), 9–184 (Ormond, 68.1 ov), 10–184 (Tufnell, 68.3 ov)

Bowling: Lee 10–3–30–1, McGrath 15.3–6–43–5, Warne 28–8–64–4, Ponting 2–0–3–0, Gillespie 12–5–38–0, ME Waugh 1–0–4–0

AUSTRALIA WON BY AN INNINGS AND 25 RUNS
Man of the Match: SK Warne

AUSTRALIA WON THE SERIES 4–1
Men of the Series: MA Butcher and GD McGrath

Australia Batting and Fielding

Name	Mat	Inn	NO	Runs	HS	Avge	S/R	100	50	Ct	St
SR Waugh	4	5	2	321	157*	107.00	56.81	2	–	2	–
ME Waugh	5	8	3	430	120	86.00	56.87	2	1	9	–
DR Martyn	5	7	2	382	118	76.40	73.74	2	2	–	–
AC Gilchrist	5	5	0	340	152	68.00	90.66	1	2	24	2
RT Ponting	5	8	0	338	144	42.25	83.04	1	2	7	–
ML Hayden	5	8	1	234	68	33.42	57.35	–	1	4	–
MJ Slater	4	7	0	170	77	24.28	61.15	–	1	1	–
SM Katich	1	2	1	15	15	15.00	31.25	–	–	1	–
JN Gillespie	5	4	1	41	27*	13.66	42.70	–	–	2	–
GD McGrath	5	4	3	11	8*	11.00	36.66	–	–	1	–
B Lee	5	4	0	24	20	6.00	37.50	–	–	–	–
SK Warne	5	4	0	13	8	3.25	54.16	–	–	6	–
JL Langer	1	1	1	102	102*	–	54.83	1	–	1	–

Australia Bowling

Name	Mat	O	M	R	W	Ave	Best	5WI	10WM
GD McGrath	5	194.2	56	542	32	16.93	7–76	4	–
SK Warne	5	195.2	41	580	31	18.70	7–165	3	1
JN Gillespie	5	174	42	652	19	34.31	5–53	1	–
B Lee	5	120.5	18	496	9	55.11	2–37	–	–
ME Waugh	5	13	1	69	1	69.00	1–40	–	–
RT Ponting	5	4	0	8	0	–	–	–	–

England Batting and Fielding

Name	Mat	Inn	NO	Runs	HS	Avge	SR	100	50	Ct	St
MA Butcher	5	10	1	456	173*	50.66	56.36	1	1	4	–
MR Ramprakash	4	8	0	318	133	39.75	47.81	1	–	3	–
N Hussain	3	6	1	177	55	35.40	48.62	–	2	–	–
AJ Stewart	5	9	1	283	76*	35.37	65.81	–	2	13	–
ME Trescothick	5	10	0	321	76	32.10	61.49	–	3	4	–
MA Atherton	5	10	0	221	57	22.10	45.66	–	2	7	–
J Ormond	1	2	0	35	18	17.50	41.66	–	–	–	–
U Afzaal	3	6	1	83	54	16.60	60.58	–	1	–	–
AR Caddick	5	9	2	101	49*	14.42	60.47	–	–	1	–
D Gough	5	9	3	82	39*	13.66	50.61	–	–	–	–
IJ Ward	3	6	1	68	23*	13.60	40.23	–	–	–	–
DG Cork	1	2	0	26	24	13.00	83.87	–	–	–	–
GP Thorpe	1	2	0	22	20	11.00	38.59	–	–	1	–
C White	3	6	1	38	27*	7.60	42.69	–	–	1	–
PCR Tufnell	1	2	1	7	7*	7.00	41.17	–	–	–	–
AJ Tudor	2	3	0	14	9	4.66	29.78	–	–	–	–
AF Giles	1	2	0	7	7	3.50	28.00	–	–	–	–
RDB Croft	1	2	0	3	3	1.50	21.42	–	–	–	–
AD Mullally	1	1	0	0	0	0.00	0.00	–	–	–	–

England Bowling

Name	Mat	O	M	R	W	Avge	Best	5WI	10WM
RDB Croft	1	3	0	10	1	10.00	1–8	–	–
MA Butcher	5	14	4	63	4	15.75	4–42	–	–
AJ Tudor	2	44.5	7	195	7	27.85	5–44	1	–
D Gough	5	155.1	24	657	17	38.64	5–103	1	–
U Afzaal	3	9	0	49	1	49.00	1–49	–	–
AD Mullally	1	30.3	10	99	2	49.50	1–34	–	–
AR Caddick	5	177.4	24	748	15	49.86	5–101	1	–
DG Cork	1	23	3	84	1	84.00	1–84	–	–
AF Giles	1	25	0	108	1	108.00	1–108	–	–
J Ormond	1	34	4	115	1	115.00	1–115	–	–
PCR Tufnell	1	39	2	174	1	174.00	1–174	–	–
C White	3	46.4	7	189	1	189.00	1–101	–	–
MR Ramprakash	4	8	0	31	0	–	–	–	–

AUSTRALIA IN ENGLAND, ONE-DAY SERIES AVERAGES

Australia Batting and Fielding

Name	Mat	Inn	NO	Runs	HS	Avge	SR	100	50	Ct	St
SR Waugh	6	4	2	200	64	100.00	77.51	–	3	–	–
RT Ponting	5	5	2	298	102	99.33	98.67	1	2	2	–
MG Bevan	5	4	2	102	56*	51.00	66.23	–	1	3	–
AC Gilchrist	6	6	1	248	80	49.60	90.18	–	3	7	5
DR Martyn	5	3	1	99	51*	49.50	70.71	–	1	–	–
ME Waugh	5	4	0	129	47	32.25	82.69	–	–	2	–
SK Warne	5	2	1	28	14*	28.00	73.68	–	–	5	–
A Symonds	5	3	0	69	35	23.00	87.34	–	–	1	–
IJ Harvey	5	2	1	19	19*	19.00	135.71	–	–	1	–
B Lee	5	1	0	10	10	10.00	55.55	–	–	–	–
JN Gillespie	3	1	0	9	9	9.00	34.61	–	–	1	–
ML Hayden	4	3	0	8	8	2.66	32.00	–	–	2	–
DW Fleming	2	1	1	22	22*	–	100.00	–	–	1	–
GD McGrath	5	0	–	–	–	–	–	–	–	1	–

Australia Bowling

Name	Mat	O	M	R	W	Avge	Best
MG Bevan	5	3.2	0	16	1	16.00	1–4
GD McGrath	5	47.5	12	141	8	17.62	2–19
IJ Harvey	5	38.1	4	153	7	21.85	2–18
SK Warne	5	45	3	232	10	23.20	3–52
JN Gillespie	3	26	6	103	4	25.75	3–20
B Lee	5	48	4	264	10	26.40	3–63
A Symonds	5	23	0	129	4	32.25	2–24
DR Martyn	5	9	0	66	1	66.00	1–45
DW Fleming	2	20	3	75	1	75.00	1–37
ME Waugh	5	8	0	27	0	–	–

AUSTRALIAN FIRST-CLASS TOUR AVERAGES

Batting and Fielding

Name	Mat	Inn	NO	Runs	HS	Avge	SR	100	50	Ct	St
DR Martyn	9	14	5	942	176*	104.66	71.58	5	3	3	–
AC Gilchrist	8	10	2	663	152	82.87	88.99	3	2	28	4
SM Katich	5	7	3	288	168*	72.00	64.71	1	1	7	–
ME Waugh	9	15	6	644	120	71.55	59.68	2	2	12	–
SR Waugh	7	11	2	583	157*	64.77	64.49	3	–	5	–
RT Ponting	9	15	1	844	147*	60.28	89.50	3	5	11	–
ML Hayden	10	17	1	636	142	39.75	65.97	1	3	6	–
MG Bevan	1	2	0	67	34	33.50	63.20	–	–	–	–
JL Langer	6	11	2	285	104*	31.66	47.02	2	–	5	–
WA Seccombe	4	5	0	157	76	31.40	51.81	–	1	8	2
SK Warne	8	10	2	237	69	29.62	74.29	–	2	13	–
MJ Slater	8	13	1	341	77	28.41	62.79	–	2	1	–
AA Noffke	3	3	0	69	28	23.00	48.59	–	–	1	–
CR Miller	5	4	1	68	62	22.66	128.30	–	1	2	–
B Lee	8	7	0	127	79	18.14	63.50	–	1	–	–
GD McGrath	7	6	3	53	38	17.66	58.24	–	–	1	–
JN Gillespie	8	9	3	94	27*	15.66	31.97	–	–	3	–
DW Fleming	5	6	0	49	20	8.16	50.00	–	–	–	–
NW Bracken	1	2	2	10	9*	–	50.00	–	–	1	–

Bowling

Name	Mat	O	M	R	W	Avge	Best	5WI	10WM
NW Bracken	1	24	5	61	5	12.20	3–29	–	–
GD McGrath	7	234.5	74	624	40	15.60	7–76	4	–
SK Warne	8	263	56	784	42	18.66	7–165	3	1
DW Fleming	5	138	32	390	19	20.52	6–59	1	–
MJ Slater	8	3.2	0	23	1	23.00	1–23	–	–
SM Katich	5	24	2	106	4	26.50	3–21	–	–
DR Martyn	9	9	1	53	2	26.50	2–38	–	–
JN Gillespie	8	228	54	801	29	27.62	5–37	2	–
CR Miller	5	157.2	37	586	18	32.55	4–41	–	–
AA Noffke	3	67.4	16	258	6	43.00	3–66	–	–
B Lee	8	186.5	30	752	17	44.23	3–17	–	–
ME Waugh	9	24	2	121	2	60.50	1–33	–	–
JL Langer	6	2	0	5	0	–	–	–	–
RT Ponting	9	7.3	1	15	0	–	–	–	–
MG Bevan	1	5	0	28	0	–	–	–	–
ML Hayden	10	11	2	44	0	–	–	–	–